BUILDING A
BETTER
TEACHER

BUILDING A
BETTER
TEACHER

How Teaching Works

(and How to Teach It to Everyone)

Elizabeth Green

W. W. NORTON & COMPANY

New York • London

For information about permission to reproduce selections from this book, write to Permissions, W. W. Norton & Company, Inc., 500 Fifth Avenue, New York, NY 10110

For information about special discounts for bulk purchases, please contact W. W. Norton Special Sales at specialsales@wwnorton.com or 800-233-4830

Manufacturing by Courier Westford
Book design by Chris Welch
Production manager: Louise Parasmo

ISBN: 978-0-393-08159-6

W. W. Norton & Company, Inc., 500 Fifth Avenue, New York, NY 10110
www.wwnorton.com

W. W. Norton & Company Ltd., Castle House, 75/76 Wells Street, London W1T 3QT

1 2 3 4 5 6 7 8 9 0

For my family: parents, brothers, and Dave.

Contents

Author's Note

All children's names in this book have been changed to protect their identities. Except where indicated otherwise in the Notes section, I provided these pseudonyms.

BUILDING A
BETTER
TEACHER

Prologue

HOW TO BE A TEACHER
(Part One)

Open the door and walk in. Remain standing. Or maybe you should sit down?

This crowded rectangular room is yours. Right now it has twenty-six chairs with attached desks, a chalkboard, and early-afternoon sunlight pouring through windows onto the tabletops. In a moment, the room will also have twenty-six fifth-graders whose names are printed on the attendance ledger: Richard, Catherine, Anthony, Eddie, Varouna, Giyoo, Awad, Donna Ruth, Tyrone, Ellie, Enoyat, Leticia, Charlotte, Karim, Shanota, Messima, Saundra, Dorota, Ivan, Connie, Illeana, Yasu, Reba, Jumanah, Candice, and Shahroukh.

Your job, according to the state where you happen to live and the school district that pays your salary, is to make sure that, sixty minutes from now, the students have grasped the concept of "rate." Specifically, if a car is going 55 miles per hour, how far will it have traveled after 15 minutes? How about after 2 hours? By the end of the year, your students should also have mastered fractions, negative numbers, linear functions, long division, ratio and proportion, and exponents. You're also supposed to teach them to become good citizens, subtly knitting into your lesson (yes, this math lesson) the principles of democracy. In whatever time is left, remember to help the children vault over any hurdles life has thrown them—racial, economic, parental, intellectual. You must bend reality closer to the dream of the American meritocracy.

Ready?

The door bursts open. With the residual energy of recess, they surge through the coat room, rearranging their clothes and jostling for sips from the water fountain. Here comes Varouna. She is from Kenya, lithe and dark skinned. Giyoo is from Japan. He is 4 feet tall and barely speaks. Catherine is studious and has her hair in braids. Eddie, freckle faced and hyperactive, takes his seat in the back. Tyrone just moved from South Carolina and prefers not to pay attention. He sits closer to you, in the front.

Don't just stand there. Teach something!

Richard sits near the front, next to Tyrone. They're both new to the school this year. On the first day, Richard introduced himself and volunteered that math was his "worse subject."

Half an hour later, the students are all askew, murmuring and chatting with each other. They've been working on a math problem you wrote on the chalkboard while they were out at recess.

Condition: A car is going 55 mph. Make a diagram to show where it will be
A. after an hour
B. after 2 hours
C. after half an hour
D. after 15 minutes

Consider how to get everyone to quiet down. Next to you, on a table, is a small bell. Do you ring it? Perhaps you should raise one hand and put the other hand over your mouth. Or what about that old line? *When my hand goes up, your mouths go shut.* You go for the bell. Thankfully, it works, and you launch a discussion.

Soon, fifteen minutes have passed, and class is almost over. So far, the students have worked on the problem in small groups of four to six. You have circulated around, peering over shoulders at their varying degrees of success, deciding when to talk and when to nod and when to hold in a laugh, letting it shake inside your chest when a student does something hilarious and adorable. And all of you, together, have reasoned your way through A, B, and C.

On the chalkboard, you've drawn a straight horizontal line, with distance represented on top and time underneath. On the far right is a crosshatch for 110 miles and 2 hours (B); halfway in the middle there is another for 55 miles and 1 hour (A); then there's one more, smaller, crosshatch halfway between 0 and 55: 27.5 miles and ½ hour (C).

It looks like this:

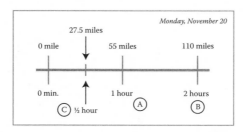

Point to the board. Ask: Can anyone show where the solution to part D should go on the diagram?

Hands shoot up. Then, right in front of you, Richard adds his. You know enough about the others to have an idea of how they understand "rate," or at least an idea of what they will be able to do with the problem. Richard, though, is something of a mystery. After the "worse subject" speech, you collected his math notebook at the end of each week along with the other students'. But he wrote very little in it and only rarely raised his hand. Now he's volunteering to answer the most difficult part of the question—and you have no idea what he'll say.

What do you do?

Look at the clock; only 10 minutes left. Do you have time to risk a wrong answer? What about Richard? What if he isn't even close? If he's wrong, will he, an African American boy in a racially diverse classroom, shut down and hesitate to participate again? On the other hand, what message does it send to the others *not* to call on him?

"Richard," you say. He stands up, turning his notebook so he can see it from the board, and walks slowly to the front. Everyone waits, silent.

D: Show where the car going 55 mph will be after 15 minutes. Reaching for the miles section, on top, he rests the chalk halfway between 0 and 27.5. "15 minutes," he writes. Below, between 0 minutes and ½ hour, he writes, "18." The board looks like this:

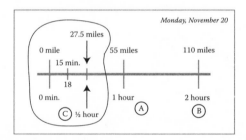

"Ummm," he says. "Eighteen."

Huh? Not only has he put time (15 minutes) where distance should go, but he has also proposed another number, 18, that makes no sense. A car going 55 miles an hour could not travel 18 miles in 15 minutes. And what reasonable computation would get you to 18? Not dividing 27.5 by 2, or 110 by 4, certainly, and not anything else related to the numbers on the board either.

What do you do?

You could quickly correct his time-distance reversal, not drawing too much attention to the mistake, on the assumption that it was a careless error. But what if it wasn't? You decide to assume nothing. "Eighteen miles," you venture, "or eighteen minutes?"

Clarify: "You wrote 18 next to minutes. Did you mean 18 miles and 15 minutes?" Richard nods, erases, and rewrites. Now the numbers are flipped: 18 miles, 15 minutes. But there's still that mystifying 18.

What do you do? Should you say, simply and directly, *That's wrong*? What does Richard mean, anyway?

Look at the class. Ask: Can anybody explain what Richard was thinking?

Another jolt of hands. Try to memorize who is asking to speak, and who is making a fan out of his pencils. Remember, you aren't just teaching Richard; the other twenty-five need to be educated too. What are they thinking? Are they learning?

Check the time. Just a few minutes left, but this could take much longer. Maybe better to give up; there's always tomorrow. But look at Richard, who still believes 18 makes sense, who doesn't know what he doesn't know.

Call on studious Catherine. "Ummmmm," she says. "I disagree with that." She pauses. Then, "Ummm . . ."

Think. She wants to give the correct answer, yet you said, can anybody explain what *Richard* was thinking, not can anybody talk about her own idea. Catherine seems to know she's out of order. That "ummm . . ."—she's eyeing you, looking for permission to disobey.

Do you grant it? Maybe you should. Nod, and the right answer will come—clear and concise, knowing Catherine, and just in time for the end of class. But look at Richard. If quick Catherine, a white girl, jumps in with the save, what effect will that have on him? On the other hand, if you don't let Catherine continue, how will that affect the rest of the class? In either case, what will the class learn about race, gender, and—oh yeah, math?

On Monday, November 20, 1989, Magdalene Lampert, a stoic, watchful woman with straight blonde hair clipped to the back of her head and more than a decade of teaching experience, made a snap decision. She pointed to the 18. "Does anyone *agree* with this answer?" she asked.

The common view of great teachers is that they are born that way. Like Michelle Pfeiffer's ex-marine in *Dangerous Minds*, Edward James Olmos's Jaime Escalante in *Stand and Deliver*, and Robin Williams's "carpe diem"–intoning whistler in *Dead Poets Society*, legendary teachers transform thugs into scholars, illiterates into geniuses, and slackers into bards through brute charisma. Teaching is their calling—not a matter of craft and training, but alchemical inspiration.

Bad teachers, conversely, are portrayed as deliberately sadistic (as with the Sue Sylvester character on *Glee*), congenitally boring (Ben Stein's nasal droner in *Ferris Bueller's Day Off*), or ludicrously dim-witted (Mr. Garrison from *South Park*). These are the tropes of a common narrative, a story I've come to call the "Myth of the Natural-Born Teacher."

Even in the rare cases where fictional teachers appear to improve—as happens in *Goodbye, Mr. Chips*, the novel-turned-film, in which a bland schoolteacher named Mr. Chips comes to "sparkle"—the change is an ugly duckling–style unmasking of hidden pizzazz rather than the acquisition of new skill. Others think Mr. Chips has become a "new man," but in fact, we are told, he has only peeled back a "creeping dry rot of pedagogy" to reveal the "sense of humor" that "he had always had."

The idea of the natural-born teacher is embedded in thousands of studies conducted over dozens of years. Again and again, researchers have sought to explain great teaching through personality and character traits. The most effective teachers, researchers have guessed, must be more extroverted, agreeable, conscientious, open to new experiences, empathetic, socially adjusted, emotionally sensitive, persevering, humorous, or all of the above. For decades, though, these studies have proved inconclusive. Great teachers can be extroverts or introverts, humorous or serious, flexible or rigid.

Even those charged with training teachers—the ones who, by definition, should believe teaching can be taught—believe the natural-born-teacher narrative. "I think that there is an innate drive or innate ability for teaching," the dean of the College of Education at Chicago State University, Sylvia Gist, told me when I met with her in 2009. The consensus seems to be, you either have it or you don't.

Before I met Magdalene Lampert, I ascribed to this view as well. My teacher friends seemed born for the blackboard. I could see it in their personalities and in how much they cared—one's earnest, unabashed sensitivity; another's confident, playful devotion. Gregarious, charming, and theatrical, they commanded attention wherever they went. No wonder they decided to teach, while I—shamefully serious, allergic to goofiness, prone to skepticism—became a journalist. They had the magical quality of "teacherness"—what Jane Hannaway, the director of the National Center for Analysis of Longitudinal Data in Education Research and a former teacher, described to me as "voodoo."

When I first met Magdalene, her talent was obvious, and it did, at first, look like voodoo. It was the winter of 2009, twenty years after she taught fifth-grade math to Catherine and Richard, and she was now a professor at the University of Michigan's School of Education. We sat in her sun-soaked office, at the far end of a long table, looking at the work of a fifth-grader named Brandon.

In the course of solving a problem about the price of party ribbons, Brandon had mistakenly declared that $\frac{7}{12}$ = 1.5. What, Magdalene asked me, could have made him think that?

This was probably the first time Magdalene read my mind, which is what she does after asking a question. She lowers her eyelids slightly, purses her lips, and peers into your soul. I had no idea how Brandon could have come up with 1.5, and she knew it.

But instead of giving me the answer, she wanted me to think about what might make sense (just as, back in 1989, she had wanted Richard to think about his answer, 18). She drew a long-division sign, that "house" that I remembered from fifth grade. She placed the numbers in the wrong spots: 12 under the house and 7 outside of it, to the left, as if we were asking how many times 7 went into 12 rather than how many times 12 went into 7. Putting 7 into 12, a student would find that it went in once, with a remainder of 5 (12 − 7). "1 R 5," he would have written, in the language of fifth grade.

When we looked at Brandon's paper, that is exactly what we saw: a house over 12, with 7 on the outside, and then "1 r 5" written next to it in green marker. Brandon, Magdalene explained, must have mistakenly translated his "1 r 5" into 1.5. (The answer is actually 1 and $\frac{5}{7}$.)

It seemed like a magic trick—how quickly Magdalene moved from noticing a problem to diagnosing its source. Instead of just looking at the final wrong answer, she had translated Brandon's notes—almost nonsensical to me—into a logical (if flawed) path, skipped backward through his thinking, and located the original point of misfire. It took her no more than a minute.

And what about all the other errors Brandon could have made as he struggled to find the price of those ribbons? What about the mistakes scattered through his classmates' papers, not to mention all the ones that weren't there, but could have been? This, after all, was just the work of one class, taken from one day out of the year, in one grade and one subject, by one student. I watched, captivated, as Magdalene worked through more papers, reading backward through the minds of the children, each prone to his own unique mistakes.

But the more I learned about Magdalene and her teaching, the more I saw that what looked like mind reading was in fact the result of extraordinary skill, not inborn talent. Her success did not depend on her personality, which—inward, pensive, and measured—was in many ways the opposite of Hollywood's mythic teachers. Instead, Magdalene's success relied on a body of knowledge and skill that she had spent years acquiring. Teaching, as she practiced it, was a complex craft.

Magdalene showed me that the illusion of the natural-born teacher is at best a polite version of the old adage attributed to George Bernard Shaw: "He who can, does. He who cannot, teaches." By imagining teaching as a "voodoo" mixture of personal charisma and passion, we are saying, essentially, *He who has intelligence, does. He who has charm, teaches.* I have come to think that this is a dangerous notion. By misunderstanding how teaching works, we misunderstand what it will take to make it better—ensuring that, far too often, teaching doesn't work at all.

"Aha!" Magdalene Lampert's decision not to correct Richard had paid off—partly, anyway.

His nonsensical answer, that the car traveling at a speed of 55 miles per hour would go 18 miles in 15 minutes, remained on the board. But after Magdalene asked the class whether anyone agreed with his answer, enduring an uncomfortable pause when nobody said anything, Richard finally broke the silence.

"Can I change my mind?" he asked her. Instead of 18, he wanted to "put thirteen and a half or thirteen point five."

Better! The calculation he should have made is that, since 55 miles corresponds to 60 minutes, and half of 55 miles, 27.5, corresponds to 30 minutes, then a quarter of 60 minutes would be half again: 13.75. He was close.

But Magdalene still didn't understand why he'd first said 18. She needed to know exactly what had gone wrong inside his head. Pointing to the place on the chalkboard where Richard had originally written "18," she asked him why he'd changed his mind.

He was back in his seat. "Because," he said, "eighteen plus eighteen isn't twenty-seven."

"Aha!" she said, permitting herself a minor celebration.

He had it—at least, most of it. Keeping her hand on the board so that it covered up the old wrong answer, 18, Magdalene pivoted so that her body faced Richard and the rest of the class. She wanted everyone to hear what she had to say. Richard had gone from stumbling to coming up with the beginnings of a proof—a mathematical argument for why 18 couldn't be the answer—and she wanted to draw everyone else's attention to his work.

This is what the board showed:

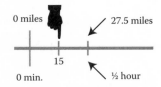

Whatever goes in this spot, she said, has to be a number that, when doubled, comes close to 27.

In the back of the room, students started murmuring. "Not close!" one shouted out. Another student threw up his hand.

Magdalene took note but did not make a move just yet. She thought about 27. The board, of course, said the correct number of miles that is half of 55—27.5, not 27. If he had been shooting for precision, Richard would have tried to find a number that, when doubled, equaled 27.5, not 27. But if they were talking about a real car, making a real trip, would it matter if he calculated a distance of 13.5 miles, rather than 13.75? It might, and it also might not. Still, learning to make approximations was an important skill, and Magdalene was happy with Richard's performance. He was estimating—proving, even—thinking mathematically.

She did not want to make Richard think he'd made a mistake, but she also wanted to help him and the rest of the class reach the exact answer. After all, if she hadn't wanted the students to deal with the tricky matter of having to divide 27.5 into two pieces, she could have picked a rounder speed, like 60 miles an hour. Then the math would have been nice and clean. But one of her objectives for the year was to have students learn to convert between decimals and fractions, and to divide each of them in their heads. She had picked 55 because she wanted the class to struggle with exactly this problem, in exactly this way.

How to acknowledge Richard's good work but also, at the same time, correct it? She surveyed the growing field of raised hands. Anthony, a small boy whom Magdalene knew loved to talk, was waving his hand in the air. Awad, a quiet boy with neat, curlicue handwriting, had his hand up too. Who would keep up her ambiguous tone: accepting Richard's answer, but expanding on it? She chose Awad.

Paradoxically, the institution most susceptible to the fallacy of the natural-born teacher is our country's public school system. And that's despite the fact that alarm—always high—over the disappointing level of our national teaching quality has recently reached a fever pitch.

"From the moment our children step into a classroom," Barack

Obama said in 2007, "the single most important factor determining their achievement is not the color of their skin or where they come from; it's not who their parents are or how much money they have. It's who their teacher is." Obama was then a presidential candidate; in office, his position only strengthened. Today, thanks to policies that his administration has advanced, school districts across the country are undergoing ambitious efforts to reinvigorate their teaching force. The debate about these reforms is fierce; many people, including many teachers, oppose Obama's efforts. But their objection is not usually with his premise. They agree that teachers matter and that the quality of their work should be improved. What they dispute is how to enact the change.

One argument—Obama's—prescribes improvement by way of *accountability*. The problem with American education, this line of thinking goes, is that we have for too long treated all teachers the same: they get the same pay raises, the same evaluations, and the same job protections whether they inspire their students like Robin Williams or stultify them like Ben Stein. But the fact is that some teachers are good and some are bad. Some help children learn while others set them back.

"They have 300,000 teachers in California," Obama explained in a speech in 2009. "The top 10 percent are 30,000 of the best that are out there. The bottom 10 percent are 30,000 of the worst out there. The problem is, we have no way to tell which is which." This, he went on, "is where data comes in." By measuring which teachers are successful and which aren't, we can reward the phenoms and discard the duds, thereby improving the overall quality of the teaching force. Following Obama's prescription, revamped teacher evaluation systems are now being rolled out across the country, along with rewards and punishments that will affect teachers' careers.

The other argument—call it the *autonomy* thesis—prescribes

exactly the opposite. Where accountability proponents call for extensive student testing and frequent on-the-job evaluations, autonomy supporters say that teachers are professionals and should be treated accordingly. Like lawyers or doctors, they will improve only if they are given the trust, respect, and freedom they need to do their jobs well. Lately, proponents of this argument have been drawing comparisons to Finland. There, a recent report by the Chicago Teachers Union described, "teaching is a respected, top career choice; teachers have autonomy in their classrooms, work collectively to develop the school curriculum, and participate in shared governance of the school." In Finland, the report concludes, teachers "are not rated; they are trusted."

As descriptions, both arguments—accountability and autonomy—contain a measure of truth. Teachers do lack some of the freedom they need to teach well, and they also lack adequate feedback. But as prescriptions, actual suggestions for how to improve teaching, the arguments fail. Neither change, on its own, will produce better teachers. Basic math makes the problem with accountability clear: Discard the bottom 10 percent and, as Obama said, that's thirty thousand teachers who will need to be replaced. And that's just in California. Nationally, the number is more than ten times that. Autonomy, meanwhile, is an experiment that many schools have tried for years, and still seen teachers struggle.

Neither accountability nor autonomy is enough, in other words, because both arguments subscribe to the myth of the natural-born teacher. In both cases, the assumption is that good teachers know what to do to help their students learn. These good teachers should either be allowed to do their jobs or be held accountable for not doing them, and they will perform better. Both arguments, finally, rest on a feeble bet: that the average teacher will figure out how to become an expert teacher—alone.

This bet is especially audacious, considering the large number of people involved. More people teach in this country than work at McDonald's, Wal-Mart, and the U.S. Post Office combined. In New York City, where I live, a corps of teachers seventy-five thousand strong makes up a workforce roughly the same size as Apple's global employee base. As Amy McIntosh, the former chief talent officer of New York City's Department of Education, pointed out, in all the five boroughs there is no building where all seventy-five thousand teachers could gather at a single time. Not even Yankee Stadium (capacity 50,287).

Of the fields to which teaching is commonly compared—those that require a college degree and are considered of reasonably high social value—none come close to matching the number of employees that teaching has. Consider a bar graph displaying the number of Americans in different professions. The shortest bar represents architects: 180,000. Farther over, slightly higher, come psychologists (185,000) and then lawyers (952,000), followed by engineers (1.3 million) and waiters (1.8 million). At the top stand the big three: janitors, maids, and household cleaners (3.3 million); secretaries (3.6 million); and, finally, teachers (3.7 million). An ongoing swell of baby boomer retirements is expected to force school systems to hire more than three million new teachers between 2014 and 2020. As the departing teachers wave goodbye to their students, they will take all their experience and skill out the door with them. These new hires will have to replace them.

One December night in 2009, I watched as hundreds of the people hoping to become teachers packed an auditorium at Chicago's Cultural Center, home of the world's largest stained-glass Tiffany dome, to hear from the city school system's director of recruitment. There were no seats available, and the sea of humanity was as diverse as it was vast. There was a cross-eyed woman with white hair and a disheveled look. There was a dreadlocked

recent college graduate with hair dangling below his belt. There
were many dozens of young midwestern ladies with their mothers, taking careful notes. There was a small woman in a Christ-
mas sweater with ornaments sewn into quadrants, including a
Velcro nameplate stuck on her left breast: RACHEL.

But even if everyone in the auditorium had signed up to teach—
the mothers along with their daughters—the crowd still would
not have filled all the available teaching slots. Each year, the city
of Chicago hires two thousand new teachers. That year, the economic downturn had lowered the number below its average. But
the district still needed six hundred new teachers. Nationwide,
nearly four hundred thousand new teachers start work at public
and private schools every year.

When all these people take their place in front of classrooms
across the country—from the overcrowded trailers in Queens,
New York, to the humid, ranch-style spaces serving Alabama
Native American reservations, to the breezy, open-air classrooms
of Cerritos, California—what will they do? What *should* they do?
And how can we make sure all of them do the best possible job?

The cold truth is that accountability and autonomy, the two
dominant philosophies for teacher improvement, have left us
with no real plan. Autonomy lets teachers succeed or fail on their
own terms, with little guidance. Accountability tells them only
whether they have succeeded, not what to do to improve. Instead
of helping, both prescriptions preserve a long-standing culture of
abandonment. Steven Farr of Teach For America described this
culture by telling me about the first time his assigned mentor
came to observe his class. The mentor was just doing her job,
but when she walked in, she apologized, as if for some voyeuris-
tic intrusion. Teaching, she told him, is "the second-most private
act." She'd rather not be caught watching someone else do it.

The sociologist Dan Lortie, in his classic work *Schoolteacher,* describes the teaching profession in the language of Victorian-era sex: a private "ordeal." Lortie traces the fundamental lone-liness to the days of the one-room schoolhouse, when teachers worked in isolation because the other adults (and some of the children) were busy farming. These days, there are more person-nel and more students associated with each classroom, but each teacher still faces a room full of pupils alone.

What do teachers do? They do what any of us would do. They make it up.

That day in November, Magdalene Lampert's gamble to call on Awad—carefully calculated, in her case—paid off. Awad played exactly the role she had hoped, correcting Richard's imprecision about 13.5 without trampling over his accomplishment in get-ting there.

"Ummm," Awad had said with his typical deliberation. "I think it's thirteen point seventy-five." Richard kept his composure, and in the minutes that followed, Magdalene untangled a series of teaching problems. She called on Anthony, who had been wav-ing his hand in the air, but didn't let him go on too long and even distilled a clear, concise idea from his confusing, if enthusiastic, speech.

She then gave the floor to a girl, Ellie, balancing the gender of speakers and thereby minimizing the idea that only boys can do math, which paved the way for an astonishing performance by another girl, Yasu, who constructed a sophisticated logical proof that recalled Richard's original insight about the relationship between doubling and halving. All this had happened in just a few minutes. But now, it was beyond time for class to end. The teacher who was to take over the room after math ended stood at the back of the classroom, giving Magdalene a look.

"You know what I think?" she said to the class, nodding at the teacher in the back. "I think that we are going to schedule a little time on remainders and division. 'Cause I think we are getting a little mix—We are mixing up a lot of ideas here and we don't have time to go into them."

She paused again. She wanted to give anyone who might be deeply confused one last chance to ask a question. The students sat before her, their math notebooks still open in front of them: Richard in the front, Awad in the back, Catherine to her right. All of them would be there tomorrow too, and the next day and the next and the next, until summer.

"Okay?" Magdalene asked, turning the statement into a slight question—a door just on its way to being closed. No one said anything.

Okay.

Both sides of the "teacher quality" debate tend to depict the challenge as a transfer problem—how to help unsuccessful, often low-income students (like the ones I cover as a reporter in New York City) to access the experiences enjoyed by their more affluent peers (like the ones I had attending public school in the manicured Washington, DC, suburb of Montgomery County, Maryland).

The accountability argument holds that suburban schools have the best teachers because, with rich coffers and newer, prettier buildings, they are able to lure top talent. To rebalance this unequal distribution, Obama has supported measures to tempt high-quality teachers back to school districts serving poorer populations. Proponents of the autonomy argument, meanwhile, contend that teachers working with the poor have paradoxically received the *least* freedom and the most restrictive working environments. Make their schools look more like those enjoyed by the children of the wealthy, and they will be able to prosper.

Again, neither description is wrong, but as prescriptions, both are incomplete. Teachers at affluent public schools do enjoy, on average, better working conditions and more flexibility. But they are also victims of the natural-born-teacher hypothesis. Indeed, the more I learned about successful teaching, the more I realized how rare it is, even in the schools with the most resources.

Not long ago, exploring the closet of my childhood bedroom in Maryland, I discovered a pink, cardboard filing cabinet that held my elementary school papers. In the best classrooms I visited as a reporter, children were reading and writing by kindergarten. My pink filing cabinet did not have a kindergarten file. What would I have put in it? That year, I did not know how to read.

The first-grade papers, meanwhile, bore little resemblance to the careful work I saw in classrooms run by excellent reading teachers. The file contained words copied from worksheets and not much original writing. By January, I had reached my peak level for the year: I was able to fill a collection of construction paper sheets, stapled together and labeled—in an adult's handwriting— "Writing Journal," with lifeless one-sentence entries:

Water is fun.
I haγt cold weather.
I like toeγs.
I like Sarah.
I like sissors.
It was fun at the show.
I haet work. It is to eyse.

No wonder I didn't read until first grade. The work *was* too easy, and as a result I didn't learn.

Even later, in the special "gifted" programs I attended from fourth grade on, how much had my teachers really taught me?

Some changed my life forever, helping me fall in love with journalism, calculus, and even quantum physics. But what about the others? Besides that fluke physics year, my memories from science classes were mainly of lethargic fruit flies. And only in my last year of high school did I figure out that history had to do with evidence and arguments, as well as memorizing state capitals and the dates of irrelevant wars.

I attended some of the fanciest public schools in the country (my school district, in Montgomery County, Maryland, has an average household income in the country's top ten), yet the teaching I received was just as inconsistent as at the schools I later visited in Newark, New Jersey, the Bronx, and San Francisco.

Yet, while I have come to see that the scope of America's education challenge is much larger than I ever imagined, I have also begun to see a path through which the challenge might be tackled. For every case I have found of the natural-born-teacher fallacy hampering progress—and I have found a lot, stretching far into the past—I have found another case of a person who thought differently.

Take Colonel Francis Parker. Born in 1837 in New Hampshire, the son and grandson of teachers, Parker believed that teaching well required intense study. Teaching was, he said, "the greatest art in all the world"; learning to do it well could take a lifetime. But it didn't take Parker long to learn that this was an unpopular view. After serving honorably in the Civil War, he was offered several prestigious jobs that would take him away from the classroom. "When I said that I was going to be a school teacher [instead]"—during the war, he had spent nights before the campfire, planning future lessons in his head, and he did not intend to give them up—"my friends were very much disgusted with me." Even another teacher called him a fool.

His fellow teachers, Parker was finding, mirrored the general public. Many of them didn't think about their work as a craft they needed to study. Later, when Parker took over a struggling school for teachers in Chicago, most of the city (including some teachers) wondered whether the school should exist at all. "The fact of the matter is, the conviction that young men and women should be trained for their work in order to teach little children existed only here and there," one of his colleagues said. "The general public was against it."

Parker died before seeing his dream of resuscitating the school and its reputation fully realized. He was, said the rabbi Emil G. Hirsch in his eulogy, "another Moses," destined to behold his promised land only from afar. The same fate befell Parker's successor at the University of Chicago, the philosopher John Dewey. Expanding on Parker's vision, Dewey had written eloquently about the "science of education" he hoped to develop—how it would help prevent the immeasurable "waste" that comes from letting great teachers' secrets live and die with them. "The only way by which we can prevent such waste in the future," he wrote, "is by methods which enable us to make an *analysis* of what the gifted teacher does intuitively, so that something accruing from his work can be communicated to others." The science wasn't to be—at least, not yet. For half a century after he made it, Dewey's prescription lay in hibernation, the victim of the same forces that Parker had pressed against.

But though Parker and Dewey both died before seeing "educational Palestine," as Emil Hirsch called it, their vision did not. Today, the natural-born-teacher illusion lives on, but thanks to Magdalene Lampert and a growing group of educators like her, so does Parker and Dewey's dream.

The educators include some people like Magdalene, longtime teachers who later became a unique breed of researcher, studying their own craft while they worked to pass it on to others.

They include, as well, people who echoed Magdalene's conclusions without ever meeting her—sometimes deliberately (as happened in the 1980s, on an island six thousand miles away from her fifth-grade classroom), other times not (as in the case of the movement of entrepreneurial educators that emerged a decade later). Together, these educators still constitute a minority. But for a variety of reasons, their chances of building Francis Parker's educational Palestine are better than any other time in history.

This book is their story. It is also the story of teaching, that hilarious and heartbreaking theater that unfolds between children and teachers every day. The work that, when done well, with trained skill, can induce in a student a near-magical feeling: the trembling sensation of beholding a new idea where nothing existed before. It begins with one of the first pioneers—a shy, industrious man named Nathaniel Gage.

1

FOUNDING FATHERS

By 1948, when he landed his first academic job at the University of Illinois, Nate Gage had already helped the army select and train radar observers during World War II; worked with the College Board to develop a new tool—the Scholastic Aptitude Test; and coauthored a definitive textbook: *A Practical Introduction to Evaluation and Measurement.* The second son of Jewish immigrants from Poland, he'd made his way from hanging wallpaper with his father to the top of his chosen field, educational psychology. At Illinois, he joined the prestigious new Bureau of Educational Research. But the breakthrough that became Nate's most important finding happened in the classroom.

Nate was serious, but also passionate and sweet. At conferences, he would transfix his colleagues with barroom storytelling late into the night. And yet, in the classroom, that chemistry somehow failed to materialize. He simply could not keep the students' attention. It was not unusual for one or more of them to fall asleep in the middle of his lectures. "He just didn't have that certain *something*," says one of his students, David Berliner. For all his success—the multiple publications in prestigious journals; the glittering title, *professor of education*—the data all pointed to one disturbing conclusion: Nate was a terrible teacher.

Distraught, Nate turned to the academic literature. Surely some of his colleagues in educational psychology had cracked the mysteries of teaching. That was when he made his second discovery: the research on teaching didn't exist. At least, the *findings* didn't. Instead of conclusions, researchers had developed a bundle of idiosyncratic hypotheses, focused mostly on teachers' personality traits. Were good teachers warmer? more enthusiastic? more organized? more interested in their subject? Maybe better teachers had similar degrees of bohemianism, emotional sensitivity, and sociability. Perhaps subpar teachers displayed radicalism, or even "worrying suspiciousness." Other studies cast their searches even more broadly, investigating traits from age and experience to eye color, clothing style, and strength of grip.

None of the studies found anything conclusive. A researcher would publish a discovery, only to have another produce exactly opposite findings. The few conclusions that could be squeezed out of the research tended to be vague and unhelpful. One set of studies suggested that good teachers should be "friendly, cheerful, sympathetic, and morally virtuous rather than cruel, depressed, unsympathetic, and morally depraved." Another study concluded that the best teachers had a characteristic called, unhelpfully, "teaching skill."

Summarizing the research in 1953, Nate wrote:

> The simple fact of the matter is that, after 40 years of research on teacher effectiveness during which a vast number of studies have been carried out, one can point to few outcomes that a superintendent of schools can safely employ in hiring a teacher or granting him tenure, that an

agency can employ in certifying teachers, or that a teacher-education faculty can employ in planning or improving teacher-education programs.

The irony was bruising. The country, at that point, had dozens of university programs devoted to recruiting, training, and vouching for America's future teachers—education schools, they were called. Yet somehow all those ed schools' professors had managed to learn nothing about teaching. And that was the professors who paid the topic any attention at all. The most prestigious among them—the elite education researchers like Nate—ignored teaching altogether.

You couldn't help but wonder. How had this happened? How had an entire field come to neglect the work at its heart?

One answer was that they did it on purpose. The tradition began with the first education professors, who taught the new education courses with undisguised reluctance. "Educational psychology?" the philosopher William James was said to have quipped. "I think there are about six weeks of it." James became the grandfather of the discipline. His student, Edward Thorndike, another foundational figure, entered the field only because he had to. After he finished graduate school in psychology in 1898, the best job offer he could find was not in psychology but in pedagogy, at the Women's College at Western Reserve University in Cleveland.

"The bane of my life is the practice school they stuck me with," he wrote in a letter to a friend soon after starting the job. Later, when he moved to Columbia University's Teachers College, he spent his first year visiting schools, but he quickly abandoned the mission, calling the trips a "bore." When asked what he would do if faced with a certain superintendent's real-world dilemma, he scoffed. "Do? Why, I'd resign!"

Instead of addressing educational problems, Thorndike took psychological ones and grafted them onto schools. He applied to human students the general laws of learning that he derived from his experiments with monkeys, dogs, and cats ("Never will you get a better psychological subject than a hungry cat," he wrote). Meanwhile, he aided the proliferation of new measurement techniques, assessing everything from intelligence to memory. But he did not study teachers.

Even John Dewey, who advocated a "science of education," wound up retreating to his original discipline, philosophy. All around him, educational researchers had followed Thorndike and abandoned the study of real schools. Discouraged, Dewey set his work in education aside.

Nate Gage, too, never intended to study education. What he really wanted to be was a psychologist. But after graduating from the University of Minnesota magna cum laude, a star student of the young B. F. Skinner, he was rejected by all ten graduate programs he applied to. "From the universities' point of view it would be pointless to take him into a graduate programme in psychology and waste resources training him, since he was Jewish," explained Minnesota's dean of psychology, Richard Elliott. Graduate programs were judged by their success at placing professors, and universities did not hire Jews. The only program that made him an offer was one he had not applied to—a new program in educational psychology at Purdue, where the young director recruited his students by scouring psych departments' reject lists.

Another reason early education professors ignored teaching was that they found it uninteresting. Learning to teach composition did not require a method, but rather a "clear head, an enduring conscience, an elastic enthusiasm, and uncommon commonsense," the English professor LeBaron Russell Briggs insisted. "There is no such thing as a science of Pedagogy," Josiah Royce wrote in the lead article of the inaugural issue of the journal *Educational Review*, published in 1891. "As for a 'philosophy of education' in any other sense," Royce added, "the lord deliver us therefrom."

Yet the subject had to be offered; simple economics demanded it. In 1890, total enrollment in US elementary and secondary schools stood at just under thirteen million. By 1920, the number was more than twenty million. In the same period, the ranks of school teachers grew by nearly four hundred thousand. Another twenty-one thousand people served as administrators. By the time Nate arrived at the University of Illinois, in 1948, the number of teachers alone was nearing one million. For a university, the calculation was clear: training teachers made financial sense whether there was something to teach them or not.

The grim history might have led another man to surrender. If William James hadn't been able to develop a science of teaching, what could honestly be expected of Nate Gage from New Jersey? Anyway, as Thorndike had proved, it was perfectly possible to make a respectable career in education research without touching the teaching problem at all. But where others might have seen a dead end, Nate saw possibility. After all, in science, the most important discoveries were born not from answers, but from puzzles. And, studying the early work on teaching, he had glimpsed a common and, he suspected, fatal flaw.

None of the traits the first researchers investigated—eye color? strength of grip?—had come from the classroom. They had looked into hundreds of variables but ignored "the primary data of the teaching process." That choice, too, belied the pattern of science's greatest discoveries. Johannes Kepler, Dmitri Mendeleev, Gregor Mendel—all began by scrutinizing phenomena close up and only *then* came up with theories to explain them. Like "Kepler in examining the orbits of planets, Mendelyeev [*sic*] in poring over the properties of the elements, or Mendel in raising his peas," Nate decided, education researchers would only unlock the mysteries of the American classroom by venturing inside of it.

Nate set out to construct a true science of teaching. He called his method the "process-product" paradigm. By comparing the process (teaching) to its product (learning), researchers could conclude which teaching acts were effective and which were not. The ambition was not unlike John Dewey's imagined science of "what the gifted teacher does intuitively." The only difference was that, while Dewey favored learning about teaching in the messy cauldron of a real school, Nate preferred formal experimentation. A successful process-product study, in his view, needed to approximate the natural classroom habitat while also controlling for extraneous variables.

In one experiment, Nate focused on explanation, the slice of teaching that, in his opinion, formed "the essence of instruction." He and his grad students recruited real teachers to teach real students, but under certain parameters. One was that the teachers could speak and use the chalkboard, but they could not invite discussion, solicit questions, or even ask students to take notes. ("For some teachers this restriction may require a difficult departure from their customary teaching style," the instructions read. "We hope that you will bear with us.") Another restriction was the content; each lesson corresponded to a preselected article from the *Atlantic Monthly* magazine. The researchers gave students a comprehension test at the end of the lesson to find out which teachers had explained it best.

Nate's students videotaped each lesson and catalogued the teachers' behaviors. One graduate student, Barak Rosenshine, had a list of twenty-seven qualities to watch for, ranging from the average length of words spoken (perhaps brevity was key?) to the frequency of "reference to pupils' interests" to the number of gestures ("movement of the arms, head, or trunk") and paces (walking from one place to another).

Another group wrote computer programs to analyze what the teachers had said. One compared the transcripts against a "vagueness dictionary" written specially for the occasion (qualifying words included *almost, maybe, generally,* and *most*). In one lecture that scored as highly vague, for instance, a teacher began by describing an author's name, which he said was "not too important." He went on:

> I will put his name up on the board anyway. It is really not very important at all. MIHAJOV [*sic*]—that is the way you pronounce that word, Uh Mihajlov wrote those articles. And someone, he has done something that is fine someone very similar had done and there was another author whose name, uh, uh, let us just remember there is another author. That one has spelling problems too. Two authors, two authors. One we know is Mihajlov, the other one wrote earlier in nineteen sixty-two. Both of them complained about conditions, especially in Russia. And this one was in prison because he wrote a book about conversations with Stalin and, I do not know if you have ever heard of the book . . .

The final step compared the recorded teaching behaviors (process) and students' comprehension scores (products). As one might expect, the students of vagueness offenders had significantly lower comprehension. Rosenshine's method yielded other strong correlations. A high number of gestures, it turned out, helped improve comprehension; so did a high level of right-to-left movement. The research might not have been quite what Dewey

imagined, but it was certainly unlike anything Nate Gage's con-
temporaries had seen.

Process-product research caught on quickly. In 1957, sharing an elevator with a colleague at the American Educational
Research Association's annual conference, Nate joked that if
the elevator crashed, then all of that year's research on teaching
would go down with it. That year, he and the colleague were the
only two giving papers on the topic. By the spring of 1963, Nate's
book collecting the available research on teaching had converted
a new generation of researchers into the fold. Officially called
The Handbook of Research on Teaching (and unofficially known
as "The Gage Handbook"), the volume sold 30,000 copies. One
chapter, outlining how to design experiments to study teaching, generated such demand that the publisher, Rand McNally,
released it separately in pamphlet form in 1966. By 1974, the
pamphlet had sold 130,000 copies.

Perhaps most important, Nate became, if not the most engaging teacher, certainly a beloved one. Graduate students devoted
themselves to him, and even the American Federation of Teachers, a union representing practitioners across the country, caught
on. "They called him the Sage Gage," says Lovely Billups, a union
official at the time, who worked with Nate to convert his findings
into usable lessons for teachers.

So when, in 1971, a pair of young staffers at the new National
Institute of Education was charged with funding the next generation of research on teaching, they went straight to teaching's
"pooh-bah," according to one of them, Garry McDaniels. Soon,
Nate was taking a leave from his university—by then he was at
Stanford—to help them launch the new round of funding with a
conference suggesting new directions for research.

There was just one twist. Created by the contrarian new president, Richard Nixon, NIE was charged not just with supporting

existing research, but with transforming it. "My assignment," says McDaniels, "was to change the field." Wittingly or not, Nate helped him do it. The draft conference agenda he circulated for feedback went to all his colleagues back at Stanford, including the man who would eventually inherit Nate's "pooh-bah" crown—a young professor visiting from Michigan State named Lee Shulman.

"Garbage," Lee Shulman said when Richard Snow, another Stanford professor, asked him what he thought of Gage's draft—the one he was circulating about the conference planning the future of research on teaching. "Same old bullshit."

Dick Snow was aghast. "Why?"

"It's nothing but a kind of testimony to the past," Lee said. "Doesn't Nate realize that behaviorism is on life support?"

It was true. Nate's process-product approach depended on a school of psychology that was falling increasingly out of fashion. Nate was a behaviorist by default and also by generation; B. F. Skinner, his old professor, had been behaviorism's seminal figure. The founder of educational psychology, Thorndike, was another lifelong adherent. Nate's rise correlated with behaviorism's most prominent period.

The behaviorists held that the only scientific way to study humans was to study their directly observable features—their behaviors and the actions ("stimuli") that triggered them. But the new generation of psychologists began to point out that by focusing on stimuli and their responses, behaviorists were ignoring the mind.

In Thorndike's model, the human mind was just an extension of the animal one. Learning meant responding to repeated rewards or punishments. If rewarded for one behavior enough times, the subject learned to keep doing it. If punished, he or she learned to stop.

But while this pattern might describe some forms of human learning, critics argued that behaviorism could never explain them all—especially not the kind of learning that went beyond simple actions (will I get food when I press my cat paw on this pedal?) to more complicated concepts (when is it useful to calculate an indefinite integral?). To explain how people learned higher-level concepts, the critics held, psychology had to reckon with cognition.

Lee, who'd begun not as a psychologist but as a philosopher, had never liked behaviorism. It rejected as unscientific the questions that he found most fascinating—questions about the mind. Early on, that opinion was unpopular. But by the time of Lee's year at Stanford, in 1973, critics—known as "cognitivists"—had broken the behaviorist stranglehold on their field. The cognitive revolution spread from one area of psychology to the next, turning attention from behavior to the working of the mind.

Lee figured the shift should apply to research on teaching too. The whole point of process-product research, Nate Gage's great contribution, was to study teaching by studying teachers' behaviors. But what about their minds?

"Why don't you write to Nate?" Snow told Lee.

"Come on, Nate *personifies* process-product research!" Lee said.

But Snow was insistent. Nate was a serious scholar. He'd listen. "So I wrote him a two-page memo," Lee says. "Probably wrote it on a typewriter, Selectric typewriter, and I made—I politely critiqued what he was doing and said, 'You don't even have one group looking at the relevance of cognitive work for the study of teaching, and my guess is that's the future of research on teaching.'"

Lee was mostly just riffing. "I mean, I wasn't really in the field at that point. I was teaching future teachers . . . But research on teaching wasn't my area." So when the phone rang a few days later and Nate asked him to use the memo as the basis for leading one of the ten panels at his conference in Washington, Lee was unprepared. He didn't think. He just said yes.

Lee Shulman's area of expertise was doctors. He'd begun studying them in 1968, at Michigan State, as an outgrowth of an idea that first struck him in graduate school.

Besides education, what Lee had always found fascinating was thinking. The technical term was *epistemology*, the occupation of thinking about thinking. Like his idol John Dewey, Lee focused on higher kinds of thoughts, the mental operations that take place when a person moves from impression to question to understanding. "The pedestrian," wrote Dewey, "*feels* the cold; he *thinks* of clouds and a coming shower."

The psychology of thinking wasn't just fascinating; it also seemed painfully relevant to education. By understanding complex thought—the process of making knowledge—researchers would not just study schools; they would help improve them. And Lee had an idea for how to study thinking in a way that could make a real difference. Other early cognitive psychologists presented subjects with problems to solve, puzzles to answer, but Lee knew that, in real life, problems didn't come prepackaged. "A problem well put is half solved," John Dewey wrote. "Without a problem, there is blind groping in the dark." To get a true grasp on how knowledge was made, Lee intended to study the blind groping in action. He only had to find the right research subjects—people for whom problem solving was part of the natural habitat.

The idea of studying doctors arrived a few years into Lee's time at Michigan State, when a man walked into his office and introduced himself as the dean of the university's new medical school. "I understand you study complex problem solving," he said to Lee. "Well," he continued, "I think that's what medicine's all about, and we physicians don't begin to understand how that really works. Would you be willing to take 50 percent of your appointment and join the medical school faculty and do research on medical problem solving?"

Doctors. Of course! "It was such an epiphany," Lee says. Doctors solved problems all day. It was the heart of their work. Joseph Bell, Sir Arthur Conan Doyle's medical school professor and a surgeon with legendary capacities of deduction, had inspired Sherlock Holmes, the greatest professional problem solver in (fictional) history.

Lee said yes, and it was a perfect fit. Observing doctors at work with his colleague and childhood friend Arthur Elstein, he overturned the conventional wisdom about medical problem solving—and, ultimately, helped improve medical education in the process. Lee and Arthur designed simulations to approximate the circumstances of daily diagnosis and asked doctors to discuss their thought processes. Students played the patients. A lab room became the doctor's office, staged like a regular exam room except for the two huge video cameras mounted on the ceiling. Three real cases provided the basis for the actors' improvisation, and Lee and Arthur concocted a "data bank" with all the blood levels and X-ray results a physician might possibly request. As the doctors worked, researchers stood behind a one-way mirror watching them "think aloud," sharing the mental considerations that usually remain private.

On the first day, Lee, Arthur, and their colleagues got a preview of what they would find. Watching their first physician, a chief of medicine, the researchers expected events to proceed as all the medical textbooks recommended. First the doctor would interview the "patient." Then he would start ordering tests. Only later, after reviewing the results, would the doctor start outlining possible diagnoses.

But the work-up had barely begun when the chief of medicine turned to the researchers to announce his first diagnosis. What was going on? At first the team figured the chief of medicine must be a maverick, an outlier who followed his instincts. But as more doctors came into the lab, each one proceeded in a similar manner, suggesting two, three, even four possible diagnoses before even taking the patient's blood pressure. The maverick wasn't a maverick at all. The majority of doctors worked this way, exactly the opposite of the meticulous decision tree that textbooks advised.

But the method seemed to work. When Lee, Arthur, and their team ran their data, they found that doctors who made their first diagnostic guess earlier in the appointment got the answer right just as often as those who waited. If anything, it looked like the more guesses were made early on, the more likely the physician was to reach an accurate diagnosis. So much for moving "from symptom to sign to syndrome to disease," as one textbook prescribed. With one modest study, Lee and his team had discovered that medical decision making was far more complex than the textbooks portrayed.

Lee thought he could take the research even further. At Stanford, that was what he planned to do—extend the problem-solving findings, fleshing out their implications for education. And that, ultimately, is what he did. He just didn't realize quite what form the transformation would take.

After the NIE conference, writing up a report based on his panel discussion, Lee's first move was to borrow from his own work, crossing out the word *physician* and writing *teacher* instead. The clinical act of medical diagnosis became the clinical act of teaching; the questions about which lab tests to run became questions about how to group the students, arrange the classroom, and select a textbook. Where Nate had thought of teachers as collections of behaviors, Lee borrowed from the medical project and called them "information processors."

Lee had no expectations for his foray into the study of teaching. Cognitive scientists had started out by studying doctors, chess masters, and investors because thinking was an obvious prerequisite of their job. How much information was processed by people who spent their days telling small children, "One, two, three, eyes on me!"?

But studying teachers by studying their thinking turned out to be surprisingly generative. The process-product findings that Nate Gage championed might have been statistically significant, but they often seemed to contradict each other. It was important that every child stay "on task," but calling on students at random—the best way to keep them focused—was not always the best path to getting a good discussion going. Similarly, after asking a question, the most successful teachers waited a few extra seconds before accepting an answer. But successful teachers also tended to be the most brisk, spending the smallest number of minutes between topics. Pulling a single, clear answer out of the process-product research was like trying to distill laws from the Bible. One passage offered perfect clarity, but the next said the complete opposite.

Lee, who had spent his grade-school years at a yeshiva, met the task as perhaps no other psychologist could. "Think about the tradition of commentaries on the Talmud—this enormously long historical tradition of interpretation in which you never get to a settled conclusion," says Gary Sykes, who worked with Lee at Stanford. "It's brilliant intellectual work with a text. Lee took as the text intellectual life in classrooms. And from there, all was commentary and interpretation."

Take the problem of timing. How could it possibly be benefi-
cial both to be fast, moving quickly from task to task, and also
to be slow, pausing beyond the bounds of comfort before calling
on a student to answer your question? Lee explored this teaching
problem by examining what he called "the anatomy of a turn."
The process-product researchers had described the visible elements of turns: teacher asks a question, time elapses, student
answers. But to really understand the turn, you had to look at it
from the teacher's perspective.

Building on others' research, especially Mary Budd Rowe's
study of "wait time"—the pause between posing a question and
selecting an answer—Lee pointed out the logic in the apparent
paradox. For a teacher, each second spent waiting for an answer
held both promise and danger. On one hand, the longer she
waited, the more time the students would have to think. This was
good. On the other hand, the sooner she broke the silence with
the correct answer, the lower was her risk of exposing the class
to a useless diversion. This was also good. The wisdom and peril
of pausing were both true, and if you thought that didn't make
sense, well, that was true too. Wait times, Lee concluded, were
"blessings dipped in acid."

The question for teachers, as for doctors, was not, What is the
best behavior? It was, How do I decide which of many behaviors
to deploy for the case at hand? It was a problem of diagnosis.
Teachers had to locate their pupils' pathologies, determine a best
intervention, and act.

With doctors, diagnosis and treatment had clear beginnings,
middles, and ends. With teachers, the questions kept coming. Since the pathologies—that is, everything the child didn't
know—were not physical but mental, how could teachers diagnose them? How could they understand what a child had failed
to learn? And if they did manage to teach successfully, how could
they confirm it?

There was also the problem of scale. "The teacher," Lee realized, "is confronted not with a single patient, but with a classroom filled with 25 to 35 youngsters." Even if a teacher could locate pathologies and somehow do it for all her students, how did she manage to deploy the correct interventions, all at once, to the entire group? "The only time a physician could possibly encounter a situation of comparable complexity," Lee concluded, "would be in the emergency room of a hospital during or after a natural disaster." Studying teachers, he realized, was just as important as thinking about doctors; in fact, "it is far more germane."

The National Institute of Education conference came and went quickly. Lee moderated his panel; submitted his summary report, advocating the usefulness of studying teachers' decisions; and soon he was back at Michigan State, working with doctors. He might have forgotten about the trip altogether, had NIE not sent him a call for proposals to build a new research and development center to study teacher thinking and decision making.

Lee knew that his proposal would be a long shot. The likely list of applicants included Stanford University and his colleague Nate Gage. And since writing his famous handbook, Nate had made Stanford into the country's leading source of research on teaching. MSU, by comparison, was a "cow college," better known for training teachers than for studying them.

But Michigan State won. Among the losers were several of the universities that had been pulling government grants for behaviorist education research for years, Gage among them. "Nate lost his grant too," says Garry McDaniels. "In the old days they always gave him the grant. But the work that he had done had been going on for so long that I was convinced that it had reached its end."

Lee is fond of quoting a line from the psychologist Jerome

Bruner about narrative. One of the cognitive revolution's leaders and an early scholar of teaching, Bruner wrote that narrative is fundamentally composed of "the vicissitudes of intention." A protagonist sets out to do one thing, but along the way something unpredictable happens, and he decides to do another thing instead.

Lee set out to study thinking. By understanding minds, he thought, he could help improve education, the work of shaping them. The thing that happened along his way—the call from Nate Gage—led him to change not his intention, but his method. Doctors had provided a neat keyhole into the mind, but it turned out that another group of professionals offered a bay window. Teachers not only had to think; they had to think about other people's thinking. They were an army of everyday epistemologists, forced to consider what it meant to know something and then reproduce that transformation in their students. Teaching was more than story time on the rug. It was the highest form of knowing.

At a university, traditionally the highest degree holders are called *master* or *doctor*. "Both words," Lee discovered, "have the same definition; they mean 'teacher.'" What was the best way to show you really understood a subject, if not to teach it? And what was the best way to use research to improve education, if not to study teaching?

Without realizing what he was doing, Lee had stumbled on Dewey's lost project. Teaching was indeed the science of all sciences, the art of all arts, as Dewey's predecessor Francis Parker had put it. And now, thanks to Nate Gage's nudge, Nixon's investment, and his own lifelong obsession, Lee was going to pick up on the work Dewey and Parker had never finished.

Lee had written in the NIE panel's concluding report that "gifted practitioners are capable of performances which our best theories are not yet capable of explaining, much less generating or predicting." Future research on teaching, then, should explore the talents of the best teachers—the "wisdom of practice," he called it. All he needed to do was find the great practitioners.

Lee Shulman was no teacher, but he became one of two seminal figures in modern thinking about policies for improving the quality of teaching. The other figure was not a teacher either. And whereas Lee focused on education after spending time inside of it (or at least inside of a school of education), Eric Hanushek came to it wholly from the outside. He would go on to have as much of an influence on education as Lee did, if not more. But he never worked at an ed school.

Hanushek became fascinated with schools in the summer of 1966. He was nearing the end of graduate school in economics at MIT, still lacking a dissertation topic, when he stumbled on a remarkable story in the newspaper:

> **Washington, D.C.**—The Johnson administration Thursday was accused of ignoring results of a Federal investigation of inequality in city school systems because of political implications . . .

> After a survey of 600,000 school children and 60,000 teachers, the report concluded that pupils from poor families left school "with greater deficiencies" than when they entered . . .

> "This report means that all our education plans—increasing spending per pupil, more and better libraries and books, education devices—won't solve the crisis in our schools," said [Connecticut congressman Abraham] Ribicoff.

Given the redistributive goals of Lyndon Johnson's "Great Society" programs, it made sense that the administration would want to cover up the report. If the study, by a Johns Hopkins sociologist named James Coleman, was right, then one of the most expensive educational interventions in history had failed. According to Coleman, giving schools additional services— including more per-pupil spending, the supposed antidote to underachievement—did not help poor and African-American students overcome the challenges of their environments.

Hanushek couldn't quite believe it. "If in fact schools don't make much difference," he thought, "why are we continually pumping more and more money into schools to try and improve them?" There had to be something else going on, a lurking variable masking the money's impact. But what could it be? Running through Coleman's data, a massive set drawing from 645,000 students and more than three thousand schools across ninety-three different variables, Hanushek found no mistakes of consequence. Nor did a working group convened at Harvard to vet the research. Coleman's conclusions largely held up.

But what about other data? Hanushek pulled together a data set from a school district in California—much smaller in scope than Coleman's national sample, but with two advantages. First, instead of capturing a snapshot of one year in students' lives, the California data followed students longitudinally. Second, the data broke down students not just by school, but by the teachers they'd had. The extra detail enabled Hanushek to get more specific than Coleman; he could go beyond whether schools made a difference and determine whether *individual teachers* had an effect as well.

The effect of teachers was no simple thing to measure, even with the better data. Countless factors undoubtedly influenced students' performance in schools, from genetic disposition to the size of their parents' vocabularies. How could Hanushek discern the teacher's influence amid all these other variables?

The education literature offered no advice, but another area of economics did: the study of industrial production. Like teachers, factories receive certain raw products (steel, coal, plastics) and then put their own unique spin on the business of transforming them into, say, a Chevy Camaro. To measure the productivity of the manufacturing process, economists had to extract the value offered by raw products from the value provided by the plant assembling them. They did this by looking for patterns. What was the value of the raw products before they came to the factory, and how much did that value rise or fall after the manufacturer had its way with them?

Applying the idea to education, Hanushek could control for the effects of nonteacher variables, from home background to past performance, by searching for deviations. "If you follow an individual kid and you see him on some learning path, and then one year, all of a sudden, he learns a lot more than in another year, or all of a sudden he learns a lot less," Hanushek explains, "that gives you a hint that maybe it's something specific about the teachers, or something specific in that year. Then, if you see that all of the kids in the one class have this jump or this fall in performance, then you start to believe that it's something in that class."

The California data was full of such jumps. If Hanushek's method was right, teachers did make a difference, and the difference was big. Later he managed to put a number to the effect. Students assigned to the best teachers, he calculated, progressed by the equivalent of a whole grade level more than students assigned to the worst, as measured by test scores.

By Hanushek's method, teachers could do what the Coleman Report suggested schools could not: they could offset the disadvantage of poverty.

Perhaps Hanushek's most influential finding stemmed from his comparison of teachers' "effectiveness" (the educational equivalent of productivity) to other characteristics, especially salary. The amounts paid to teachers were based on how many years of experience they had and on how many degrees they had earned; a master's won a salary bump, and every additional graduate class won another. Yet the salary inputs seemed to have no bearing on the output: teacher effectiveness. Experience did matter, but only up to a certain point. In productivity terms, there was no difference between a teacher who'd been teaching for three years and a teacher who'd been teaching for thirteen.

Writing his final dissertation, eventually published as a book called *Education and Race*, Hanushek turned the observation into a suggestion—one that would reverberate for years into the future. If school districts stopped rewarding graduate study and experience, then they could redirect their investments into something more efficient: "Teacher Accountability," he called it.

Accountability would draw on the statistical method that Hanushek had adapted from studies of factories. "This procedure," he explained, "allows the ranking of teachers on the basis of teaching ability." Ranking and then rewarding teachers according to their effectiveness might create some problems—including, he suggested, "problems arising from attempts to 'teach the tests.'" (Held accountable for how their students performed on tests, teachers might emphasize the exam material to the exclusion of other, equally important lessons.) But, Hanushek wrote, "while we may not be at a point now where we trust standardized tests to hold up under concerted attempts to foil them, conceptually the problem appears soluble." A decade later, Hanushek gave his method a name: "value-added."*

In the same book, *Education and Race*, Hanushek made one more intriguing point. Like Coleman, he had only examined educational investments and their effects—comparing, in economic parlance, education's "inputs" to its "outputs." He had not studied education's vast middle. "The black box of the production process," he called it. That is, classroom teaching and learning. He had, in other words, followed the trail that Nate Gage and Lee Shulman were blazing, looking not just at schools but at teachers, yet he had followed them only so far. He looked at teachers' effects, but not at their work—at teachers, but not at teaching.

Hanushek made the observation as an aside, but the decision to overlook teaching's "black box" would prove just as influential as his "value-added" innovation. By studying teaching, Lee Shulman and his colleagues were about to explode many common ideas about how it worked, including the myth of the natural-born teacher. Hanushek, meanwhile, ignored teaching and, as a result, ignored how teaching worked. He could read his value-added research and draw the simplest conclusion, the one that matched what everyone already believed: some teachers were bad, most were fine, and a few were wonderful—as if they'd been born that way.

---

* The other researcher with a claim to having invented value-added calculations of teacher effectiveness is the statistician William Sanders, who developed the Tennessee Value-Added Assessment System (TVASS).

2

A TEACHER IS BORN

Deborah Loewenberg Ball arrived at the Spartan Village school in East Lansing, Michigan, in the fall of 1975. Technically still a college student, Deborah had never taught her own class before. Barely a decade separated her from the fifth-graders. But it did not take long for the other teachers to size her up. Mindy Emerson, who taught across the hall, could tell almost immediately.

As Mindy saw it, there were two types of teachers: those who chose to teach and those who were born to it. For the latter, teaching was not a job; it was a calling. (Mindy, for her part, decided she would be a teacher on her first day of kindergarten. "I walked in, I smelled the chalk, and I knew I was home," she says.) From Deborah's first day, Mindy could see that she, too, had been called. Deborah had finished high school early, and by the time she turned twenty years old, she spoke four languages. "She could have been whatever she wanted to be," Mindy said. But she was visibly giddy at the chance to teach, and her gift was undeniable.

Deborah had joined Spartan Village as a member of Michigan State's Elementary Intern Program, a teacher-training course that culminated in a one-year, immersive classroom experience at a local elementary school. Other new teachers went through a predictable litany of challenges. They couldn't get the students to listen, they tried too hard to be the students' friends, they doubted whether all the children could really learn, they struggled to feel comfortable in the new role. In one memorable case, one of Mindy's old classmates at MSU came back from her first classroom experience in shock: "The children are *touching* me!"

Mindy couldn't blame them. Teaching, after all, wasn't like other jobs, where new hires take on new responsibilities only after they've mastered simpler ones. "With us, when the kids walk in the door, you're on," Mindy said. "It doesn't matter if you've taught one year, ten years, or thirty years. You're on." And you are alone. "You feel like the lone ranger."

But if Deborah felt any of the typical jitters, she did not show it. She had a calm, gentle way with the children, connecting even with the ones who came unable to speak English (and there were many of them at Spartan Village, a public school literally on the wrong side of East Lansing's tracks, with more than the usual share of immigrants). Her discipline struck that rare balance, leaving the children both happy *and* well behaved. Mindy had never seen better penmanship: neatly lined print and cursive that made the discriminating heart flutter. And her lesson plans! Organized and comprehensive, they left nothing to chance. All Mindy could think was, *Wow.* "A natural-born teacher," she said confidently, thirty-six years later.

Even the new principal, a young woman named Jessie Fry, had to admit that there was something extraordinary about Deborah. And if Jessie had seen any weakness, she would have pointed it out. Jessie was strict. The teachers made no secret of their frustration with her mandates. Lesson plans turned in a full week in advance; goals and objectives outlined for every single child;

visits to every family's home by Thanksgiving; unannounced classroom observations, and always followed by a pointed note "FROM THE DESK OF JESSIE J. FRY."

Deborah was different. "Great!" and "Thank you!" and "You are coming along nicely," Jessie wrote, because when she watched Deborah teach, she couldn't think what to improve. Her only advice was to *slow down.* "She was animated, and she talked very fast, very fast," Jessie says. "I said, 'Okay, Deborah, you got to slow this down!'" By the end of her first year, Jessie had violated an unwritten law of the Elementary Intern Program. Tradition held that interns left after graduation to find a permanent job; that way, another intern could have a chance to teach the next year. But Jessie asked Deborah to stay permanently. Within two years, Deborah was petitioning her to create an unheard-of first-, second-, and third-grade combination class with another teacher. And, call Jessie naïve, she heard herself saying yes.

The staff slipped the custodian a little something extra, and he tore down the wall separating the two classrooms. Deborah, meanwhile, dragged in a working refrigerator and stove off of the street. For cooking lessons, she explained. (In high school, she had worked in a bakery; that was where she had met her husband, Richard, whose mother decorated the cakes.) She used baking as a teaching opportunity and also to help raise the money needed to take her students on a train trip to visit the Kellogg Cereal factory in Battle Creek. Together, she and her second-graders opened a "dessert restaurant"—staffed, of course, by eight-year-olds.

Some of the older teachers, already annoyed with Jessie, began to grumble. Why didn't every classroom have a stove? And how could they be sure that this special combination class wouldn't skim off all the best students? If Deborah is so creative, they suggested, Jessie should give her the troublemakers. But as the years passed, the grumblers became acolytes. They rearranged schedules so that their students could use Deborah's stove. They requested subs so that they could leave their own classrooms and watch Deborah teach. And sometimes, they invited her to join them in theirs.

By 1980, only one person in all of Spartan Village doubted Deborah's gift. That was Deborah.

Mindy, Jessie, and the others had one thing right. Teaching had become Deborah's passion. But she did not find it easy. To the contrary, her favorite part about teaching was how hard it was. Before deciding to become a teacher, she'd majored in French, taking classes in phonology and culture and philosophy. She seemed to enjoy courses in direct proportion to their difficulty. She also needed to study something that would lead quickly to a decent job. (Rich, the baker's son, was her high school sweetheart. Once they married, at nineteen, Deborah no longer had financial support from her parents.) The Elementary Intern Program offered both an intellectual challenge and a job.

She became particularly fascinated by the puzzle of how to teach children to read—a mystery for any literate adult, but especially so for Deborah, who had learned to read at age four and could not remember a time when words weren't synonymous with sounds and meanings. The job of a teacher was to explain to others what you already knew by heart. To teach children to read, Deborah had to understand all the things that make reading hard. Adults know intuitively all the different ways that "ea" can be pronounced, depending on the context. But teachers needed to be able to explain that *break, beak, read* (present tense), and *read* (past tense) all make different sounds. Same with the "r-controlled vowel." Few adults could explain it, but children certainly noticed the confusing way that "r" can transform a vowel from its usual sound to something entirely different—so that the "e" in *her* is nothing like the "e" in *hen*. Those children's teachers had to know how to help them figure that out, selecting specific words for each student to work on: *milk, store, lot, her; say, ran, down, right; laundry, laundromat, iron, fall, bag, them, from, girls*. Each group of words had a purpose, carefully selected to match exactly what the children needed to learn.

The next challenge was science, the other subject Deborah taught in that first year at Spartan Village. (The school was organized into departments, like a high school, with different teachers handling different subjects.) The Elementary Intern Program had no science equivalent to its reading course, and Deborah's own knowledge of science was limited to what she had learned in high school, where her teacher had staged a debate on the topic of whether evolution should be taught in school. (The teacher's position: no.) At Spartan Village, Deborah had to learn the content and pedagogy simultaneously. How did electric circuits work, again? What was the difference between a closed and an open system, and how did this apply to the systems that her students were supposed to study (weather, electricity, and heat)? What should she expect out of a third-grade science fair project? And why did the textbook think it was a good idea for third-graders to grow cotyledons and brine shrimp?

For every teaching problem Deborah conquered in those early years, a new one seemed to emerge. The greatest arose in 1980, when, teaching fifth grade, she discovered that her students were struggling with math. And not just a few of them. All of them. One day, twenty-five notebooks would fill with perfect little number houses as she walked them through the steps of long division. The next day, left to reconstruct the steps alone, the children would flounder. Weekends were her worst enemy. "My students would go home on Friday able to solve a long division problem and on Monday no longer seem to remember how to begin," she wrote, reflecting on the experience in an essay.

Worst of all, the students' misunderstandings included even the simplest ideas. Trying to subtract a number like 55 from a number like 72, the students would subtract up, taking 2 from 5 instead of 5 from 2, and decide the answer was 23. Deborah handed out bundles of sticks to represent tens and ones and repeatedly explained the idea of "borrowing"—take ten from the 7, carry it over to the 2—but her students would still make mistakes. Reading a word problem like "So-and-so has 12 and so-and-so has 20. How many more does so-and-so have than so-and-so?" the students would see the word *more*—and decide to add. But the question was asking how *many* more: the *difference*. A child who added because of seeing the word *more* either didn't understand the meaning of addition or hadn't read the words.

It did not escape Deborah's notice that a sizable number of these clueless students came from the very same first-, second-, and third-grade math classes she had taught with such apparent success a few years before. What had she been doing when she thought she was teaching? What had they been doing when she assumed they were learning?

Deborah's first move was to ask other teachers for help. But almost everything they suggested, she had already tried. She followed the textbook, divided the children into "skills groups" (the Triangles, the Diamonds, the Circles, they were called), constructed clear explanations, and used paper cutouts to illustrate key ideas. Yet when her tests came back, they told the same story. The children had not understood.

Stumped, she took her problem to a professor back at Michigan State's College of Education. The professor suggested that she try out a new experimental curriculum for elementary school math.

"Experimental" put it mildly. For first grade alone (Deborah had moved again after teaching fifth), the teacher's guide filled more than seven hundred pages. The curriculum was strange, suggesting that lessons move forward according to scripted discussions about, in one case, an elephant named Eli. ("There is an elephant named Eli who lives in the jungle and is always very hungry. What do you think is Eli's favorite food?" the guide suggested teachers ask, as a way to begin a lesson on negative numbers.) But the baffling methodology began to make sense when Deborah steered the students through the "dialogues" that punctuated each lesson.

On its face, the idea of a math lesson as an extended conversation, rather than a set of ideas and related practice problems (subtraction with regrouping, say, or counting), was as unusual as using an elephant story to teach math. Deborah had held discussions in reading, where students could talk about stories— discussing the characters and what the students thought might happen next—and in science, where they could guess the results of an experiment. But she had never led a discussion about math, and despite the assurances in the teacher's guide, she wondered whether her students would really have much to say. 2 + 2 always equaled 4. What was there really to discuss?

Yet when she tried it, the curriculum began to show its wisdom. Eli the elephant, for example, turned out to love peanuts— and his peanuts took two forms: regular peanuts and "magical" ones, which were like negative numbers. When a regular peanut and a "magical" one met, it was like adding 1 and –1: both disappeared. Following the story, Deborah's first-graders quickly picked up the idea of negative numbers—a concept that often befuddled much older students.

In discussions, meanwhile, the challenge wasn't in getting the students to talk, but in making sense of all they had to say. The deeper into the math the students got, the more questions they presented to their teacher. For instance, are there "afinidy" possible ways to use a 24-story building's elevator to get to the second floor—or are there 25?* What exactly did it mean to add a negative number? What about to subtract one (for example, 3 minus –5)? Even rudimentary ideas now raised complicated questions that Deborah felt unprepared to answer. Talking about math was surprisingly interesting, but for the talking to lead to learning, it seemed the teacher needed to know something more.

Once again, Deborah turned to Michigan State, this time not to the College of Education, but to the Department of Mathematics. As an undergrad, she had tested out of math completely. Now she started from the beginning, venturing through elementary algebra, geometry, and calculus while her students studied addition, subtraction, and fractions. The courses produced some exciting aha! moments, as when the details of limits and integrals helped her steer students through a problem about area.

The most important revelation arrived in her final course: Number Theory. Taught by the chair of the math department, a professor named Joseph Adney, the class addressed a mathematical subject Deborah hadn't studied before (one deeply relevant to an elementary school teacher). And, even more important, Adney taught it in a new way. Instead of marching methodically through a list of concepts, he invited his students to discover the ideas for themselves. He'd write something on the board and then ask, with a straight face, "Is that always true?"

Deborah found herself thinking about these problems for

---

*The correct answer depends on the problem's assumption, which wasn't given. If the passenger can stop only once, then there are only 25 ways to get to the second floor. If trips can include multiple stops, then the number of possible trips is infinite.

hours. Sometimes the writing on the board took the form of a statement: a "conjecture," Adney said. A conjecture was like the mathematical version of a hypothesis, a question without a question mark. The sum of two odd integers will always be even, for instance, or the sum of an even and odd integer will always be odd. *Is that always true?* When the students came up with arguments—proofs—he would present everybody's attempt without prejudice. Then they'd have to defend their reasoning before the class. If anyone could find a counterexample, then poof! The conjecture would explode.

Deborah had seen proofs before. But she had never been asked to make one from scratch, and she'd never realized how many different proofs could support a single statement. Adney took special interest in oddball proofs (Deborah, with her abbreviated math background, was a connoisseur of these). The more diverse ideas they could pull together, the richer was their exploration of the math.

Discussions in Adney's class were not just fun ways to pass the time. They were vital to the work of *doing math.* By talking about math—puzzling over problems, making conjectures—they practiced it. In the process, Deborah—the classic humanities type, who never took a single left-brained class in college—fell in love with the subject. The math she'd learned in school was dull, rote, blah—"uninspiring at best, mentally and emotionally crushing at worst," she wrote not long after taking the class. The procession of rules and procedures flattened any latent pleasure in the neat finality of the right answer. (*"How many more"* = *subtraction*, she'd reminded her students at Spartan Village just a few years before. *Subtract the ones first.* And always *subtract down.*) Sometimes the procedures made sense. More often, they were just a predetermined path to the right answer. Adney presented a different subject altogether. In his class, math was powerful, rich, even awe inspiring. For days, a problem boggled. But then someone would offer another way of looking at it, and suddenly it would make sense.

What would it look like to teach elementary school children math in the way she was learning it? Adney, who taught undergraduates, could take her only so far. Deborah needed another resource.

A few years after her classes with Adney, Deborah decided to teach a summer school section outside her usual repertoire. She'd just taken a class on research methods, and the material had struck her as potentially powerful for eight- and nine-year-olds. In particular, she wanted to teach inferential statistics, a kind of math in which students use tools like curves and intervals to draw conclusions about data. But, finding no research or curriculum on how to teach the subject to young children, she'd had to create the course from scratch. This proved more challenging than she anticipated, so she decided to recruit help. Not a coteacher—the class had only eighteen students, a perfectly manageable number for one person. What Deborah needed was another brain. Better yet, a dozen of them.

Recruiting teachers was simple; by participating, they could cross off a required professional development session. Every day that summer, before the children arrived, the group walked through the lesson Deborah had drafted, trying out problems, imagining how students might react, and discussing what Deborah might say in response. When the lesson began, the other teachers served as extra eyes and ears, studying each child and noting what they did and did not understand. At the end of each day, Deborah had the students leave their notebooks behind so the teachers could study those too. Then they all sat together and talked about what had just happened. What did everyone think about what this or that student had said? What ideas did the class still not seem to grasp? What should Deborah do tomorrow?

In a way, this method was no different from her normal practice. At Spartan Village, she frequently pulled other teachers into her class to help her solve problems. But at Spartan Village, moments like these were merely friendly favors offered by busy colleagues. At the summer program, the group's focus was sustained, the tone serious; it was as if they were not in an elementary school, but in a laboratory. Or maybe, Deborah thought, a surgical theater.

Technically, only Deborah taught the children. But really she was the group's surrogate—a kind of "pedagogical daredevil," she decided, trying out ideas on everyone's behalf. "Whatever we decided to do," she wrote later, "I was the one who had to try to make it fly." The group, meanwhile, formed her safety net, making sure the students didn't become casualties of the experiment.

The students learned, and, just as importantly, so did Deborah. Looking back, she says it is impossible to recall any one moment of epiphany. Her teaching was evolving quickly, and she hadn't yet begun to make records capturing each lesson and the discussions that followed. But similar public lessons, held years later, at the annual program known as the Elementary Math Lab, shed light on what she and those first co-conspirators must have seen that first summer in 1984.

During a lesson in July 2012, a group of observers took notes from bleacher-style seats as Deborah asked a class of rising sixth-graders to consider a rectangle. The rectangle looked like this:

What fraction of the rectangle, Deborah asked the students, is shaded? The first student she called on, a girl named Anya, gave the correct answer, ¼, explaining how she had drawn an additional line to help her solve the problem:

But when Deborah asked for comments on Anya's answer, a boy named Shamar, with puffy cheeks and long dreadlocks, said something curious. "I think the answer was one-half and a one on the side of it," he said. The mysteries multiplied when Deborah brought him up to the board to explain. "1 ½," he wrote. But he kept saying the number backward, as if reading from right to left: one-half first, then one, which he called the "remainder."

What was he thinking? Under what assumptions might 1½ make sense? Scrutinizing Shamar's responses during the debriefing Deborah held after the lesson, once the students had left, one group of observers pieced together a hypothesis. Perhaps he had flipped the question. Instead of looking at the fraction of the rectangle that was shaded, he focused on the fraction that was empty. He might have even seen the image as its inverse:

Others focused on Shamar's description of 1½ as "one-half and a one on the side of it"—more like ½ 1 than 1½. Maybe he had transcribed the inverse image into the numbers that it resembled: ½ on the left, 1 on the right. If you saw math as a set of rules and procedures, as so many children were taught, then you did not think about fractions as holding meaning. They were simply numbers with lines through their middles.

Whatever his exact thought process was, Shamar had clearly become confused about an idea that stood at the heart of fractions—one that, over the years, Deborah and those who joined her at the lab had come to see as a typical stumbling block for children (and many adults): the idea of the whole. To answer any fractions problem, you had to define the thing that you wanted to know a fraction *of.*

In this case, the whole was the largest rectangle, the one that also happened to be a square. Shamar's answer suggested that he had defined a different rectangle as the whole—the one that, with its longer sides, looked more like a child's idea of a rectangle. (Children often do not understand that all squares are rectangles too, just with equal-length sides.) If you defined that slimmer rectangle as the whole, and you accepted Shamar's inversion of the shaded and empty space, then 1½ made sense.

The misunderstanding offered an opportunity. Encountering the math through the students' eyes, the group could figure out what needed to be clarified. Then together, these observers could figure out what Deborah might say and do to get Shamar to understand the importance of defining the whole.

There were many possible paths into the material: questions to ask, explanations to give, problems to assign. Over the course of many teaching labs, the most productive methods and problems made themselves clear. One good approach was to have students with different ideas present them to the class. Some of them undoubtedly shared Shamar's misunderstanding, in one form or another. (Even adults in the room could forget sometimes that a fraction was meaningless without its unit.) Listening to their peers could help the confused students sort out their ideas. When a boy named Eduardo jumped in to clarify, Shamar seemed to understand his own idea better too. Then, when Eduardo explained why he agreed with Anya anyway about ¼, Shamar decided to change his answer.

The lab group also studied turns—which students Deborah called on, in what order, and what she asked each of them to do. Her decisions had come to hold more significance over time, as she learned the many different types of turns, each with varying dimensions of both academic difficulty (offering a math fact versus offering an interpretation) and social risk (giving an answer even though you hadn't raised your hand was moderately risky; coming up to the board and offering a detailed description of your incorrect answer, much more so).

Other considerations mattered too. To make sure everyone participated, it was advisable to call on the three students who had not spoken yet, but this might not be a good strategy if all three had the same answer. Order also made a difference. In certain cases, there was wisdom to calling on, say, Anya before Shamar. Shamar's answer had assumed an idea that Anya's, by drawing in the previously invisible line, made explicit—that fractions made sense only if they formed *equal* parts of the whole. The discussion would go better if Deborah could get Anya's idea on the table before tackling Shamar's confusion.

Over time, more conventions emerged. It was crucial, for instance, to make sure that students did not talk just to Deborah, but to the entire class. Everyone had to learn everyone else's name. Then, instead of saying "that weird idea about one-half and one beside it," they could simply say "Shamar's idea" or, if Shamar posited an argument, "Shamar's *conjecture.*"

Deborah came to see these named conjectures as "fence posts" for a productive conversation. The students could peer backward over the landscape of their evolving understanding and name the key turning points. And when another part-whole misunderstanding inevitably arose, they could undo it more quickly by thinking back to Shamar's idea and the reasons it didn't hold up.

The precise wording of questions also mattered, and the lab

group spent hours debating Deborah's constructions. That same year, hoping to introduce students to the concept of infinity— one of those dazzling ideas that could spin in a student's mind for days—she had presented a problem with endless answers. Then, asking the students to guess how many solutions they could come up with, she added an extra question, apparently as an after-thought. "After you write down your answer," she asked, "can you write how long it will take [to come up with all the solutions]?"

The lab group devoted several minutes to considering the value of that extra question. By asking the students to write down how long writing the solutions would take, hadn't Deborah suggested that writing them all down was actually possible? And so, argued a teacher from Chicago, hadn't the question inadvertently tilted the students away from the correct answer? But the question had done exactly the opposite, another group of teachers argued. "We could be doing this *forever*!" the students might realize, thereby jumping closer to the key idea.

The group dissected the problems Deborah selected too. On the day of Shamar's misunderstanding, another confusion had arisen—this one not about the whole, but about the parts. Count-ing the shaded part and then counting the total number of parts, some students had called the fraction ⅓. They had missed what Anya saw about drawing a line to make the parts equal. The class discussed why dividing a shape into equal parts was important, but some lab observers wondered whether all the students really grasped this idea. One person offered a proposal. In the next class, why not present a problem that forced the students to draw even more lines? Something like this:

The next day, Deborah added the problem to the warm-up.

Back at Spartan Village, the lessons from the early summer labs—which began in 1984 and continued for years after—were combining with the new curriculum to create a kind of magic. Now that the students conjectured, reasoned, argued, and proved, they were building one idea on top of another. They sometimes forgot what they'd learned, like all students do. But now, when they stumbled, they could pick themselves up. Deborah saw it happen one day a few weeks into the fractions unit, when two third-graders were puzzling over a problem about cookies that involved the number $\frac{4}{2}$.

"How can we have this?" Betsy asked Jeannie, pointing to the confusing fraction.

"I don't know," Jeannie said.

"Four *twoths*?" Betsy asked.

"We take something and divide it into two parts . . . and take *four* of those parts?" Jeannie asked.

"I'm confused," Betsy said.

"Me too," Jeannie said.

Just then, Sheena walked up. "Four *halves*, isn't it?"

"Yeah!" Betsy exclaimed. "Four *halves*! Halves are two parts. So . . ."

"So we need two cookies and cut them each in half, then we have four halves," Jeannie said. "One, two, three, four. Twoths. I mean halves."

While Deborah worked on the puzzle of how to be an effective teacher, another question pulsed in the back of her mind: Why hadn't she learned any of this before? As a double major in French and elementary education, she'd taken a methods class, supposedly about how to teach math. Later, of course, she'd taken nearly the entire strand of university-level math classes. But none of these classes had prepared her to help children learn math. That class did not exist.

The trouble, she suspected, lay in the kind of knowledge one needed to teach well. It fit in neither the category of general education nor that of pure math, though both kinds of knowledge were helpful. In addition to the math itself, she reasoned, math teachers needed to know the kinds of activities and tasks that turned a student's slippery intuition into solid understanding. Not only did they have to master procedures, concepts, and the special cycle of conjecture to argument to proof, but they also had to know the students: how much they were capable of; the iterative, circling way in which they learned; and the kinds of representations—the particular configurations of pictures, numbers, and blocks—that best helped them to understand.

No wonder the class did not exist. It would have had to teach a subject with no name. Even Deborah—who was now both a teacher at Spartan Village and the special "math helping teacher" for all East Lansing elementary schools, not to mention a doctoral student at Michigan State's College of Education—could not articulate the parameters of this knowledge. But that began to change in the mid-1980s, when she decided to study teachers' mathematical knowledge as part of her dissertation.

Her hunch was that Michigan State was still not equipping future teachers with the knowledge and techniques they would need. But to be sure, she devised a test, a short set of teaching problems that she thought math teachers should be able to answer, and gave it to education majors about to graduate.

One question described a group of eighth-grade teachers who "noticed that several of their students were making the same mistake." When multiplying large numbers, like 123 × 645, their students "seemed to be forgetting to 'move the numbers.'" Their work looked like this:

```
    123
x   645
    615
    492
    738
   1845
```

when it should have looked like this:

```
     123
x    645
     615
    492
   738
   79335
```

"While these teachers agreed this was a problem," Deborah's question went on, "they did not agree about what to do about it." She turned the question to the future teachers. "What would you do if you were teaching eighth grade and you noticed that several of your students were doing this?"

To answer the question well, Deborah decided, teachers would need to identify the ideas the students lacked. Two were particularly important. One was the concept of place value, the convention that gives integers different values depending on where they sit, so that the second 3 in 79,335 actually means 30, whereas the first one represents 300. The second missing idea was the distributive property, which explains why the common procedure depicted in her second picture worked—why, in order to find 123 × 645, you could add up the results of three multiplication problems (123 × 5, 123 × 40, and 123 × 600). By not moving the numbers over, eighth-graders showed they had followed a procedure blindly, and then fallen over the inevitable cliff. To help them understand the steps that *did* make sense, a teacher would have to acquaint them with the reasons why the algorithm worked.

As it turned out, of the nineteen future teachers Deborah interviewed, only five mentioned either idea. Most described how they would remind students of the right steps, especially what a teacher named Teri called "shift[ing] things over." Some referenced the idea of place value, but obliquely, without remembering its name, meaning, or why it was important. "Since you are working with such a large sum," explained a teacher named Rachel, "you have to know how to work in the thousands, you know, to keep your numbers that way."

They had taken classes in both education and math, but the Michigan State students didn't have another kind of knowledge required for teaching—"pedagogical content knowledge," Lee Shulman called it. Not just teaching methods or the intricacies of the subject, but the perfect mix of the two.

Even future high school teachers with a joint major in math struggled to produce clear explanations. More often, like a teacher named Barb, they remembered the reason for the procedure only in the course of trying to explain it, and then stumbled through it. " 'Cause you're going to take 5 times that, and you take 40, and then 600, and you can see where those zeroes come from," Barb told Deborah. Deborah could see, but would Barb's student?

Other questions were as puzzling to the math majors as to everyone else. One query asked the future teachers to come up with a way to represent a common part of the curriculum, division by fractions. Deborah picked a specific problem: 1¾ ÷ ½. Math teachers, she reminded her interviewees, often try to explain problems by relating them to real-world situations or "models that make clear what something *means*." Could the interviewee think of a situation or model for 1¾ ÷ ½?

A good answer would help the students visualize what it

means to figure out how many ½'s go into 1¾. In her dissertation, Deborah described one possibility: "A recipe calls for ½ a cup of butter. How many batches can one make if one has 1¾ cups of butter?" The answer was 3½ batches, because 1¾ cups of butter contains 3½ half cups. The story not only represented the problem; it clarified the concept, offering the students one way to imagine division (as creating groups of a certain size) and cutting through the confusion of defining the whole by making the unit clear. 3½ whats? 3½ halves.

Once again, of the nineteen interviewees, only five came up with representations that Deborah could call mathematically correct. And of those five, only one made up a representation that was decipherable, though it lacked the crispness of the butter example. (The teacher said she would use a number line to mark off 1¾ and ½, and then ask the students how many ½'s went into 1¾.)

The other four teachers-in-training offered examples that, while correct, strained even Deborah's imagination, like one by a young man named Terrell. He said he would have students imagine getting three pizzas: one whole pizza, ¾ of another pizza, and ½ of a third. Then he would ask them to imagine placing the ½ pizza on top of the first and then the second pie, each time taking away that amount of pizza. How many times would they perform this strange ritual before there was no pizza left?

Deborah asked Terrell to explain what the answer, 3½, would mean in this story. Terrell stumbled. "The answer," he said, "would be how many times you got a whole half (if you want to say that). Of the . . . whatever's left over, what part of it is *of* the half, I guess you could say." He obviously knew what fractions were, but when it came to explaining the idea to another person, he was at sea.

Another five future teachers came up with stories or diagrams that did not actually represent the problem. Several made up problems that divided 1¾ "in half"—that is, by 2 instead of by ½. The remaining eight came up with nothing.

Deborah didn't extrapolate the finding in her dissertation, but the reader had to wonder: Besides Deborah herself, how many people at the College of Education could have answered even one of those questions correctly? How many teachers at Spartan Village?

In 1984, MSU announced the arrival of a new professor with a unique joint appointment. Magdalene Lampert (or Maggie, as everyone called her then) was to serve as both assistant professor of education at Michigan State and, simultaneously, math teacher for grades four and five at Spartan Village. She was both a researcher of education and a practicing math teacher. And, as Deborah soon learned, not only could she have breezed through all the questions on Deborah's quiz; she could have written a better one.

Magdalene came from Cambridge, Massachusetts, but she might as well have sprung from Deborah's imagination. Here, in silk blouses and pulled-back blonde hair, was Deborah's special teaching knowledge personified. Magdalene spoke about problems the way a potter talked about clay, turning them over to see just what they could do and then saving them for the perfect opportunity. The best problems, the ones that really pushed students into just the right mathematical territory, Magdalene deemed "rich," "open," "productive." In class, she infused lessons with the ideas and also the habits of math, teaching her fifth-graders to "confer," "conjecture," and "prove." Confronted with a student's wrong idea, she often spied the hidden misunderstanding faster than anyone else.

And just like a good math problem, she gave nothing away. With lips pursed, her face was perfectly opaque. "Nobody knew what the right answer was for Maggie," said Thom Dye, whose fifth-grade classroom at Spartan Village became her home (and the place where she eventually taught Awad, Ellie, and Richard about "rate," helping them see how far a car going at 55 miles per hour would travel in 15 minutes). "She's very stoic. And so the students had to look to themselves for the correct answer . . . They couldn't just say, 'Oh, it's the right answer because the teacher said so.'" Magdalene gave them no other choice. They had to think.

The fact that Deborah hadn't met Magdalene until she came to MSU made the resonance between their work that much more incredible. What did it mean that two people, living hundreds of miles apart, had stumbled on the same approach—Deborah's still nascent, Magdalene's far more developed, but in spirit the same? In time, as they began collaborating—Deborah learning from Magdalene—the work they were doing, the specific *kind* of teaching, began to demand a name, an easy tag for referencing in discussion, like one of Deborah's students' fence posts. Unable to come up with something adequately distinctive, the Michigan State faculty settled on a compromise: "This Kind of Teaching"—TKOT (pronounced *tee-kot*)—or, sometimes, "teaching for understanding," though no one really liked that term. ("What other kind of teaching is there?" someone would inevitably ask.) More specific labels simply didn't fit. *Progressive*, for instance, was a political movement, not a pedagogical approach; *constructivist*, meanwhile, had to do with a theory of learning, not teaching. So they stayed purposefully, playfully vague: "This Kind of Teaching" would do fine.

Deborah protested the impulse to name; the teaching she and Magdalene did, she insisted, was simply *teaching*, not a special subset or approach. They taught so that children learned. Wasn't that the whole point? For her part, Magdalene acknowledged that her teaching was a kind of "existence proof": living evidence that it was possible to teach math in the way Deborah aspired to teach it.

A graduate of one of the country's most prestigious ed schools—the Graduate School of Education at Harvard—Magdalene Lampert had eschewed a conventional academic path. After getting her doctorate, she'd taken a job teaching elementary school math at Buckingham Browne & Nichols, a private school in Cambridge, Massachusetts, that also doubled as a teacher-training program, working with students from nearby Lesley College. There, her classroom, a loft space shaded by trees, became her laboratory. Her daily journal entries chronicled the room's happenings—her own ideas as well as her students'. At Harvard, she'd read the formal research on teaching, but none of it harmonized with her own experience. Between lessons at BB&N, she took careful and thorough notes, reassembling the day's events into an account of what teaching really entailed.

She was happy at BB&N and had no desire to leave. But with the grant he'd gotten from the National Institute for Education, Lee Shulman had built Michigan State a new research group that suited Magdalene perfectly: the Institute for Research on Teaching (IRT). Charged with exploring what Lee called the "wisdom of practice," IRT professors were expected not just to do research and not just to teach future teachers, but also to teach school. In other words, at Michigan State, Magdalene could do everything she'd been doing at BB&N, except with the support of a full research university. She was sold, and soon she had conscripted Deborah into her cause—the transformation of Spartan Village into a full-fledged teaching laboratory, a project that came to transform both women's careers.

Magdalene first got the idea from a former colleague, who made a career of teaching school, teaching teachers, and writing about his teaching, all at once. To help unlock her own hidden teaching expertise (the pedagogical content knowledge behind her TKOT), Magdalene had turned her classroom into a petri dish open for study. At BB&N, back in Cambridge, her observers had been the cohort of teachers she worked with. At Spartan Village, a small army of teachers-in-training, grad students, and fellow professors followed her turns. On any given day, two dozen or more ed school students left Erickson Hall and drove past the football stadium and over the train tracks to the Spartan Village school. There they crowded into the back of Magdalene's classes (and, soon, in Deborah's too), taking notes.

But Magdalene quickly found that her observers failed to see the subtlety of her methods. It was as if their microscopes were smudged. They saw only the least important details. After all, Magdalene's most important work, her moment-to-moment decisions about what to do, lived only in her own head. If she interrupted her teaching to make them visible—to think aloud— she stopped teaching. Deborah had used the metaphor of a surgical theater. But unlike surgery, the act of teaching took an entire year. In that way, it was more like a novel. Skipping one chapter meant missing everything.

An MSU graduate student offered a suggestion. Why not videotape an entire year in her class, starting with the first day and going all the way to the last? It was a "wild idea," Magdalene reflected later. But it was the mid-1980s by then, and technology was improving fast. (The grad student had come to MSU by way of a new company called Apple Computer.) Magdalene and Deborah both already kept diligent journals, but video would expand their data dramatically—and help convey it too. Video, after all, could be paused as well as rewound. To review a particularly productive or confounding turn, all an observer would have to do was click a button.

Working with Deborah, Magdalene drafted a grant application, and by the 1989–90 school year, the two of them had recruited two teams of graduate students—the Lampert team and the Ball team, they called themselves—to do the filming. Careful schedules outlined which days the grad students would man the cameras and which days they would take notes. Each student was on a quarter-time appointment, which paid enough for just ten days of work per month. But after a while, the students began giving up their days off because they didn't want to miss anything. This Kind of Teaching, TKOT, might have a ridiculously vague name, but it was riveting.

"They couldn't keep us away," laughs Kara Suzuka, who was on the Ball team. "It was just hard not to be there. You know, the story continues! I mean, class just ends, and they still don't have a resolution. Kids are still confused. Or they *just* came up with an incredible conjecture, and you don't know what's going to happen with that. You know, are they going to use it? What's the next thing? . . . It was just a very compelling story." Just how compelling, they had no idea.

Hyman Bass first watched the videos in 1996, after a package of VHS cassettes arrived in his campus mailbox at Columbia, where he was then a tenured mathematics professor.

Sixty-four years old, having worked in math for decades already, Hy was known professionally for expanding a new field of algebra. But he had also taken a late-career interest in the way children learned his subject in schools. As far as he was concerned, math was not just beautiful and fascinating, but vital. "One of the noblest expressions of humanity," he said. Yet, instead of encountering the beauty of the discipline, children slogged away at a mere facsimile.

This was hardly a new worry. Math education's woes had

always drawn extra attention in the United States. Partially, this had to do with the country's belief in the economic power of the so-called STEM fields (science, technology, engineering, and math). Another factor was poor test scores. US students regularly ranked behind Canada, Germany, and Japan, reflecting a math aversion that plagued many of their parents too. As a country, it seemed, Americans simply were not "math people."

Hoping to make a difference, Hy joined policy groups, math education boards, and advisory panels. Despite the progress being made by Lee Shulman and his colleagues at Michigan State, the most prominent education reforms in the 1980s stemmed from economist Eric Hanushek's ideas about accountability— an attention to outputs rather than inputs, production rather than process. "The conventional wisdom about public schools is that they face serious problems in terms of performance and that improving schools requires additional money," Hanushek explained in a 1981 article. "However, the available evidence suggests that there is no relationship between expenditures and the achievement of students." Instead of investing in traditional remedies like lower class sizes or better teacher training, he wrote, "more attention should be given to developing direct performance incentives."

The attention to incentives manifested as a movement to craft more demanding educational standards. The tragic flaw of the public school system, standards advocates argued, was that it had neither attended to the outputs of its students nor defined what those learning goals should be. Of course the schools wasted money; the system literally had no standards!

Following the trend, Hy's early forays in education focused on writing better goals. He was serving on a board devoted to just this task when he met Deborah Ball. Deborah was unlike anyone else Hy had met in math education. While he believed in the power of standards, the efforts to write them felt disconnected. Everyone seemed to have an idea of what better math learning could look like, but no one could describe it, and they had certainly never seen it. Deborah was the first person he met who actually seemed to know something about the school side of the equation. She was also the first person to imagine a way that Hy himself, with his extensive math background but limited knowledge of classroom teaching, might be helpful. So when she asked him to review the videotapes that she and a colleague had made, Hy said sure.

Now, popping the tape into his VCR, he knew his instinct had been right. The video opened on a classroom that looked, at first glance, ordinary. At the front was a long, green chalkboard with little posters pasted on either side; in the middle stood the standard beige desks with smooth, laminate tops and built-in storage below. And of course, there were children—nineteen of them. As the video opened, one child stared listlessly at the floor, her head slumped onto the back of her chair; another perched his chin on his hand, pensive; a third pulled her desk open, super quick, and grabbed a pencil. The scene couldn't have been more mundane. Yet the class was unlike anything Hy had ever seen.

The first voice to break the silence was Deborah's. "More comments from the meeting?" she asked from the side of the room, out of the camera's sight. A transcript explained the context. The day before, the third-graders had held a meeting with a group of fourth-graders who'd taken Deborah's class the previous year. The "Conference on the Number Zero," the fourth-graders had called it, lining up their desks in an authoritative row to present their findings on a question the third-graders had only just begun to puzzle over. Was zero even, odd, or, as some children argued, neither one?

Now it was a day later, and Deborah was giving the third-graders a chance to debrief. The discussion, she figured, would last only a few minutes. They'd talk quickly about what they had learned (zero is even),* and then they'd move on to the real plan for the day, an activity Deborah had been anticipating for weeks. A few days earlier, working on a problem she'd designed specifically for this purpose, the students had come up with conjectures about the properties of even and odd numbers. An odd number plus an odd number, they'd noticed, always seemed to equal an even, while two evens always made an even. Now, she wanted to see if they could do what no third-graders she knew had ever done before. She wanted them to prove the statements true—not just for the numbers they'd tried so far, but for *all* numbers.

It wasn't to be—not that day, anyway. Before she could get through the discussion, Deborah found her plan hijacked by a tall boy named Sean. She wouldn't regain control for another several days.

"Sean?" she'd said, noticing his hand.

"I don't have anything about the meeting yesterday," he said, "but I was just thinking about six. I was thinking that it can be an odd number too, 'cause there can be two, four, six, and two—three twos—that'd make six."

"Uh-huh . . ." Deborah said.

"And two *threes*. It could be an odd and an even number. Both! *Three* things to make it and there could be *two* things to make it."

Deborah jumped in. "And the two things that you put together to make it were odd, right? Three and three are each *odd*?"

"Uh huh," Sean replied, "and the other, the twos were even."

Maybe, she thought, Sean was responding to the earlier com-

---

* Like all even numbers, zero can be divided evenly by 2, is surrounded on either side by odd numbers, and when it is subtracted from an even number, produces an even result.

ment about how even numbers can be made up of two even numbers. Maybe he wanted to point out that some even numbers, like six, were actually made up of two odd numbers instead.

Knowing they'd get to all that in just a few minutes, Deborah decided to let the idea rest. "Other people's comments?" she asked, returning to the debriefing.

But Cassandra, a tall girl with a yellow hair clip, who raised her hand next, was stuck on 6. "I disagree with Sean when he says that six can be an odd number," she declared, rocking her chair back on its legs. "Because—"

Hy watched Cassandra stand up and walk to the board, where she picked up a long pointer. "Look," she said, directing the pointer at the number line high above the chalkboard and landing it on zero. "Six can't be an odd number, because this is, um"—she pointed to zero—"even." She walked through the rest of the numbers, "Odd, even, odd, even, odd," until she landed on six. "*Even.*" She turned back to Sean. "How can it be an odd number?" But Sean persisted. "Because," he said, "because six—because there can be three of something to make six, and three of something is, like, *odd.*"

Next came Keith, who threw up his hand. "That doesn't necessarily mean that six is *odd,*" he said, to a chorus of agreement from the class. "Just because two odd numbers add up to an even number doesn't mean it has to be odd."

Hy marveled as the video continued. These third-graders—not a gifted class, but average, public school third-graders from, Deborah said, a wide range of backgrounds and ability levels—were having a real mathematical debate. One of them had made a claim, and then the others were trying to prove him wrong. Cassandra's proof followed a classic structure. First, she had invoked one definition of even and odd—the fact that integers alternate between the two types on a number line—to show that six could only be even. Then she had drawn out a counterargument. To be odd and still fit the alternating definition, she'd shown, zero would have to be odd too. But, she'd concluded with a flourish, they had just decided the other day that zero was even. QED: Sean's conjecture was impossible.

Deborah had asked Hy to watch the video for important mathematics. Well, here it was: a third-grader doing a fairly sophisticated mathematical proof.

More proofs followed, none of which helped Sean articulate his idea. Jeannie reminded her classmates of their working definition of an even number—one "that you can split up evenly without having to split one in half." Sean had agreed that, yes, 6 fit that definition. Later, from Ofala, a girl from Nigeria, came a derivation of a definition the class apparently had not made before, for odd numbers—"my conjecture," Ofala called it. If even numbers were those that could be split evenly in twos, without any left, then odd numbers were those that also "have two in them, except they have one left." Drawing out six lines, she showed, there were none left. "I already *have* all the twos circled," she said.

But the most intriguing proof belonged to a little girl in a purple headband, the one who'd started the day staring at the floor: Mei. "Oh!" she'd exclaimed, out of nowhere, not long after Deborah had declared herself confused. "*I* think I know what he's saying! . . . What he is saying is that—you have three groups of two, and three is an odd number. So six can be an odd number and an even number." That is, it could be even because 6 is broken into groups of two, but odd because the number of groups of two is odd. "Is that what you're saying, Sean?" Deborah asked. Finally, it was!

Mei was not done. She had clarified Sean's argument, and now she intended to destroy it. "I *disagree* with that," she said, when Deborah asked her opinion. "Here." She was already halfway out of her seat. "Can I show it on the board?" Before her teacher could say yes, Mei was pushing in her chair and marching to the board. Sean, still standing at the board, took a step to the side to make room. "It's not according to, like, how many groups it is," Mei said, her long, black hair wagging from side to side behind her as she reached the board and grabbed a piece of chalk. Her head barely reached Sean's elbow.

She explained. "Let's see if I can find . . ." she said, pointing her chalk at the green board and staring ahead, deep in thought. Her voice was high, even for a nine-year-old. "Let's say ten." She began drawing a line of circles. "One, two," she counted. She drew ten in a row. "And here are ten circles," she said.

Sean stood with his back against the board, watching Mei press down her chalk again. "And then you would split them," she was saying. "Let's say I want to split them by twos. Go one, two . . ." She drew vertical lines between every other circle. The board looked like this:

"Well, look!" she said, gaining speed as she tapped each pair with her chalk—"one, two, three, four, five!"—and turned to face Sean, who now had his entire body facing hers.

"Then why do you not call *ten*, like—a—," Mei stopped for a moment, and Sean said something, but she didn't hear it. She had turned to face the rest of the class, and she was throwing her hands out to either side of her, summing up her case like a trial lawyer reaching the climax of a closing statement. Just as 6 divided by 2 produced an odd number (3), 10 divided by 2 was 5—another odd number. Why didn't Sean call 10 "an odd number *and* an even number?" Mei asked. She dropped her hands to her sides and stepped back, scratching her nose. Case closed.

Mei had missed the key sentence, but it had not escaped Hy.

Right in the middle of her crescendo conclusion, Sean had mumbled the following four words: "I disagree with myself." To Hy, all this was stunning—an extraordinary episode of mathematical reasoning, enacted entirely by nine-year-olds. First, Mei had pulled off something that is often challenging, even to mathematicians. She had listened to Sean's confusing argument, and she had translated it into an impeccably clear explanation of his own thinking. Mei's analysis helped the class, and it also allowed Mei to articulate to the whole group why she disagreed.

What she did at the board was even more amazing. Until that point, all the arguments against Sean had followed the same pattern: Sean made his claim, and then the students attacked the conclusion, offering up different proofs of why 6 was actually even. Mei took a much more sophisticated stance. Instead of challenging his conclusion, she challenged his reasoning. And in the process, she took a leap Sean had not yet made or even seen. Six, she showed him, wasn't the only number that met his odd-groups-of-two criteria; 10 did too, and possibly others.

"What about *other* numbers?!" Mei had said. "Like, if you keep on going on like that, and you say that other numbers are odd and even, maybe we'll end it up with *all* numbers are odd and even. Then it won't make sense that all numbers should be odd and even, because if all numbers were odd *and* even, we wouldn't be even having this *discussion*!"

Sean seemed to have no choice but to fold. Except, that's not what happened. After a pause—Mei staring at Sean, Sean staring at Mei, Mei scratching her nose, Sean rocking back and forth—Sean extended his gratitude. "I didn't think of it that way," he said, smiling. "Thank you for bringing it up. So, I say it's—ten can be an odd and an even."

Instead of quieting Sean, Mei had unleashed him. Not only that, but soon other students were joining his cause, deriving more numbers that fit his criteria (not just 6 and 10, but also 14 and even 2!). When Deborah tried to steer the conversation to a close—one more idea, she allowed, "but then I think maybe we're going to have to stop with this"—it was no use. The children, Hy thought with delight, had been ignited.

Not only were they constructing proofs. They had invented an entirely new category of numbers. "Sean numbers," Deborah christened them a few days later, deciding to turn the diversion into an opportunity to enhance a point she'd been trying to teach, about how to make mathematical definitions. (A point, she had to admit, that the Sean detour had offered multiple chances to underscore, what with Ofala's new definition of odd numbers and Jeannie's restatement of the definition of an even number.)

When the video came to an end, Hy considered the question Deborah had asked him. What math could he see in the videos? He'd seen math in the kids, of course, but also in Deborah. Upon reflection, it was the teacher, not Sean or Mei or Ofala, who had provided the kids with two critical turning points. Deborah had directed them back to their "working definition" of an even number, laying a foundation for discussion. Sean, in calling 6 "even and odd, both," was actually positing an entirely different definition. And then there was the moment, right after Mei suggested that 10 fit his criteria too, when Deborah suggested that the children consider 14—the launch point that had sparked a girl named Riba to derive another mathematical definition. In fact, Riba had shown that, if you followed Sean's logic, every fourth number on the number line could be called "odd and even."

Another mathematician might look at "Sean numbers" as a mistake. After all, numbers that met the boy's criteria were, ultimately, even. But Hy knew that math was all about definitions— coming up with the specific rules and restrictions that made one number positive and another negative, or one prime and another composite. The usefulness of these definitions determined which ones stuck and which ones mathematicians discarded. The concept of Sean numbers would ultimately end up in the dustbin, but by inventing the numbers in the first place, the students had learned something fundamental about how to think about math, something they certainly wouldn't have gotten just from learning the difference between odd and even.

Deborah amazed Hy. He had viewed only what she had done on this particular day. But what about everything she had to know to get to this point? The problems she'd had to pick, the habits she'd had to teach, the decisions about when to let a detour happen and when to shut it down? Every amazing student epiphany in a TKOT classroom reflected an equal capacity on the part of the teacher orchestrating it. And Deborah's capacity was unlike anything Hy had ever seen. "Watching Deborah teach," he said, "is like listening to chamber music."

He liked it so much that, not long after watching that first tape, he handed in his resignation at Columbia and moved to the University of Michigan, where he took a joint appointment in the math department and the education school. Standards, curriculum, and assessments were important. But math education, he had realized, could not change unless the teachers could turn those tools into everyday lessons. He and Deborah began a formal inquiry into the kind of knowledge required to teach math well. Soon, they had a definition of their own—and a name: Mathematical Knowledge for Teaching, or MKT, "the mathematical knowledge, skills, habits of mind, and sensibilities that are entailed by the actual work of teaching." The math version of Lee Shulman's pedagogical content knowledge. The wisdom of expert practice.

Some parts of MKT overlapped with knowledge held by any educated adult, but other parts, like knowing how to analyze incorrect or nonstandard solutions, identifying the student thinking that might have produced an incorrect answer, anticipating likely student errors, and understanding what kinds of representations offer the best explanations, did not. Even Hy, a professional with decades of experience, did not possess these parts of MKT. And later, administering a test of MKT, he and Deborah saw that neither (to the subjects' horror) did other mathematicians.

In time, the Sean episode went viral, playing at conferences from California to Korea. Magdalene Lampert's class, meanwhile, was featured in *Life* magazine and eventually came to inspire an entire television show on PBS: a math program for young children called *Square One TV* in which noir detectives George Frankly and Kate Monday of "MathNet" worked to solve a new case each week. (In addition to the cases cracked by MathNet, recurring sketches offered the two-minute television equivalent of Magdalene's problem of the day. In the "Bureau of Missing Numbers," distressed citizens reported absentee numbers to an FBI-style investigator, who hunted them down by interviewing witnesses about their characteristics; "Prime Club" depicted a nightclub that admitted only prime numbers; a musical number parodied "Climb Every Mountain" in a song about counting to the highest number.)

The two teachers—Deborah Ball and Magdalene Lampert— were a form of proof themselves, evidence that a different kind of teaching was possible. If two women in Michigan could teach this way, people began to wonder, why couldn't everyone?

3

SPARTAN TRAGEDY

It was one thing to prove that excellent teaching was possible, quite another to teach it to people without the extraordinary skill of Magdalene Lampert and Deborah Ball. In 1982, after Lee Shulman left Michigan State University for Stanford, the woman who took responsibility for that task was Lee's original IRT partner in crime, a Michigan native and former teacher named Judith Lanier.

Judy modeled her reform efforts on two of the schools where she'd been trained herself—*lab schools*, they were called. Even back then (she started teaching in the late 1950s), the schools had been the last of a dying breed. Lab schools, in turn, were the offshoots of another antiquated institution, the "normal" school, a college alternative that thrived in the early twentieth century before universities took over the job of training teachers.

Aimed both at training future teachers and inventing better ways of teaching, normal schools served two kinds of students: kindergarteners through twelfth-graders and, simultaneously, the college students who wanted to learn how to teach them. Each normal school was really two schools: the "normal" part, for teacher training, and the lab, or "practice," school, where K–12 kids learned while the future teachers watched and, eventually, stepped in to try out teaching themselves.

John Dewey's lab school at the University of Chicago, which he inherited from his mentor Francis Parker, fashioned itself on this model. Judy's own experiences—first at a lab school in Paw Paw, Michigan, and later at a school in Milwaukee, Wisconsin— showed her the model's power. In Paw Paw, she and her fellow teachers learned to keep detailed logs of their daily practice. Later they met with researchers to go over what they'd done, receiving lectures in a building adjacent to the school. The lab school in Milwaukee even had an upstairs viewing area, a glassed-in catwalk raised around the classroom's perimeter, from which education students could sit and observe, opening the glass window to eavesdrop on the lesson without interrupting its flow. Afterward, the students and their professor would go over teaching problems together.

Working at the lab school changed Judy's view of teaching. Originally, she'd taken up the work by default. (When she finished high school, in the early 1950s, women seemed to have only three choices: nursing, secretarial work, and teaching. Since Judy disliked blood and found office work boring, teaching was it.) But after the experiences in Paw Paw and Milwaukee, teaching was no longer a job she had settled for. It was, she saw, a craft—one that a person could spend a lifetime mastering.

As the years passed, however, the lab schools, and the view of teaching they supported, became increasingly obsolete. The main trigger was universities, which began to add the lucrative teacher-training business to their repertoires, putting normal schools out of work. But in taking over teacher training, universities marginalized it. Instead of training, their professors—men more like the psychologists William James and Edward Thorndike than like the former schoolteacher Francis Parker—focused on research that offered "hardly a nod toward the public schools," Judy later wrote. At the university, "schoolteachers and young learners, who should be the focus," became a "sideshow to the performance in the center ring."

An Oxford professor named Harry Judge, touring American ed schools at the request of the Ford Foundation, described the university approach as "the doctrine of Anything-But." That is, ed schools were "anything but schools of pedagogy," an ed school professor told Judge.

The doctrine of Anything-But began with professors. In his final report, Judge described how faculty recruitment happened at a fictional university he named Waterend—a composite representing the elite ed schools he'd toured:

> The dominant tactic was to make a foray into the disciplines, to track down a scholar of achieved distinction or of sparkling promise, and to carry him triumphantly through the gates of Waterend. Thereafter, the professor would be careful to explain that this was the first appointment he had ever held in a school of education, that he was unsullied by contact with the lower worlds of educational practice, that he was first and foremost a Waterend Professor—with at least a courtesy appointment in another department as well.

At land-grant universities like Michigan State, which Judge satirized as a fictional place he called HSU, the same practices ruled, but on a larger scale. Instead of a handful of unsullied psychologists, he observed, HSU's ed school hired sixty.

At both Waterend and HSU, education professors tended to feel more loyal to their discipline of origin than to the study of education. Among the subjects of interest, Judge recounted, a professor of education might study "the history of the family, the role of the media in the formation of public opinion, the structure of higher education, the changing shape of macroeconomics, or the evolution of organisational theory" before ever visiting a classroom. The neglect was sometimes benign (for example, Lee Shulman studied doctors before his encounter with Nate Gage), but often it was outright hostile. One professor told Judge how happy he was not to have to work with "dumb-assed teachers."

Fueling the doctrine of Anything-But were the perverse pressures of tenure. Even those with good intentions learned that the work that led to that ultimate academic accolade did not also lead to good schoolteaching or teacher training. A young professor might be a masterful trainer of undergraduate teachers, but her CV needed to list publications like "Sex Stereotypes of Secondary School Teaching Subjects" if she wanted a job after grad school.

Judge concluded that the tradition, while "indefensible," was nevertheless unchangeable. The universities depended on ed schools for tuition and thus suppressed reform. The ed department became "our dumping ground," one professor told him.

When Judy Lanier arrived there in 1964, as a graduate student, the MSU ed school epitomized the doctrine of Anything-But. It was a "good old boys' paradise," Judy told one historian. The reigning clique of big-thinker types met regularly in the lounge on the top floor of Erickson Hall, where they spent hours smoking their pipes, sipping coffee, and generally infuriating the rest of the faculty, who noted with aggravation that they rarely strolled in before 10:00 a.m.

These "good old boys" had little interest in research on teaching. When Judy first described her dissertation idea—a study of the features that separated excellent teaching from mediocre cases—several senior faculty told her that the project was impossible. They were unimpressed by her proposed methodology: surveying principals, teachers, and parents and videotaping the teachers with the best reputations. This was the mid-1960s, pre–Nate Gage, and most studies had failed to identify any common ingredients of good teaching. The faculty doubted there was any way for Judy to identify the best teachers, much less to discern what made them succeed.

MSU's "teacher educators," meanwhile, formed a distinct, marginalized group. While the "good old boys" enjoyed light teaching loads and ample time for research, the teacher educators endured monumental class sizes, heavy loads, and slim to nonexistent research budgets.

As for teacher preparation itself, rigorous tracks like the Elementary Intern Program that fed Deborah Ball into Spartan Village were rare. A typical American undergraduate, Judge's report had observed, could pass through the courses necessary to become a teacher even if she suffered "a prolonged fit of absentmindedness."

Rather than closely guided classroom experiences, the average MSU education student followed a three-part curriculum. First, there was the overview of the academic subjects, basic survey courses, taught by what Judy considered the department's lightweights. Then came the "foundations" courses in the psychology, history, and philosophy of education, taught by the most junior of the "good old boy" types (including, when he first arrived, the young educational psychologist Lee Shulman). Finally, there were the methods classes, taught by the teacher educators. In theory, these focused on the craft of teaching, the "how" rather than the "what." But more often they reflected what Judy called the "boots and galoshes" vision of teaching—"the idea," according to Francesca Forzani's history of the period, "that all teachers needed to learn was how to help children dress for recess."

Next, future teachers embarked on the student teaching experience, ten weeks in a classroom buoyed only by whatever limited guidance their host teacher could provide. Sometimes, Judy observed, schools assigned student teachers to their weakest staff members—the ones who struggled to keep the children in order and could use the help. During her own student teaching, at Western Michigan University, she'd wound up doing more of the teaching than the host teacher did.

In 1980, when she became dean of the ed school, Judy upended the doctrine of Anything-But. Instead of dallying in other disciplines, professors would spend their time mining the secret wisdom of teachers, modeling for the entire school the approach that she and Lee Shulman had perfected at the IRT. They would transform MSU into a modern version of her lab school in Paw Paw. Michigan State would set an example for universities across the country, raising the level of teaching nationwide.

Judge's scathing report to the Ford Foundation in 1981 might as well have been Judy's blueprint. First came housecleaning. Judy cut ed school spending by 40 percent. In return, she extracted a promise from the provost: a 25 percent *increase* for future initiatives focused on her mission. Then she went in search of new hires. Just as she and Lee had done at the IRT, Judy recruited professors whom other ed schools might have ignored, faculty who were expected to conduct research about teaching and to train teachers. The goal was not just to do teacher education, but to transform it. Judy even convinced Harry Judge to join the cause. For five years, he served a joint appointment, working at both Oxford and MSU.

She capped off her hiring spree in 1984 with Magdalene Lampert. Magdalene had sworn off ed schools long before then, banishing herself instead to the classroom at Buckingham, Browne & Nichols. Her experience at the Harvard Graduate School of Education had thoroughly disenchanted her. Of all the listings in Harvard's course catalogue, only one had the word "teaching" in its title—and she ended up marrying the professor, David Cohen. But even David, a historian by training, had never taught school himself. He had only recently moved from studying education policy and history to observing classrooms. "Crouching," he called it.

Not only that, but Michigan State was a cow college. When Magdalene and David first visited MSU, one of the first departments they passed had a sign that announced, in bold MSU green and white, "DEPARTMENT OF SHEEP TEACHING AND RESEARCH." Another: "SWINE TEACHING AND RESEARCH." Erickson Hall, home of the education school (human teaching and research), sat on a street called Farm Lane, less than a minute's drive from a long stretch of cornfields. Finally, they passed a sign reminiscent of home: "AI School," it said. "Well, in Cambridge, that's MIT, and that's artificial intelligence," David says. At Michigan State, "AI" meant artificial insemination.

But Judy Lanier took what was most foreign about the Midwest—that staggering flatness, the swine—and spun it as an advantage. As the country's first land-grant university, Michigan State prided itself on its commitment to producing knowledge for the field, literally. In the nineteenth century, it was a professor at MSU who first devised a procedure for hybridizing corn, helping to modernize agriculture.

The education school, Judy explained to Magdalene and David, could do the same for teaching. With such a huge student body, their experiments might change the lives of thousands of student teachers in classrooms throughout Michigan each year. Equip them with the right ideas and skills, and they could change education.

How could Magdalene say no?

Judy Lanier's ambitions were not novel. Efforts to transform teaching stretched back to the early nineteenth century. In a speech to a gathering of school leaders in 1830, an educator named Warren Coburn announced that he wanted to extinguish what he called "the old system." In that approach, "the learner was presented with a rule, which told him how to perform certain operations on figures . . . But no reason was given for a single step," Coburn wrote. "As he began in the dark, so he continued; and the results of his calculation seemed to be obtained by some magical operation rather than by the inductions of reason."

But the "old system" was still current in 1911, when the mathematician Alfred North Whitehead described the "road to pedantry" offered by most school math. Poorly taught, with a focus only on brute memorization and not any of the subject's more intricate concepts, he said, the great science became like the ghost of Hamlet's father: "'Tis here, 'tis there, 'tis gone." Nor had much changed by 1957, when the competitive panic wrought by the Soviets' *Sputnik* launch inspired a fresh curriculum called the "New Math"—a program of study that, Suzanne Wilson summarized in her history of American math reforms, would help "any normal human being [to] appreciate some of the beauty and power of mathematics." The state of math teaching as Deborah Ball and Hy Bass encountered it in the 1990s showed how well that had gone.

Math got the most attention (not to mention more research dollars), but it was not the only school subject to inspire, and then resist, calls for change. Studying classrooms in Portland, Oregon, in 1913, a survey team found pedantry everywhere. In geography, "the questions, almost without exception, called for unreasoning memorization of the statements of the book." In grammar, much of the work "had little meaning for most of the children." In history, "there was not the slightest evidence of active interest in the subject; the one purpose seemed to be to acquire, by sheer force of memory, the statements of the assigned text." Yet in 1970, the journalist Charles Silberman was still diagnosing "mindlessness" across the board. This was the story and, perhaps, the destiny of American schoolteaching: always admonished, never changed.

But Judy Lanier benefited from good timing. Like-minded comrades might have come and gone before, but none had arrived at a moment as auspicious for teaching reform as the 1980s. One advantage was the emergence of academic research that, for the first time, bolstered (rather than ignored) educators' notions that learning was more complicated than Nate Gage's behaviorism suggested. Studying the inner workings of the mind, the new breed of cognitive scientists had found that learning did not respond to common teaching techniques.

One study examined the math capabilities of child street vendors in Brazil. Selling coconuts and watermelons on the street, the children tabulated prices and counted out change with impressive facility. But when the researchers transferred the problems the children had encountered on the street to paper, the children floundered. Over and over again, the researchers watched them miscalculate in the same way: by incorrectly following procedures they had learned—and completely misunderstood—in school. They were more than capable of complex computation. School just seemed to conspire against their ability to do it.

The pattern repeated itself again and again. On the street, a child would improvise mental math to figure out his customer's price. Then, on paper, he would switch off that part of his mind—the part where multiplication and division represented real transformations—and instead do his best imitation (often incorrect) of the steps he'd been taught to memorize in school. It was as if the two problems were completely separate: one an actual manipulation of real numbers, the other a series of steps performed to please a teacher.

A twelve-year-old boy who had just fluently calculated the price of 4 coconuts at 35 *cruzeiros* a coconut, 140 *cruzeiros*, was flummoxed when researchers presented him with the exact same problem on paper. 35 × 4? Instead of following the same calculation he'd done a minute before in his head ("Three will be 105, plus 30, that's 135 . . . one coconut is 35 . . . that's 140!"), he tried to walk through the multiplication procedure he'd learned in school, stacking one number on top of the other:

$$\begin{array}{r} 35 \\ \times \quad 4 \\ \hline \end{array}$$

He got the main pieces right, correctly multiplying the 4 by 5 to get 20 and then carrying the 2. But instead of waiting to multiply 4 by 3 before adding the carried 2, he added the 3 and 2 and *then* multiplied by 4. He produced his answer for the researchers—200—apparently without wondering about the difference from his first calculation. School, the study suggested, not only failed to help students learn; it actually seemed to confound them.

In addition to the cognitivists, an even more powerful group had begun to influence schools in the 1980s—the business and political elite. Alarmed by new international tests showing that US students were falling behind their counterparts around the world, these CEOs, elected officials, philanthropists, and advocates worried about what the apparent downturn might mean for the national interest. After all, the economy was shifting from moving and making physical objects (cars, food, coal) to constructing what economists called "information products" (software, video games, cell phone calls). Floundering American students did not seem poised to participate in this new economy.

One CEO, Alfred Taubman, a billionaire businessman whose empire included the A&W restaurant chain, became alarmed about schools after a major product flop. Hoping to challenge the famous McDonald's Quarter Pounder, he'd released the A&W one-third-pound burger—at the same price. But though the A&W burger beat the Quarter Pounder in taste tests and value, the one-third-pounder did not sell. Only after hiring a market research firm to mount customer focus groups did Taubman understand why. Half the participants in the focus groups believed that A&W had overcharged. "Why should we pay the same amount for a third of a pound of meat as we do for a quarter-pound of meat at McDonald's?" they asked. Some customers actually thought that a third, having to do with the number 3, was less than a fourth, having to do with 4.

The math abilities of customers augured poorly for those of workers. "When companies have to spend billions of dollars providing remedial instruction in reading, simple math, and problem solving," Taubman concluded, "that's a double tax." They paid once for the official education system, through government taxes, and then, when the schools failed, they paid again for their own.

Economic competitiveness was on the mind of President Reagan's first secretary of education, Terrel Bell, when he commissioned a study of American schools in 1981. Titled *A Nation at Risk*, the report described the deteriorating condition of the American education system. Of special concern was the fact that even students with basic competency failed at the "higher order intellectual skills" that would be vital in the postindustrial economy. The *Nation at Risk* report launched dozens more. One history concluded, "Within a few years, it was no exaggeration to speak of a 'movement' for school reform."

Reformers waged their fight on many fronts. Over time, the

most prominent was the push for standards. After *A Nation at Risk*, governors began meeting to plot new learning standards—a development that sowed the seeds for the No Child Left Behind law two decades later. Judy Lanier, meanwhile, used the budding concern to build an impressive coalition around her reform agenda: transforming the study and training of teachers. When Terrel Bell announced the *Nation at Risk* report, Judy traveled to Washington, DC, for the occasion. Later, Bell visited Michigan State, where he gave an award to Judy and to the Institute for Research on Teaching. Judy's advisers also included Alfred Taubman, Jim Blanchard (the Michigan governor), and the leaders of several national philanthropies. Rallying the reform movement to her cause, Judy didn't have to persuade the establishment about the importance of training better teachers. For the moment anyway, she *was* the establishment.

But, Magdalene Lampert would later ask, exactly what did teachers need to learn, and how were they going to learn it? Not long after Magdalene agreed to come to MSU (she signed on for a provisional two-year stay, short enough for David to keep the option of returning to Harvard without losing his tenure, and long enough for her to give MSU a real shot), a teacher named Ruth Heaton came to embody the challenge of teacher education.

A first-year graduate student, Ruth first met Magdalene midway through the school year in a state of distress. She'd come to grad school to become a teacher educator, but despite nine years of experience in elementary school classrooms, her confidence was suffering at MSU. All around Erickson Hall, she heard people diagnosing the pitfalls of the traditional math classroom. And, with horror, she realized that for nine years she had been perpetuating those same mistakes.

Magdalene took Ruth on as her new student. She put her on

the Lampert team, the group of grad students who came to watch her teach during the year of the videotapes. The following September, Magdalene installed Ruth in a fourth-grade class right next door to her own. Ruth became the math teacher for that class, as well as Magdalene's unofficial apprentice. Twice a week, Magdalene sat in Ruth's classroom, watching and composing comments. In the years that followed, both women taught each other; Magdalene taught Ruth how to teach math, and in turn, Ruth taught Magdalene how to teach teaching.

One early lesson started off simple and then got more complicated. Watching Magdalene and Deborah teach, Ruth had grasped the importance of getting her students to talk. In her math lessons, she dutifully plied the fourth-graders with questions, often imitating Magdalene and Deborah word for word. "How do you know that?" "What do other people think about that?" But although she asked the right questions, she wasn't sure what to do with the students' answers. As a result, class discussions felt less like explorations and more like a series of dead ends. Each comment fell with a thud—the sound of no one thinking.

In one typical sequence, Ruth introduced a lesson on functions. She was using the same experimental curriculum that Deborah had tried with her first-graders. Following the teacher's guide, Ruth had the class make up a list of numbers that fit a simple function: $f(x) = x + 10 + 2$. Plug in any number for x, and what would you get? The students came up with a list easily: 99 and 111, 8000 and 8012, 250 and 262, 4988 and 5000, and so on.

Next, Ruth was supposed to ask them what patterns they saw in the numbers. The teacher's guide described the rich dialogue that would ensue. The students would make sharp observations—if the number on the left is even, then so is the number on the right; the number on the right is always bigger than the number on the left—and then, as in one of Magdalene's or Deborah's lessons, they would move from noticing to verifying ("Is this always true?") and from verifying to a deeper understanding. Who knew, maybe they'd even invent a new class of numbers!

Instead, it was another dreary parade of dull ideas marching nowhere. There are two "80s," one student offered, pointing to 8000 and 8012. Another pointed to 8000, 111, and 5000. "Here is three zeroes in a row and three ones in a row, and then three zeroes in a row," the student, a boy named Richard, said. What was the pattern? Ruth asked hopefully, and he said it again: "000, 111, 000."

Ruth was despondent. "I felt like I was floundering today," she told a colleague later that afternoon. But where Ruth saw failure, Magdalene saw room for improvement. Ruth knew her students needed to talk about math. She just didn't know how to turn the talking into learning. That was what Magdalene would have to explain.

To teach math to a child, the best strategy was to design a productive problem. To teach TKOT, Magdalene needed a parallel opportunity, a *teaching* problem to help Ruth see the difference between her solution (repeating the question from the textbook) and other, better possibilities (a more fertile way of responding to students' ideas).

A productive teaching problem arose one day in late September, when Ruth assigned the fourth-graders a problem of the day:

What whole numbers could be put in the boxes?
$$26 - \square = \square$$

Instead of plunging into the problem, like Magdalene's students always seemed to do, Ruth's diverted. "What's a whole number?" one girl asked her. Thrown off guard, Ruth tried to answer the question quickly and move on. She directed the girl to the number line on the wall, which displayed a list of whole numbers. But instead of returning to the problem, the same student piped up again. "I don't understand," she said. "What's *not* a whole number?" Frustrated by this waste of time—they needed to be coming up with solutions, not debating the directions!—but also trying to listen to the students, Ruth paused one more time, helping the students list more examples of whole numbers.

Watching from the sidelines, Magdalene saw a classic teaching problem. Ruth seemed to have missed what the girl was asking for. She didn't want *examples* of whole numbers; she wanted a *definition*. That was why she asked the second question, "What's *not* a whole number?" There was no easy solution to this problem (or to any teaching problem, for that matter), but Magdalene could help Ruth think more carefully about her response. She could, for instance, help Ruth see the value in listening to what students were asking her for. Sometimes, a teacher needed to steer students away from questions that threatened to take them off on tangents because, sometimes, the tangents *were* a waste of time. But in this particular case, clarifying the students' confusion about whole numbers was core to helping them work on the task. They needed to know what a whole number was before they could think of whole numbers to fit in the boxes.

Magdalene could also help Ruth devise a better response by helping her understand the math she was dealing with. Her decision to point to the number line had its merits, as it gave the students a ready and visible list of possible numbers to try. But Ruth had confused the whole-number numerals written on the line with the line itself, which represented not only whole numbers but also all the fractions in between. Magdalene understood the confusion. "Within *mathematics* the importance of the number *line* is that it represents *continuity*," Magdalene wrote in a note to Ruth. "That is, it represents the idea that there are always more numbers *in between* the other numbers." The challenge for teachers was to walk the line between these two equally important uses of the number line—a stock of discrete numbers to draw on, and also an expression of continuity—without confusing the students or being incorrect.

Reading over Magdalene's note later, Ruth felt relief. There was no magic bullet that took students' ideas and created a rich conversational environment. But there were better and worse ways of making sense of their comments—and better and worse ways of responding to them. For instance, had Ruth done a better job of listening to what it was the students actually wanted—a *definition*—she could have focused her efforts on helping them generate one. And to get them there, she could have elaborated on a move that Magdalene pointed out approvingly, when Ruth suggested that a student discuss the meaning of *whole number* with other students at her table. Instead of just letting them talk, she could have steered their conversation toward the right answer. The key to moving a discussion forward was to listen to students' questions, figure out what they needed to understand, and construct a response to pull them there.

When Ruth finally managed to pull this off, she didn't even notice she'd done it until Magdalene pointed it out to her. Magdalene always scribbled comments right after watching a lesson and then gave them to Ruth to read before they discussed them in person. This time, Magdalene's note underlined a certain moment, when Ruth had told the students, "I want to show you something." "Did you get some kind of 'bright idea' about how to pull all this together when you said [that]? Or were you following the script?" Magdalene wrote in her observation note that day. "It seemed to me as if you were more engaged here, more thinking about the kids and the subject matter and the representation rather than reading the manual."

At first, reading the note inside her car in the Spartan Village parking lot, Ruth had no idea what Magdalene meant. "Did I get some bright idea? What moment was she referring to?" she thought. At home that night, she opened the audiotape she had made of the lesson, found the "I want to show you something" moment, and hit play. The lesson had begun like so many others, with Ruth throwing out questions and the students handing back duds. They plodded on like this—nothing interesting, no grist for exploration—until, more than half an hour into class, a boy named Arif stepped to the front. The problem was $2 \times (3 \times x)$, and they were trying it out with different numbers standing in for x. In this case, x equaled 35, and another student had offered the solution, 210, counting out the calculation with checkers. Arif volunteered to do the problem another way.

But now he stood at the board, stuck. Ruth listened again to the awkward silence that followed. "I am confused," Arif said. "Why?" Ruth asked. "Because over here we added three of them [35] and we got 105," Arif said, "and I thought over here we were supposed to add two more of them." He meant two more of 35, but the other student had added two more 105s, not two more 35s.

Ruth could remember the moment now, and Magdalene was right—she had been struck by a "bright idea." While preparing for class, she herself had misread $2 \times (3 \times x)$ as $3 \times x + 2 \times x$. She had soon realized her error; the problem actually called for multiplying, not adding—for tripling x and then doubling the product. This was a common misunderstanding of multistep multiplication. When Arif said he thought they should add two more 35s, Ruth could tell he'd made the same mistake. "Does anybody have thoughts for Arif about this?" she asked the class.

A student named Bob jumped in, but Ruth heard herself cut him off. She remembered why. Knowing exactly where she wanted the discussion to go—a point about order of operations and the properties of multiplication—she had seen almost immediately that Bob's answer wouldn't take them there. He hadn't understood Arif's confusion, so his comment wasn't going to move anything forward.

That was the moment when she said those words—"I would like to show you something here." She walked the class back through their steps, starting with $35 \times 3 = 105$. "Now," she heard herself saying, "and this is what some people were having problems with, I want to double this." "This" meant the 105—not, she was making clear, the 35. She drew an arrow from the 105 and wrote "$2x$" over it, the class's symbol for multiplying a number by 2.

A chorus of "Ohhhhhhhh" filled the room.

Listening to the tape, Ruth experienced her own aha! moment—not about math, but about teaching. "I did see what they needed," she wrote in her own journal. "The point was to see the connection between addition and multiplication . . . They were missing the point and I could see that."

In her notebook that night, Ruth paraphrased the lesson she took from Magdalene's comment. "Things came together in that moment because I was thinking about the subject, listening to the students and trying to make sense of what they were saying," she wrote, "and then I acted." Discussions wouldn't work if she simply let the students talk on their own. The best exchanges actually happened when she figured out what the students needed to understand and guided their conversation to a place where she could teach it to them.

By the end of the year, the challenge was not how to get a discussion going but how to end it. (Class often went on straight through the bell, stopped only by the cries of other children making their way to lunch.) Ruth still had a lot to learn, but the success was undeniable. Now her only question was, "How do I keep it up?"

At Spartan Village, Ruth wasn't the only one mastering the techniques of TKOT. Down the hall, a veteran teacher named Sylvia Rundquist was studying with Deborah Ball the same way Ruth watched Magdalene—and changing her own teaching in response.

Sylvia was nineteen years older than Deborah, and her teaching experience dated back to the 1960s. She taught third grade but gave her class over to Deborah for math. Sitting in the back of her own classroom during Deborah's hour each day, she became a student herself, full of questions. Was zero odd or was it even? Why wasn't -7 prime if 7 was? Did 7×4 really mean something different from 4×7? One morning each week, she and Deborah met outside of school, talking over the answers. (Zero is even; negative numbers aren't prime because they're all divisible by -1 as well as 1; and yes, though they both have the same answer, the difference between 7×4 and 4×7 is an important concept for math teachers to know.)*

* Though it's true that the two expressions are equivalent (both equal 28) math teachers need to see that 4×7 and 7×4 represent different ideas: one means four groups of seven; the other, seven groups of four. (Imagine, for instance, seven cars with four wheels each versus four cars with seven wheels each; both have a total of twenty-eight wheels, but through very different means.)

The distinction grows even more important in division. The corollary of the idea that 7×4 is different from 4×7 is the fact that there are two ways to understand the meaning of $28 \div 4$. One, called *partitive* division, asks questions like, If we have 28 wheels and 4 cars, how many wheels can we give to each car? Another, called *quotative* division, asks, If we have 28 wheels, and we know we need 4 wheels per car, how many cars can we fit with new wheels? In both cases, the answer is 7, but again, the configurations look very different.

Watching Deborah teach made Sylvia question her own teaching. Midway through the year, she began to refer to her old habits as BDB, "Before Deborah Ball." One day, attending a required professional development training on math, Sylvia found herself following along easily—and even, in some instances, catching errors. "[The leader] simply announced that 3 × 4 and 4 × 3 were the SAME!" she wrote to Deborah in an e-mail later that night. "Val and I strongly disagreed with her, and she agreed that they were different, but the end result was the same . . . Amen and thank you! (It's working.)"

One major challenge for Sylvia was managing her fear. Deborah always looked so calm and serious. When Sylvia opened up a discussion for children's thoughts and ideas, her heart raced, her stomach got tight, and her face grew warm. What if a student asked a question she didn't know how to answer? TKOT obviously worked, but it was also scary. To do it well, Sylvia didn't just have to learn about math and how children understood it. She had to muster a kind of confidence she hadn't previously thought to find.

Sylvia found herself changing the way she got ready for class. "Whereas when she used to go in on weekends it was to clean up and to correct papers," Sylvia and Deborah wrote in a summary of the experience, "now she looked for materials, read, and organized areas of the room. She tried to imagine various paths the students might want to take in investigating what was going on with their plants, or their bread mold cultures, or their magnets.

Armed with this understanding, Sylvia no doubt would have been able to answer the division-by-½ problem that stumped so many MSU undergrads. Dividing by ½ makes no sense from the perspective of the most common conception of division (how can you make ½ number of groups?) but it makes perfect sense conceived quotatively (you can easily make groups of size ½).

She looked for books. She gathered magazines and newspapers. In short, she realized that she was *preparing*, rather than *planning*, for teaching."

Like Ruth, Sylvia became more comfortable over time. She never taught a full math lesson, but the effects of what she saw trickled over into the way she taught science, reading, and English. She stopped using a basal reader, one of those textbooks with pre-prepared passages, and started having the class read complete works of children's literature. "What do the rest of you think?" she'd ask, moving from the usual ask-tell ping-pong to something looser. "Facilitating," she called it.

Sylvia and Ruth weren't the only ones learning from Magdalene and Deborah. Every day, Magdalene invited MSU undergrads to sit in the back of her fifth-grade classroom and observe. Every week, she met with a small group of Spartan Village teachers to work on math problems and talk about teaching. Deborah, meanwhile, continued playing pedagogical daredevil, teaching mini-lessons in other teachers' classrooms.

At first, the visiting undergrads' reactions traced the same superficial territory that had inspired Magdalene to make the tapes. "The teacher doesn't say much—she doesn't do anything to reinforce the kids who are getting it right," one student said. "I wonder if this is a gifted class," said another. "Most third graders can't talk like this." And, noting that the students worked on just one problem a day, another wondered, "Don't they need to get through everything they are supposed to learn in third grade? How can they do that if they work so long on one simple problem at a time?"

By the end of the year, after watching videos and also practicing the material on their own (writing and solving fraction problems, for example), their opinions had changed. They noticed the ways that Deborah and Magdalene did give feedback, if not by simply decreeing each answer right or wrong. They saw that in the space of one problem, the class often touched multiple parts of the curriculum. And they watched as misunderstandings that the teacher seemed to ignore one day were taken up and obliterated the next. They even shed their ideas about their own math abilities. "I'm just not a math person," they'd said at the beginning. By the end, one such student wrote, "This course has enlightened me to a whole world."

As the years went by, Judy Lanier's ambitions grew. She gave the model that Magdalene and Deborah were creating at Spartan Village an official name, the "professional development school," a modern-day lab school. And with a grant from the Michigan state legislature, she began creating more of them. By the mid-1990s, more than a dozen MSU professors had made home bases of local schools and embarked on new teaching research.

These professors were just the first wave of the recruits Judy and Lee Shulman brought in. In 1986, two years into their hesitant tryout, Magdalene and her husband, David Cohen, had decided to stay, making David perhaps the first tenured Harvard professor in history to leave Cambridge for East Lansing. With David on board, Judy began persuading professors from all across the country to come to Michigan State.

Judy needed the extra faculty members because she was eyeing an even bigger expansion. The same year Magdalene and David decided to commit to MSU, Judy launched a national campaign with fellow disaffected ed school deans. They called themselves the Holmes Group after a maverick Harvard dean who was committed to training teachers. Their first report urged ed schools to better prepare teachers or "surrender their franchise." Among the group's recommendations: create more professional development schools. By the end of the year, to everyone's surprise, membership in the group included more than a hundred deans from colleges and universities all across the country.

It was hard not to feel like MSU was the center of a new universe, ground zero for a new national reform movement. The sense had been underlined in 1985, when the California Department of Education announced its intention to adopt "teaching for understanding" in math classes throughout the state. A year later, David and a group of young MSU researchers boarded a plane for California. The group included Deborah and Ruth, though not Magdalene, who preferred to study teaching rather than policy. They were excited. What would it look like if an entire state committed to teaching math with more than just rote exercises and memorization? They were about to see for themselves.

Over the next several years, the group observed classrooms across the state, watching elementary school teachers teach math. They saw some promising changes. One teacher who viewed the reforms with suspicion nonetheless used the new method of teaching fractions and reported being "amazed" by what the students achieved. "He never had imagined that his fifth graders could think and reason in such advanced ways," the team wrote in one report. Another teacher, a woman David called Mrs. Oublier (a pseudonym), proudly declared that her classroom had undergone a "revolution" as a result of the new ideas.

But on closer inspection, the MSU team wondered how extensive California's changes really were. Mrs. Oublier's "revolution"—which David observed from the back of the room, crouched among the second-graders—seemed to have real limits. Following the state's decree that math lessons "involve concrete experiences" with numbers, Mrs. Oublier had replaced her pen-and-paper worksheets with "manipulatives"—little dried beans and drinking straws. Instead of seating the children in rows, she arranged them in clusters of four or five, in line with the state's new emphasis on "cooperative learning groups." And she zeal-ously incorporated new topics that the state said were important, like estimation.

Yet each adjustment did little to achieve the state's goals. "Concrete experiences," for instance, were supposed to help chil-dren "develop a sense of what numbers mean and how they are related," according to the state's new math framework. Yet Mrs. Oublier paid more attention to the activities themselves than to the math they were supposed to teach. In one activity that David observed, the children used beans and cups to model place value. But Mrs. Oublier focused most of her time on whether the children were holding the beans correctly, sometimes physi-cally moving their arms to make sure they made the motions as she'd instructed. When she got to the activity's key mathemati-cal point—the moment when the students had to enact subtrac-tion with regrouping, effectively taking a larger number from a smaller one—she flew right past it. They did the exchange and they moved on—no emphasis or discussion.

The supposedly cooperative learning groups, meanwhile, were intended to give Mrs. Oublier's students opportunities for "spec-ulating, questioning, and explaining concepts in order to clarify their own thinking." But David never once saw students speak to each other about math. "Indeed," he wrote, "Mrs. O specifi-cally discouraged students from speaking with each other, in her efforts to keep class orderly and quiet." As far as David could tell, she used the groups only as a means to call on individual children to come up to the board (for example, so that they could note their response to a yes-or-no question for use in a graphing activity), to pass out or collect papers or materials, and to dismiss the class for lunch and recess. "She would let the quietest and tidiest group go first," David observed.

Another lesson David sat in on had to do with estimation. Like the place value lesson, the activity had potential. Mrs. Oublier asked the students to guess how many paper clips it would take to line an entire edge of her desk, and then, after they wrote down their ideas, she collected each student's guess on the chalkboard, asking each time if the class found the guess "reasonable." But instead of discussing what makes a guess reasonable, or helping the students to discriminate between more or less reasonable estimates, Mrs. O treated all the guesses equally—even some that were obviously far off.

Mrs. O wasn't the only one whose revolution fell short. The team visited the classrooms of nearly three dozen teachers and, wrote one researcher, "To a one, we never saw radical change." The teachers sat children in groups and even assigned each group member a "cooperative learning" role, but the roles didn't translate into conversations about math. They emphasized the importance of knowing the "why" of a procedure, but only accepted one kind of why as correct, even when more existed. And when students presented explanations that teachers didn't understand, instead of digging into the ideas, the teachers steered away.

Deborah watched that particular drama play out in a lesson focused on one of her own old teaching challenges: subtraction with regrouping. After explaining "Mrs. Turner's law of math"— "Never subtract the top number from the bottom number"—the teacher harped so much on the importance of regrouping, or "borrowing," that one little boy borrowed on every subtraction problem, even when it wasn't necessary. But instead of unpacking the child's misunderstanding, Mrs. Turner (a pseudonym) seemed to brush it aside. After asking him a short series of stacked questions and getting the desired response ("You have 4 cookies. Can you eat 3 cookies? . . . So there's no reason to borrow there."), she moved on.

What explained these poor choices? Some might argue the

problem was an active resistance to change. And there might have been some teachers in California who did resist the ideas in the new California math framework. One MSU researcher reported visiting a teacher who swapped the problem-solving pages of a new textbook his district had adopted for old worksheets. Another scoffed at the term *teaching for understanding.* "What do they think we've been doing—teaching for *mis*understanding?" the teacher asked the MSU team.

But many teachers, like Mrs. Oublier, plainly embraced the changes. What stopped them from implementing the ideas more effectively wasn't a lack of will, but a lack of clarity about what to do. Like Ruth and Sylvia, the California teachers were struggling to understand students' ideas, figure out what the students needed to know, and then use that information to respond. They thought that simply giving students a chance to talk was enough. But without the mathematical training to respond to students' comments, they weren't able to translate confusion into understanding.

Change was also difficult without good models. In the absence of proper coaching, many like Mrs. Oublier believed they had undertaken a revolution. And with many visible changes in their classrooms—more children talking or playing with blocks—they had reason to believe the revolution was real. Yet when David asked Mrs. Oublier if she had actually read the state's manifesto outlining the changes, she couldn't remember. That response was repeated over and over again. Outside of a small group of math specialists, who had their own worn copies of the math framework, teachers told the MSU researchers that they'd either never read the document or didn't even know it existed. The teachers did receive new textbooks, but the books had not actually made the changes that California education officials hoped for. Despite hard lobbying by the state's Department of Education, publishers' revisions were minimal. According to Suzanne Wilson's history of the period, *California Dreaming*, state officials "estimated that 90 percent of the texts had remained essentially the same."

Professional development sessions, meanwhile, made matters worse. Wilson watched one session in which an instructor, explaining the new focus on open-ended rather than multiple-choice problems, emphasized that students must communicate their ideas clearly but failed to mention that teachers also need to make sure the students' answers are correct.

For her part, Mrs. Oublier relied on a book written before the framework came out, a teacher's guide called *Math Their Way*. Reading it, David found that the book centered on a strange idea. Young children can't actually understand abstract numbers, it argued. But if they work enough with physical representations of numbers—beans, say, or straws—then when they are old enough, numbers themselves will come quite "naturally." The process, the book said, would be "effortless."

To MSU researchers, Mrs. Oublier's decision to use *Math Their Way* was hard to understand. The book was not part of the state's reforms. Indeed, its magical thinking directly contradicted psychologists' findings about how much abstract math young children are capable of doing.

But Mrs. Oublier's decision had its own logic. As Ruth and Sylvia had found, changing the way you taught was a major undertaking. A teacher had to revise everything from the kinds of questions she asked to her very understanding of the subject she was teaching. Implementing the activities in *Math Their Way*, meanwhile, was more like what Mrs. Oublier did with the desks: a redesign, but not an overhaul. The same old wine in new bottles, David said. She could carry out the activities without rebuilding her core beliefs.

More than that, nobody had challenged Mrs. Oublier or any

of the California teachers on their fidelity to the reforms. Mrs. Oublier's principal admired the changes in her classroom and even called it a model for others. Instead of really teaching Mrs. Oublier, giving her opportunities to learn, and noting what she did and did not understand, the state simply said, here's the framework; good luck.

Back at MSU, Judy Lanier's plans were faltering too. Support for overhauling the ed school had never been universal. But in the beginning, Judy's supporters had usually drowned out the skeptics. Now the balance began to flip. Hiring education researchers who also did teacher education and taught in a school classroom was a lovely ideal, but difficult to carry out. Magdalene's and Deborah's positions at Spartan Village had grown organically. Building new relationships with new schools took time. According to a history of the period by Francesca Forzani, one faculty member had to spend a year "hanging out" in a school before a teacher finally agreed to collaborate with her.

Time spent in a professional development school, meanwhile, meant time away from the usual tasks of being a professor, like doing original research and joining professional groups. According to Forzani, several young professors scaled back their involvement in professional development schools to focus on boosting their academic résumés.

Harry Judge, the observer from Oxford, had predicted this: the American practice of tenure, historically determined not by the number of days spent working in elementary schools, but by the number of publications in peer-reviewed journals, would undermine ed school reform efforts. Judy Lanier swore that those who followed her into the classroom would not be punished, but, according to one professor, young faculty "saw the writing on the wall in terms of the productivity expected for tenure."

Instead of relaxing her goals, though, Judy sped up. Even with more professional development schools under way, a majority of MSU undergrads still did their student teaching at schools selected essentially at random. There simply weren't enough professional development schools to accommodate every trainee.

Judy's ambitions were also influenced by the people whose support she spent more and more of her time courting—potential donors who might provide the money needed to expand her operations. Especially influential was Alfred Taubman, the billionaire A&W proprietor, who began to brainstorm with Judy about how to take the professional development school idea statewide—a "scaling" project that he modeled on his own experience growing supermarkets and chain restaurants. The spiraling plan called for building fifty or sixty professional development schools all across the state. "M.S.U. has only 140 faculty members and the numbers doing teacher education are even smaller," a faculty member told Forzani. "That's just not enough people to make it work." For her part, Judy (known today as Judith Gallagher) points out that she pursued the expansion only at the insistence of some of the same colleagues who later questioned it. Whatever the source of the plans' ambitions was, though, the gap between what Judy and other faculty members believed was needed in both Michigan and the rest of the country and what the resources at hand made possible was undeniable.

According to a faculty member interviewed by Forzani, Judy came to think of her job as analogous to the queen Scheherazade from *One Thousand and One Nights*. Just as Scheherazade had to tell the king a new captivating story every night to stay alive, Judy felt that she constantly had to spin better and better plans before potential funders. "You had to propose a grand vision that is [in fact] cockamamie," the faculty member told Forzani. "I mean, people in this place would read Judy's plans and say, 'What is she thinking?!' But that's what it took in the corporate community; that's the story you've got to tell."

Fed up, other faculty members aired their frustrations publicly, publishing a newsletter filled with "enraged and sometimes satirical essays about Judy as well as cartoons that depicted, for example, the dean smashing hammers and other instruments over the heads of her colleagues." By the early 1990s, a group of particularly frustrated faculty members—many of them members of the old boys' club Judy was trying to change—began holding regular meetings to discuss how to resist her plans.*

Even if Judy and company were unable to reform the university system and the ed school institution, Spartan Village might still have offered an example of what professional development schools could do on their own. It's true that Deborah's, Magdalene's, and Ruth's relationships with the school had been forged through MSU, but much of their work could have continued even without an ed school to support it.

But the work at Spartan Village proved unsustainable too. Though she never mentioned it to Deborah, Principal Jessie Fry caught a lot of complaints from teachers who didn't want to visit each other's classrooms. At first, Deborah's unique powers of persuasion and Jessie's own iron will kept the changes intact. But as they sought more ambitious reforms, Jessie began running into roadblocks more formidable than veteran teachers' skepticism.

The evolution of the staff meeting told the whole tale. Tradi-

---

*Judy, for her part, disputes the account that building resentment against the reform work at Michigan State was targeted at her personally. She remembers support for the reforms staying strong until after she took time off as dean in 1989. (Judith Gallagher, interview by Jessica Campbell, November 2013.)

tionally, the meeting existed for the purpose of exchanging business unrelated to teaching: the state of the school budget, applications for supplies, news from the district, building concerns, fire drills, tornado drills, parent-teacher conferences, schedules, upcoming events. But as the school began to change, the meeting did too. "I would say, 'So-and-so, I was sitting in your room and I saw what you were doing,'" Jessie described. "Would you kind of share what you were doing with so-and-so little kid?" Teachers started out shy, but over time, more and more of them shared, until eventually, the staff meetings had so many non-"business" items that Jessie ran out of space. The meeting simply wasn't long enough to deal with both school business and teaching practices.

Finding another time to meet was not easy. According to all the official district policies, the teacher and teacher's aide contracts, and the school calendar, the school week was full. The Spartan Village school also had no physical space to meet. The school already used a tiny hallway alcove as a library, and the room where they met for staff meetings doubled as a classroom. So Jessie had to negotiate. Through meetings with both relevant unions, as well as the school district and the school board, she won permission to change the school's calendar, eventually building in extra time for "professional development."

The agreement solved the meeting-time problem, but not its corollary. Teachers wanted to observe their colleagues but had no one to step in and watch their own classes. Determined to give them more chances to observe, Jessie negotiated a separate arrangement to bring more substitutes to Spartan Village—and, because her teachers wouldn't leave their students with just anyone, Jessie had to negotiate something even trickier: permission for her teachers to screen their subs, something the district had not previously allowed. Grants, meanwhile, paid for additions to the school building. She built a new library and a new room just for teachers to meet. Improving teaching, it turned out, required not only new job descriptions for the teachers, but also a new floor plan.

After all of these acrobatic feats, Jessie still faced another hurdle. Like the staff meetings, Jessie's own official schedule allowed for only the "business" part of her job. She alone was responsible for writing the school's budget, ordering supplies, managing the maintenance staff, and dealing with parents. Working with teachers on their teaching—the schedule simply didn't allow for that. Jessie began working even more overtime than usual. During the school day she moved from one classroom to another, watching teachers work, leaving notes with feedback, and thinking of which teachers might benefit from talking together. At night, she played official principal, filling out the endless paperwork that kept the school humming. Most nights, she didn't leave school until 8:00 or 9:00 p.m.

The arrangements worked for a while, but over time, strains began to appear. Each time a new superintendent arrived— Jessie was principal through at least four—she had to defend the Spartan Village exceptions. Every time budgets grew tight, the school board always seemed to turn to Spartan Village. Did that training school across the tracks really need to exist? The long hours and rising stress strained Jessie's private life. Her marriage ended, and her health declined.

Teachers, meanwhile, came to resent the growing demands on their own schedules as more MSU professors sat in on their new professional development meetings. Some refused to attend the meetings at all. Others joked about being "bugged"; to study the school's transformation, MSU researchers had begun videotaping the school's meetings. A few teachers even refused to let Jessie watch them teach. "There were a couple of people that, they didn't want anything to do with the professional development school," Jessie says. "They didn't want to meet extra hours or anything. They wanted to just stay in their classrooms, do their teaching. They would do everything else I required, the lesson plans and all this. 'Nope! Don't want you to come into my room.'"

When Judy Lanier asked Spartan Village to become not just a professional development school, but a demonstration school, teaching not just future teachers but other schools, Jessie and the staff said no. It would be too disruptive. "You've got to remember," Jessie says, "that this is the university." She held out one hand. "Here's us out here." She held out another, way over to the other side. "The two don't meet. So we had to learn to work together and to share our knowledge and our own expertise. We are on one side, we're a team, and they're on the other side, and it's like us and them, us and them. We weren't all together. We grew together."

Until they didn't.

Soon, David and Magdalene had announced their plans to leave MSU for the University of Michigan, beginning a wave of departures. By 1992, the self-described faculty "mutiny" against Judy Lanier had expanded to include even Taubman, who told Judy she needed to become more realistic about what she could accomplish, according to Forzani's account.

That October, Judy resigned as dean. A few years later, she moved to Flint, Michigan, to work with the distressed city's public schools. Seven years later, when those reforms crumbled under opposition too, she left education altogether and moved permanently to Beaver Island in Lake Michigan, the most remote inhabited island in the Great Lakes. She has lived there ever since.

4

KNEAD AND RISE

Creating a country full of teachers like Magdalene Lampert and Deborah Ball might have failed in the United States, but that didn't necessarily mean it was impossible. Magdalene learned this lesson one day in 1985, after giving a talk at the University of Chicago. She'd opened her remarks with a warning. The videos the audience was about to see, taken in her classroom at Spartan Village during a series of lessons on multiplication, would depict teaching that deviated markedly from traditional math class culture. As far as she knew, no other teacher in the world taught in quite the same way.

That last comment stuck in the mind of one member of the audience as he watched the videos. James Stigler, then a young psychology professor at the University of Chicago, knew that Magdalene was only partially right. Yes, her teaching did look different from that in most American schools. But, as Stigler told Magdalene later, she was not, in fact, the only teacher in the world who taught that way. Indeed, a whole group of teachers taught almost exactly like she did. They just happened to live in Japan.

Stigler knew because he'd seen them do it, starting when he was in grad school at the University of Michigan. He'd gone to Japan with Harold Stevenson, a psychology professor who studied children in Japan and China who struggled with reading. By comparing how children learned to read in different languages, Stevenson and Stigler hoped to get a better sense of the process in general. But the pair's focus shifted when they ran a test of students' math achievement.

Comparing reading abilities, they had found some discrepancies between countries. But, says Stigler, "the reading differences were minor compared to the math differences." Japan stood out most of all. Comparing children from Minneapolis, Taipei, and Sendai, they found that 73 percent of Japanese six-year-olds scored higher than the average American child. The advantage grew even larger as children got older. Among ten-year-olds, the percentage of Japanese students scoring higher than the average American was 92. Even the Japanese ten-year-olds with the lowest average math scores in Sendai scored better than those with the highest scores in Minneapolis.

Stigler and Stevenson's finding echoed a growing set of international comparisons that put statistics behind deepening anxiety about America's educational standing, especially in matters of science and math. One study funded by the US government compared achievement across twelve different countries (not just the United States and Japan, but also Israel, Sweden, England, and others) and found that the average Japanese student scored as well on a math test as the top 1 percent of students around the world. Another, comparing high school students in Illinois and Japan, found that the average Japanese student performed better than roughly 98 percent of Americans. A third study, commissioned by the *Dallas Times Herald*, found that out of eight countries, Japan ranked number one in math achievement, while the United States ranked number eight. "There is no doubt that the Japanese . . . have built up their educational system in a manner comparable to the heralded 'economic miracle,'" a *New York Times* reporter visiting Japan concluded, just after the release of the *Nation at Risk* report.

With concern mounting about American schools' performance, explanations for the gap proliferated. Some commentators pointed to cultural factors, noting the Japanese emphasis on effort above ability. Stevenson and Stigler themselves argued that home life had to play a role; in Japan, they found, 98 percent of fifth-graders had a desk at home, while the percentage among their American counterparts was 63. Others speculated that Japanese children had inherently higher IQs, though Stevenson and Stigler could find no significant differences when they gave children a test of cognitive ability.

Reviewing the math results, Stigler thought the extracurricular factors must be important. But he doubted that they could completely explain the difference. "It's not like your parents sit you down and teach you algebra," he says. "You go to school, and your teachers are teaching you these things." What the Japanese teachers did in the classroom had to matter too. Each time he visited a Japanese school, he began to ask the local hosts a favor. Would they mind taking him into a classroom to watch a lesson or two?

On early visits, Stigler had noticed superficial differences. Instead of the one-floor buildings common in America, in Japan elementary schools were all three-story concrete palisades, with the hallways wrapping around the circumference like a multilevel motel. (Indeed, every elementary school had a full swimming pool, although not usually on the ground floor.) Children snapped between opposite poles of activity, shrieking and running chaotically one minute—the boys on stilts twice their size, the girls on unicycles—and silently studying the next. At the front door, everyone exchanged their shoes for slippers (as is standard everywhere in Japan). Schools used heat sparingly, creating a constant chill. And when the principal received visitors, he always served them hot tea.

But it was only when he started visiting classrooms—not just poking a head in, but sitting through an entire lesson—that Stigler noticed the deeper differences. Japanese math teachers led class with a different pace, structure, and tone than did other countries' teachers. Instead of a series of problems, the teachers used just one, and instead of leading students through procedures, they let students do much more talking and thinking.

Watching Magdalene's videos in Chicago transported Stigler back to those classrooms in Sendai. She had the same slow, methodical way of studying students' work, asking a question, and channeling their replies toward the desired conclusion. How had such uncannily similar pedagogy evolved in teachers an ocean apart? And how had the Japanese managed to do what eluded Americans, training what appeared to be the entire profession to use TKOT?

In the years after meeting Magdalene, Stigler could only guess. The number of Japanese classrooms that he'd visited was tiny compared to the total number of schools in the country. His knowledge of what happened inside American classrooms, meanwhile, was also imperfect. Many people thought they knew how most American teachers taught math, but no one had ever mounted a large-scale scientific study to confirm it.

Stigler's opportunity arrived in the early 1990s, when the group behind the new international tests was preparing its third and largest comparison study yet: the Third International Mathematics and Science Study, or TIMSS. This time the participating countries (a group that had now swelled from twelve to more than forty) agreed to examine not only scores on achievement tests, but also other measures that might shed light on international differences—including a variable to account for classroom teaching.

Applying the sampling methods that had been used to compare achievement, TIMSS could build the first-ever study of international classroom teaching, using video cameras to capture teachers and students at work. Because video technology was still relatively expensive, they narrowed the recording to just three countries. In addition to the United States, TIMSS organizers picked Germany (a major economic competitor) and Japan (the reigning king of the international tests).

They selected James Stigler to lead the study.

Stigler guessed that he would find differences across countries. But he didn't anticipate just how similar teachers would turn out to be *within* the countries. Common lore, of course, held that a wide gap separated the best American teachers from the worst. But compared to their German and Japanese counterparts, even the two most disparate Americans looked identical.

The consistencies stood out most when Stigler got people from different countries in one room to watch the videos together. One day early on, a Japanese researcher abruptly stopped a video of an American classroom right in the middle of the lesson. "What was that?" he asked. The teacher in the video had been demonstrating a procedure at the chalkboard when an invisible voice interrupted him. "May I have your attention, please," the voice said. "All students riding in bus thirty-one, you will meet your bus in the rear of the school today, not in the front of the school. Teachers please take note of this and remind your students."

The Americans had barely noticed the public address interruption. "Oh, nothing," they told the Japanese researcher, pressing the button to start the video again. But the Japanese researcher persisted. "What do you mean, nothing?" he said. Stigler wrote:

> As we patiently tried to explain that it was just a P.A. announcement, he became more and more incredulous. Were we implying that it was normal to interrupt a lesson? How could that ever happen? Such interruptions would never happen in Japan, he said, because they would ruin the flow of the lesson. As he went on, we began to wonder whether this interruption was more significant than we had thought.

Later, going over all the videos, they found that the researcher was right. Thirty-one percent of the American lessons contained some kind of an interruption, either a PA announcement or a visitor walking in to deal with administrative business (like collecting the lunch count). Zero of the Japanese lessons did. But they never would have thought to count interruptions, had the observer not singled out that moment. Sometimes the most distinctive features of a country's teaching were also the most difficult for natives to notice.

One striking example was the way teachers structured their lessons. American teachers rarely talked about lesson structure—the way class proceeds from a beginning to a middle to an end—and yet, watching each individual teacher at work, Stigler felt as though they'd all read the same recipe. "A cultural script," he called it. The American and Japanese scripts were the most different from each other—a limerick versus a sonnet. Some American teachers called their pattern "I, We, You": After checking homework, teachers announced the day's topic, demonstrating a new procedure—*Today, we're going to talk about dividing a two-digit number by a one-digit number* (I). Then they led the class in trying out a sample problem together—*Let's try out the steps for 24 ÷ 6* (We). Finally, they let students work through similar problems on their own, usually by silently making their way through a worksheet—*Keep your eyes on your own paper. If you have a question, raise your hand!* (You).

The Japanese teachers, meanwhile, turned "I, We, You" inside out. You might call their version "You, Y'all, We." They began not with an introduction, but a single problem that students spent ten or twenty minutes working through alone—*24 chocolates to be shared with* x *number of people (no leftovers); come up with as many solutions as you can* (You). While the students worked, the teacher wove through the students' desks, studying what they came up with and taking notes to remember who had which idea. Sometimes the teacher then deployed the students to discuss the problem in small groups (Y'all). Next, the teacher brought them back to the whole group, asking students to present their different ideas for how to solve the problem on the chalkboard. *Give the answer and the reason for your answer.* Finally, the teacher led a discussion, guiding students to a shared conclusion—*What did you learn from today's problem, or what new questions do you have, if any?* (We).

The patterns didn't dictate everything each teacher did, of course, and the researchers found some cases of departures. But even departures happened inside the spirit of the scripts, which encouraged some moves more than others. Take the kinds of questions each country's teachers asked. Americans asked a lot of simple questions and sought quick answers. *1 – 4: What does it equal?* Japanese teachers, working at the slower pace provided by a single focused problem, used questions not simply to understand whether the child had the right answer, but to peek into her mind, discerning what she understood and what she didn't: *Who had the same thinking? Anything to add to this way of thinking? Did anybody else use another way?*

In a ministudy of four lessons, two American and two Japanese, Stigler counted the types of questions that arose in each one. In the Japanese lessons, the most common question took the form of what he called "explain how or why": *How did you find the area of this triangle?* for instance, or *Why is the area here 17?* Problems, meanwhile, seemed to be designed with great care: they were generative enough to fill one or two forty-five-minute lessons each, and carefully selected to lead students not just through interesting math but to an important new idea. They tied lessons together like daisy chains, with the fruits of one day's problem leading directly to the task of the next. On its own, the task of deriving a formula to find the area of any triangle would be a lot to ask of a fifth-grader, but coming right on the heels of a lesson on parallelograms, children could use the formulas they'd derived just days earlier (often conveniently pasted to a wall for easy review) to come up with that day's answer.

Stigler called the second most common question in the Japanese lessons "check status": *Who agrees?* Japanese teachers often asked, tallying up whether other students had been persuaded by a classmate's idea. Or, checking whether students were following the progression of thoughts: *Is anyone confused?* In the American lessons, meanwhile, the most common question was what Stigler called "name/identify": *What kind of triangles have we studied so far?* the American teacher might say in her version of review, or *What is the length of this shape?* The second most common question was "calculate": *What is 90 divided by 2?* Neither of the two Japanese teachers asked a "calculate" question, and neither of the Americans asked a "check status" question.

The different sorts of questions led to different forms of participation. The Japanese students spoke more often and said different things. For instance, they were much more likely than the Americans or the Germans to initiate the method for solving a problem. Whereas students initiated the solution method in just 9 percent of American lessons, in Japanese lessons that number was 40 percent, Stigler's team found. Students in different countries also did different kinds of work. The researchers found that 95 percent of American students' work fell into the category of "practice," while Japanese students spent only 41 percent of their time practicing. The majority of work fell into a category the researchers termed "invent/think." A solid 53 percent of Japanese lessons included formal mathematical proofs. In all the American lessons collected, the researchers found zero mathematical proofs.

The TIMSS study revealed vastly different approaches to teaching exactly the same material. Lessons on the difficult problem of adding fractions with unlike denominators (for example, ½ + ⅓) exemplified the gulf. American teachers were encouraged to build up to the challenge step by step, starting with like denominators (⅕ + ⅖), and then moving on to the simplest unlike ones (½ + ¼). They did this only after warning students of the importance of not adding the denominators and demonstrating exactly what to do instead. Japanese teachers, meanwhile, gave students unlike fractions without commentary. When students inevitably made mistakes (adding denominators together, for instance), the teachers embraced the error as a chance to see why converting to like denominators makes more sense.

Even the architecture of the classrooms reflected the national predilections. To supplement their lessons visually, for instance, US teachers usually used overhead projectors, but in Japan, every observed teacher used the chalkboard. At first it seemed like a trivial difference. But on closer inspection, the researchers could see that each device created a specific mood. In the American classrooms, where teachers seemed to value attention more than any other form of participation ("Eyes on me!"), the overhead forced light onto everything the teacher wrote. A strategically placed sheet of paper, meanwhile, covered up everything but the latest problem. Guiding students step by step, teachers brought all eyes to the immediate idea—and prevented any reflection on what came before. In Japan, where teachers cared more about the attention students paid to the ideas as they unfolded, a chalkboard that could hold the full trajectory of forty-five minutes' worth of insights served teachers better.

Taken together, the findings confirmed Stigler's hunch. American teachers reported in large numbers that they knew about the new math reform ideas that David Cohen and Deborah Ball had tracked in California. Like Mrs. Oublier, many reported that they were adopting the ideas in their own classrooms. But the videos disputed their accounts. In some cases, the reforms actually made matters worse. One eighth-grade teacher, following directions to use calculators for problems where practicing computation wasn't the point, guided her students to use the machines to find the answer to 1 − 4. ("Take out your calculators," she said. "Now, follow along with me. Push the one. Push the minus sign. Push the four. Now push the equals sign. What do you get?") No wonder parents and some mathematicians had begun protesting that the reforms constituted "fuzzy math." In the warped way teachers interpreted them, they *were* fuzzy.

One surprise finding did not appear in the videos or even in Stigler's final report, but in informal interviews with Japanese teachers and education leaders. Asked when and how they had learned to teach this way, they all responded the same way. The changes, they said, began in the 1980s. Before that, math classes were more like what Stigler saw in the United States: rote, mechanical, dull. After the reforms, Japanese teachers took inspiration from three main sources: John Dewey, the American philosopher; George Polya, a Stanford mathematician whose writing about problem solving had influenced Magdalene Lampert; and "*NCTM*," the acronym for the standards produced by the National Council of Teachers of Mathematics—the ones inspired by Magdalene Lampert and written in part by Deborah Ball. How did Japanese educators learn to teach this way? *You*, they'd some-times tell Americans more simply. *We learned from you!*

The exchanges reminded Stigler of a confusing conversation repeated often during his first visits to Japan. Asked to explain the success of the country's thriving companies, Japanese would pronounce with reverence the name of a management expert: De-Ming. "Gee," Stigler thought. "I wonder if this guy's work has ever been translated into English!" Only later did he learn that "De-Ming" was William Edwards Deming, an Iowa-born statis-tician and management consultant who had begun his career in the United States after World War II, but whose ideas had gained traction only in Japan. (Later, after word spread of Deming's fame in Japan, American companies paid hefty fees to seek his advice about how to compete with their Asian counterparts.)

Like Deming's work, the NCTM standards had a more loyal following in Japan than in the country that birthed them. Not only had the Japanese discovered the American math standards; they'd accomplished what California never could. They'd taken a population of earnest but ordinary teachers and produced a country full of Magdalene Lamperts.

How had they done it? While Stigler pondered that question, Akihiko Takahashi found himself obsessed with another. The son of a Tokyo police officer, Akihiko himself had stumbled into teaching. Then, in the fall of 1991, he and his wife found them-selves in Chicago, halfway across the world.

Officially, Akihiko had moved under orders from Japan's Min-istry of Education, which sent teachers abroad to work at the Japanese schools serving the children of traveling businessmen— in Akihiko's case, the Futabakai School in Chicago. But in fact, he'd asked for the assignment. During twelve years of teaching in Japan, he'd become a careful student of American educators, especially George Polya, John Dewey, and the NCTM. Now he wanted to see the schools they'd built. With the ministry order, not only did he get to go to the United States; he got to go to Chicago, the home of Dewey's original lab school at the University of Chicago.

At the Futabakai School, Akihiko had to teach classes, of course, but he also received permission from the principal to spend part of his time visiting American schools. It didn't take long for the other teachers to grumble. *Why is Takahashi always traveling?* The truth was he was searching for the classrooms he'd read about in books.

Mecca did not reveal itself. At an elementary school outside the city, the teacher kept saying "Shh!" There must have been one hundred "Shh!"s. "I thought, well, that's only this class," Akihiko says. "I came to the wrong class." But "Shh!" turned out to be the rule. Math classes, his specialty, were nothing like what the NCTM had described. They were rote, tedious, and full of mistakes. A member of the Japanese Ministry of Education, traveling in America a few years later, watched a math teacher calculate that $2 + 3 \times 4$ equaled 20, first adding 2 and 3 to get 5, and then multiplying by 4. Astonished, the ministry official wondered for a minute whether perhaps Americans followed a different order of operations, in which addition preceded multiplication. (He quickly confirmed that math is indeed the same all around the world.)

Even the Chicago lab school, the one that Akihiko had read so much about, betrayed no trace of its founder. "I was shocked. Like, I read John Dewey!" Akihiko says. "But they don't do anything like that." The Americans produced wonderful intellectual work on what teaching could look like, but they had failed to implement any of it. He'd told the principal he needed time off to do research on the American classroom. But, he says, "rather than findings, there were a lot of puzzles. Good documents and good research and good materials . . . but somehow it disappears in the classroom. So how does this happen?"

Not long after the lab school visit, Akihiko took a trip to the University of Illinois campus in Champaign. A colleague in Japan had introduced him to a professor there and his wife, Jack and Elizabeth Easley. Elizabeth was Japanese American, and ten years earlier the two had spent four months embedded in a Tokyo elementary school, with Elizabeth translating while Jack observed the Japanese teaching style. The visits to Japan had inspired Jack to improve math and science teaching in the United States, but he had not been able to import the ideas into actual schools. The problem, he thought, was a lack of communication between the two worlds: researchers and teachers. So, with a few colleagues, he'd created a new group to bridge the gap. Dialogues in Mathematics Education, he called it, or DIME—a regular workshop for professors, teachers, even principals. When he connected with Akihiko, he invited him to join DIME for a meeting.

The meeting fascinated Akihiko. People from all around the Midwest presented work they were doing in classrooms, generating rich conversations. But one thing stood out: the DIME meeting seemed to be each participant's only chance to discuss her work, and as far as Akihiko could tell, the group met only twice a year. Could this really be the United States' best mechanism for translating ideas into practice? Most stunning of all was the fact, confirmed to him by members of the group, that the conversations were just that—talk. The teachers described lessons they gave and things students said, but they did not *see* the practices. When it came to observing actual lessons—watching each other teach—they simply had no opportunity. Indeed, the researchers and teachers viewed it as a triumph that they were meeting together at all. To Akihiko, the unusualness of the affair spoke volumes. What happened in Japan as a matter of everyday business (meetings between professors and teachers) was, in the United States, a revolutionary act.

The realization helped explain something else that had been puzzling him. Almost every time he tried to visit an American classroom, he would get the same frustrating response. Instead of letting him watch quietly while they taught, teachers would halt the lesson to welcome their guest from Japan. Dozens of minutes would disappear as he introduced himself and fielded questions. Afterward, his conversations with the teachers imitated the distraction. Any question he asked about the actual content of the lesson got batted away in favor of something completely unrelated to education. It was as if, instead of colleagues in the same profession, they were strangers meeting at a dinner party. What do you think of the United States? Where do you live? Social questions, not professional talk. When a conversation did veer in an interesting direction—How do you teach this topic in Japan? a teacher might ask, beginning the discussion Akihiko longed to have—it always ended too quickly.

The experience would have been unbelievable if it had not repeated itself so many times. After visiting more than a handful of math classes, he understood. The teachers didn't let him stand in the back of their classrooms quietly to watch because *nobody* ever stood in the back of their classrooms and watched. The same went for conversation. They didn't talk about their teaching with him because they didn't discuss their teaching with anyone.

They had, he realized, no *jugyokenkyu*. Translated literally as "lesson study," *jugyokenkyu* is a bucket of practices that Japanese teachers use to hone their craft, from observing each other at work to discussing the lesson afterward to studying curriculum materials with colleagues. The practice is so pervasive in Japanese schools that it is like the PA interruption to Americans:

effectively invisible. For a Japanese observer like Akihiko, asking if schools had *jugyokenkyu* in America would be like asking if they had students.

And here lay the answer to his puzzle. Of course the American teachers' work fell short of the model set by their best thinkers—Polya, Dewey, and the NCTM. Without *jugyokenkyu*, his own classes would have been equally drab. Without *jugyokenkyu*, how could you even teach?

Akihiko was not a natural-born teacher. He had become a teacher mainly because the university that had accepted him, Tokyo Gakugei, specialized in education. Even in his final years of college, he was indifferent to teaching. But during the second semester of his junior year, he stepped into the classroom of Takeshi Matsuyama at the Setagaya Elementary School, and everything changed.

The school stood at the end of a curving cobblestone driveway in Tokyo's affluent Setagaya Ward, a residential neighborhood famous even in inscrutable Tokyo for its mazelike streets. The grounds were unusually large for a center-city school, but the building was ordinary: three drab concrete stories, practical wood floors, drafty, and cold. Setagaya, however, was different from any other Japanese elementary school. A *fuzoku* school, meaning "attached"—as in, part of the university, or, in American parlance, a lab school—Setagaya conducted its hiring with the thoroughness of a corporate recruitment office, combing the country for the best teachers. They had to be true masters because, as *fuzoku* teachers, they were responsible for educating both children and future teachers. For three weeks each autumn, these college students trooped into the Setagaya school, breaking into groups of five per teacher. They lined the back of the classroom, notebooks in hand, unsure of what to expect.

Among the masters, Matsuyama stood out. His public lessons attracted so many teachers that to make room for them all, he had to hold class in the cafeteria. This made the job of his student teachers especially daunting. In order to graduate, education majors not only had to watch their assigned master teacher work, they had to effectively replace him, installing themselves in his classroom first as observers and then, by the third week, as a wobbly five-person approximation of the teacher himself. It worked like a kind of teaching relay. Each trainee took a subject, planning five days' worth of lessons in language or math or science or history. Then each took a day. To pass the baton, you had to teach a day's lesson in every single subject: the one you planned and the four you did not. You had to do this whether or not the teacher before you made it through the full material the day before. And you had to do it right under your master teacher's nose. Afterward, everyone—the teacher, the college students, and sometimes even another outside observer—would sit around a formal table to talk about what they saw.

During the observation week, the trainees stayed in Matsuyama's class until the students left at 3:00 p.m., and they didn't leave the school until they'd finished discussing the day's events, usually around eight o'clock. They talked about what Matsuyama had said and done, but they spent more time poring over how the students had responded: what they wrote in their notes; the ideas they came up with, right and wrong; the architecture of the group discussion. The rest of the night was devoted to planning; some days, these teachers-in-training didn't go home until 10:00 p.m. It was intense, exhausting, terrifying—and thrilling. Watching Matsuyama teach, with all the intellectual rigor that entailed, was inspiring. The trainees began to come up with their own ideas. Akihiko saw for the first time what it meant to be a teacher. He was hooked.

For his focus, Akihiko selected math, which was Matsuyama's specialty too. This was 1977, and Matsuyama, a student of John Dewey and George Polya, was an early proponent of the changes just arriving in Japanese math teaching. His technique tantalized Akihiko. In grade school, Akihiko had loved math but hated math class, where teachers always acted as if there were only one correct way to solve a problem. Matsuyama offered the exact opposite. He not only rewarded students who came up with their own solution methods; he depended on them.

Admiring Matsuyama's teaching style and carrying it out, of course, were two different things. Akihiko's first lesson, which he would still remember thirty years later, began easily enough. That week, sixth-grade classrooms across Japan were introducing the concept of proportional relationships—as in, if 5 cookies cost 300 yen, then how much do 2 cookies cost? A traditional lesson might have introduced the topic and then demonstrated how to calculate the unit rate (60 yen per cookie) and use that to find the answer (120 yen). But under Matsuyama's guidance, Akihiko had devised a problem that guided the children to map a set of relationships that would turn out to be proportional. Then he led the students in a discussion of the line they had drawn, showing the relationship between the number of cookies and how many yen they cost:

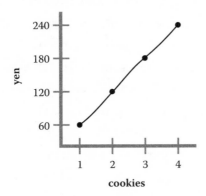

Everything was going well enough, when a student raised his hand with a question. Why, he asked, couldn't they connect the line all the way down to zero? Another student asked a different question: What does the line connecting the dots mean?

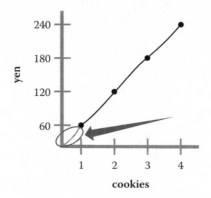

Akihiko was stuck. He knew that, in general, a graph representing proportional relationships should connect zero to all the other data points. However, the quantities in the cookie problem were discrete; the case of buying less than one cookie or even zero cookies for zero yen simply did not exist. But how could he explain that to the sixth-grader? "I still remember the feeling," Akihiko said. "Even though I knew, I could not explain it. I felt like my back is to a cliff, and I cannot go back anymore." He had no answer, but having no answer was not an option. Like a student called on to talk about a book he hadn't read, he bluffed—and felt that everyone could tell. In that moment, he knew. Teaching wouldn't just be his college major, something to study before finding his real profession. He was going to make it his life's work.

Over the next six years, as he graduated and went to work at another nearby elementary school, Akihiko experimented with more Matsuyama-style lessons. He knew enough not to try the approach every day. Veering from the textbook's suggested lesson plan required more preparation than he had time to do, and there was no guarantee of success. Instead, he deployed it in select cases, always remembering to spend as much time imagining how students might respond to a problem as he spent inventing it. Still, no matter how late he stayed at school, planning, the lesson would begin with a leap into the unknown. The students loved to surprise him. He took to keeping a journal; he wanted to remember every lesson. When parents complained about the young new teacher experimenting on their children, he turned his notes into a newsletter, sent to parents first once a month and then, by his third year, every day. If they were going to support their children, and support Akihiko, the parents needed to know the math as well.

Year by year, the lessons got better, and the parents' confidence grew. By his fifth year, he was teaching almost every lesson in the single-problem style. By his sixth, he received unexpected news. Back at the Setagaya *fuzoku* school, Akihiko's old mentor Matsuyama had just received a promotion from the school district. The new job meant that his position as master was now empty, and the district officials had asked him to suggest a replacement. He had named Akihiko.

To an American, Akihiko Takahashi seemed like another diamond teacher in the rough, the precocious counterpart to the *madogiwa* ("window gazers"), as weak employees are called in Japan. By the time he arrived in Chicago, he'd become as famous as Matsuyama, giving public lessons that attracted hundreds, and, in one case, an audience of a thousand. He had a seemingly magical effect on children.

But Akihiko knew he was no virtuoso. "It is not only me," he always said in English. "*Many* people." After all, it was his mentor, Matsuyama, who had taught him the new approach to teaching math. And Matsuyama had crafted the approach along with other math teachers in Setagaya Ward and beyond. Together, the group met regularly to discuss their plans for teaching differently, a Japanese version of TKOT; at the end of a discussion, they'd usually invite each other to their classrooms to study the results. In retrospect, this was the most important lesson Matsuyama taught Akihiko: not how to give a lesson, but how to study teaching, using the cycle of *jugyokenkyu* to put his work under a microscope and improve it.

Those three weeks of student teaching at the Setagaya *fuzoku* school had been a *jugyokenkyu* cycle in miniature: early planning based on the curriculum and potential student response; the observation of another teacher (first Matsuyama, then each student teacher); teaching a public lesson; and finally, a discussion of observed events. Each public lesson posed a hypothesis, a new idea about how to help children learn. And each discussion offered a chance to determine whether it had worked.

The typical postlesson discussion began at school, around tables arranged in a U, a cup of tea at each seat, and continued over beers at the local *izakaya*. In addition to his own notes, each observer had a copy of the teacher's lesson plan. The plan explained what the teacher intended to do and why, describing the advantages of 12 − 7 instead of 13 − 6 to introduce subtraction with regrouping. It also offered context. So far, all students have mastered subtraction *without* regrouping except Sayaka, the plan might say. Beneath that detail would be a list of techniques all the students had mastered—for example, counting on fingers, using manipulatives, or breaking up the numbers mentally.

In the discussion, the best comments were microscopic, minute-by-minute recollections of what had occurred, plus commentary. These ranged from pragmatic tweaks—since the students were struggling to represent their calculations visually, why not arrange the tile blocks in groups of ten rather than individual blocks?—to insights that spilled outside the bounds of the lesson.

After a lesson on finding the area of a rhombus, for instance, an observer recalled a powerful moment when one student had asked another *why* she calculated the way she did. Usually, teachers struggled to persuade students to talk not just to the teacher, but to each other. They often had to force the issue by having students stand at the board and present their ideas to the class or by asking one student to respond to another's confusion. But this kind of spontaneous discussion—one student asking another about her thinking—proved much harder to engender. What was it about this class's culture, the observer asked, that had taught the children to communicate so well?

The group reviewed the evidence, searching for occasions when the teacher said or did something to encourage this kind of dialogue. In transitioning the students from working on the problem independently ("You") to conferring with a neighbor ("Y'all"), for instance, the teacher had been very deliberate in her language. Instead of describing the step of finding a partner or talking to a friend—a common pattern, and one that could feel forced—she'd focused on the exchange itself, telling students to "look at each other's papers." "Maybe," she'd said, "you will find an idea you never knew!"

Someone else pointed to the way the teacher had begun the discussion part of the lesson ("We"). Like other teachers, she had her students record their ideas on pieces of paper that they then tacked on the chalkboard for the whole class to see. And like other teachers, she divided the different students' ideas into groups: triangle method here, square method there, parallelogram method here. But she added one unusual twist: instead of grouping the ideas herself, she delegated the task to the students, thereby forcing the thinking work onto them too. In the rhombus lesson, a spirited discussion had ensued as one little boy picked up a piece of yellow chalk, unprompted, and began dividing the board into four different sections for each type of idea, leading the others to scramble as they figured out the section to which each idea belonged. By creating a simple, predictable routine—after we have our ideas, we arrange them on the board in groups—the teacher had inculcated a spirit of ownership.

Another routine cemented the culture. Each time, after sharing an idea with the class, a student asked the same question: "Who thinks the way I am thinking?"

On its own, each of the routines might have felt forced. Indeed, teachers observing the lesson recalled other classrooms where similar exchanges fell flat. But together, the routines formed a powerful combination, getting students to ask each other earnest questions—without having to be told.

Other postlesson discussions focused more on the subject matter itself, noting, for instance, which part of the material the students misunderstood and whether all children struggled with that same difficulty. In a lesson about angles, for instance, an observer commented about the inherent challenge in seeing angles as not just shapes but quantities—a more difficult stretch than making the same mental step for area.

Problems, too, could come under scrutiny. The same lesson on angles stemmed from a question asking students to come up with as many angle combinations as they could, given two triangles—without using a protractor. But instead of leaving it at that, a basic math problem, the teachers who designed the lesson embroidered the question into a story about an imaginary king who loved to wear hats of all different angle sizes. ("One day," the story began, "there was a country without a protractor.") The story made for some fun moments in class, as when one teacher playfully anointed a boy king of the class, directing questions to him. ("King, is this okay?" the teacher asked, prompting another boy to ask, of no one in particular, "How did he become the king?") But in the postlesson discussion, the observers noted that mostly the story seemed to leave students confused. Angles just don't look like hats. By the end of the lesson, the teacher had spent so much time clarifying the bounds of the question that the students hadn't gotten to dig into much math.

The power of *jugyokenkyu*, from the planning process to the discussion afterward, lay in the fact that no teacher worked alone. To solve the puzzles that teaching posed, teachers needed the push and pull of other people's opinions.

Jugyokenkyu pervaded Japanese elementary schools. But how directly each teacher participated in it was up to the individual. After graduating from Tokyo Gakugei University, Akihiko took two steps to become a power user: he made a vow to perform (not just help plan) one public lesson a year, and he joined a volunteer study group of math teachers in the area. The math group operated under the sway of American documents that kept coming out in Japanese translation. Though he'd first read John Dewey and George Polya in college, it was with this group that Akihiko really delved into those Americans' writings for the first time—and discovered just how complicated it was to apply their ideas every day in the classroom.

Take Polya, the mathematician whose problem-solving manual *How to Solve It* became like a bible to the group. Polya argued that the process of solving a problem had four key steps. At first, the Japanese teachers followed Polya's recipe faithfully, guiding their students to begin by first understanding a problem, then planning a solution, and only then attempting to implement the plan. (The fourth step advised students to look back on their work, checking for mistakes and thinking about the solution's implications.) But when the teachers in Akihiko's study group tried using the steps with their students, nobody ever followed step two: "devise a plan." They always jumped straight to step three: "carry out a solution." Again and again, the teachers tried to get the students to follow the steps, without success, until it emerged in their discussions that perhaps they didn't need step two at all. Three steps were enough.

Akihiko's teaching group formed at about the same time that the National Council of Teachers of Mathematics released its standards. As with Polya, Japanese teachers took the NCTM standards not as a recipe book, but as a guideline. Instead of following the ideas step by step, they thought carefully about the goals, tried out ways to achieve them in their classrooms, and compared notes on what worked.

Nobody expected progress to happen immediately. Akihiko followed other teachers' advice when choosing subjects to approach with the single-problem format. Area lessons, for instance, were a natural fit: students could play around with shapes, experimenting with different methods for finding the area of a parallelogram or a triangle, and then, by comparing methods, they could derive a formula that would work for any such shape.

As Akihiko worked on the lessons, the rest of the group looked at his plans and offered feedback, guiding him through changes. He especially treasured public lessons, held on special days in the Japanese school calendar when teachers were released from their regular teaching loads to travel and only the students of teachers giving a lesson stayed in school. With public lessons, Akihiko learned as much from the ones he taught as the ones he attended. Visiting a school in Nagano one year, he watched a teacher do something intriguing. One component of teaching that Japanese teachers often discussed was *bansho*, or "board writing"—the art of writing on the chalkboard in a way that helps students learn. Each teacher had her own style, but over time, intricate conventions evolved. Usually, a title went in the upper left-hand corner; the problem of the day, right underneath. The writing on the board then proceeded in columns: selected students' solution methods, then thoughts about how to connect them, followed by a concluding statement (a final formula, definition, or observation). The key was to make the space a visible representation of the lesson's unfolding ideas.

Carrying this out, of course, posed all kinds of problems. Not running out of space was a big one. If the teacher paced herself just right, she recorded all the important ideas, right up to the conclusion, without having to erase any that had come before. But one too many notes could throw off the whole balance. When students suggested lots of great ideas, teachers needed strategies to keep them from getting lost in the dense progression.

The Nagano teacher had found a novel solution to this *bansho* challenge. On the right-hand side of the chalkboard, the class kept a collection of magnets, each inscribed with a different child's name. When a new idea emerged, the teacher wrote it out—and attached its author's name magnet above it.

The innovation served multiple purposes. On an aesthetic level, it helped set off the students' proposed solution methods from the other parts of the board. It also made discussion smoother. Talking about the area of triangles, it was easier to refer to "Nori's hypothesis" than it was to constantly summarize its crux. Teachers already used students' names to mark ideas this way, like Deborah's fence posts, but labeling them with a magnet made the process even more efficient. Finally, appending an idea with a name magnet rewarded students for sharing thoughts, equipping teachers with a new weapon in their continual war on shyness.

Akihiko took up the idea, and soon he was seeing other teachers do the same. By the time he returned to Japan after his stay in Chicago, you could hardly go to a classroom without seeing a collection of name magnets dotting the right side of the chalkboard.

The one-problem approach to teaching math took hold just like the magnet idea. Akihiko wasn't the only teacher to observe and emulate Matsuyama. As the number of teachers experimenting with the approach expanded, so did the number who saw it during a public lesson or just while walking down the hall of their own school. Often, all it took was one lesson to be persuaded that the approach was worth trying. Many teachers could still remember the exact lesson that had opened their eyes.

Not every attempt succeeded, of course. The difference was that, in Japan, a teacher who treated group work as merely an end in itself, or tried so hard to engage the children with a fun story problem that she distracted from the content, was likely to hear about it from her colleagues. And then, after learning what she needed to work on, she didn't have to come up with a solution all by herself. She could observe other teachers' classrooms with that problem in mind and learn something.

Take a second-grade teacher's lesson on bar graphs. To get the students engaged, the teacher, Mr. Hirayama, didn't come up with a goofy fairy tale. He simply designed a version of the textbook's suggested lesson—survey students about a preference, then have them plot the results on the chalkboard—around a topic he knew the students were interested in. They'd been talking about growing plants in the classroom, and the teacher decided to use the bar graph lesson as step one in their planning process.

Hirayama began not by announcing the lesson's mathematical purpose (today we will learn about bar graphs), but by telling the children that today they would decide which plants to grow.

First, he solicited ideas. What might they want to try? When almost everyone had shouted out their preference, Hirayama—a young, tall man with a smiling, calm demeanor—wrote the final list along the lower part of the chalkboard, left to right: potatoes, carrots, okra, sweet potatoes, tomatoes, cucumbers, green peppers, cosmos. Then he announced the next step. The students would vote, placing their magnetic name cards next to the plant they wanted to grow. The opportunity caused a minor ecstasy, with some children making a choice quickly and defending it and others mulling until the last minute, engendering a small mutiny from cucumbers to sweet potatoes right before the deadline.

Between shrieks, Hirayama paused to ask questions. Which plant has the most votes? Which has the least? How do you know? When all the children had entered their final votes, he asked the question that steered them closer to their secret purpose. "Did you realize," he said thoughtfully, putting his hand on his chin, "you piled up your names on top of each other?" Indeed, above each plant name stood a little makeshift bar line made of name magnets. Inspired by the discussion about which plant had the most votes, they'd started to sort them out. With the help of Hirayama—conveniently more than twice their height—the name magnets made columns stretching toward the top of the board. Without being told the idea of a bar graph, the second-graders had come up with it intuitively.

Now Hirayama just needed them to notice what they'd done and think about why they'd done it. "You didn't have to do that," he said. "Why did you do it that way?" The students threw out ideas, and the teacher listened calmly, waiting for the one that would take them closer to grasping the purpose of arranging data in a bar graph. Finally, a boy named Ano gave him the opportunity he was looking for, not in the form of an answer, but as a question. Why, Ano asked, did Hirayama make some categories line up in a single column when others had two columns per plant?

The question turned into a debate. "I don't really see the reason of making it two," another boy retorted. "Maybe in your head, Ano, you're thinking 2, 4, 6, 8?" He mimicked counting by twos.

More comments followed. Using two columns might help the second-graders reach the name cards more easily, and it also helped them count by twos. But what about the plants that received an odd number of votes? Running out of time, Hirayama abandoned his original plan. He'd expected to have the students replace the name cards with circles, solidifying the transition from data collection to chart making. Instead, he let them pursue their discussion about columns. He didn't regret the decision. Even if he had insisted on moving to the circle technique, they probably wouldn't have grasped it; their attention was somewhere else. He could always make the transition in the next day's math lesson.

For the moment, Hirayama concluded the Ano debate with a poll: How many students thought that arranging the votes in single columns made the most sense, and how many agreed with Ano about two? A consensus emerged. One column, they decided, was the best way to help them see which plant had received the most votes. A quick experiment confirmed the hunch; arranging the votes in single columns, they all sang out the winner in unison. "Potatoes!"

Just as the second-graders learned more by sharing their thoughts with each other, the fluid exchange of ideas accelerated progress among teachers too. The beauty of watching multiple teachers at work was that you could see the many different facets of a single practice. Sometimes the different solutions built on each other.

Take the challenge of ending each lesson with a neatly summarized main point, or *matome*—and getting all the students to really consider it. One *matome* innovation involved adding a new minisegment to the very end of the lesson, in which the teacher asked the students to scribble down what they had learned that day. "Today unlike the other days we talked about plants and we compared the heights and I'm happy," one girl wrote in her notebook at the end of Hirayama's lesson. "Today we did graphs for the first time. I didn't know about it so it was fun," a boy wrote.

Another group of teachers expanded on the idea, not only asking students to write a summary for themselves, but then asking certain students to share with the group. Sharing had multiple benefits. Students with excellent summaries got recognition, and they also served as models, giving others a chance to discreetly revise their notes. And everyone got a few minutes to revisit, record, and (the teacher hoped) remember the key thing they'd just learned.

A third group of teachers took a slightly different approach, replacing summaries with a competition to give the lesson a title. Usually, the title to a lesson was written in the upper left-hand corner of the chalkboard as soon as the students sat down. In this approach, the teacher left that part of the board blank. Then, at the end of the class, she asked students for nominations about what to fill in. Like summarizing, title writing helped tie the lesson together. "Times 2 and divided by 2 are brothers!" one little boy suggested after a lesson on division, in which the class had noted a pattern connecting products and dividends. The teacher encouraged the idea, but it was the more descriptive suggestion—"The relationship between the answer and the number to be divided"—that won a space at the top of the blackboard (and in every child's math notebook).

Even teachers who didn't observe these methods in classroom visits found the new ideas entering their classrooms. Leading teachers in Japan not only attracted crowds to their lessons; they also took jobs with textbook publishers, helping to write the texts they had to teach. And so the math textbooks, too, started to take up the new ideas, gradually centering each lesson around a single problem. They refined the problems over time as they tried them out in lesson studies, finding out which ones were most productive. Akihiko was the author of several textbooks; so was Hirayama's mentor, a colleague of Akihiko at Tokyo Gakugei named Toshiakira Fujii.

Take subtraction with regrouping. The numbers 1 through 19 produce thirty-six different problems that introduce the idea, from $11 - 2$ to $18 - 9$. But over time, five of the six textbook companies in Japan converged on the same problem: $13 - 9$. Other problems were likely to get students discovering only one solution method. For example, taking on a problem like $12 - 3$, the natural approach for most students was to take away 2 and then 1 (the subtraction-subtraction method). Very few would take 3 from 10 and then add back 2 (the subtraction-addition method). But Japanese teachers knew that students were best served by understanding both methods. Knowing two methods would come in handy when students encountered new problems that worked better with one or the other. And in general, seeing two paths to a solution helped students understand just how subtraction worked.

That was why $13 - 9$ almost always came out ahead. When tackling that problem, teachers knew, students were equally likely to devise subtraction-addition (break 13 into 10 and 3, and then take 9 from 10 and add the remaining 1 and 3 to get 4) as they were to devise subtraction-subtraction (take away 3 to get 10, and then subtract the remaining 6 to get 4). Because both approaches were likely to be tried, they could count on the class to come up with the most productive path to understanding.

The layout of the textbooks evolved too. Traditionally, a new unit would begin with the point of the lesson in bold letters at the top—how to make proportional relationships, say. Units also usually began on the left side of a two-page spread, so that the next page, with the formula or concept spelled out, was immediately visible to a reader. But this format, of course, gave away what should have been a delightful and important discovery. So, the textbooks began opening units on the right-hand page, leading off with broader topics and a single problem, so as not to spoil the ending—or, more important, to make sure children understood it for themselves.

One could also get ideas from the essays teachers published after a lesson study, describing their plan, what had actually happened, and then discussing what they had learned from it. Magazines full of these essays lined the shelves of local bookstores, offering everything from ways to introduce a particular concept to transcripts of the lectures on school culture given by elementary school principals each month.

The education system was no utopia, of course. Japanese teachers rolled their eyes at Ministry of Education bureaucrats as much as teachers anywhere else do. And just like in the United States, official ministry-run professional development sessions, usually held outside of classrooms, could feel disconnected and pointless—wastes of time to teachers for whom time was a scarce resource. Indeed, one idealistic official hoping to breathe new life into the sessions traveled all the way to America, only to be told about a Japanese practice called "lesson study." And while teaching evolved impressively inside elementary schools, high school teaching changed more slowly because the teachers were bogged down by the pressure of preparing students for the cutthroat college admissions contest, not to mention the requirement of spending their after-school hours running extracurricular activities.

Meanwhile, lower-income students received more struggling teachers and fell behind their peers in achievement, just like in the United States. And citizens worried about falling behind in the international achievement race, as other countries inched ahead on global tests—some of them, like Singapore, by deliberately adopting Japan's approach to *jugyokenkyu*; others, like China, by using their own native *jugyokenkyu*-style traditions (*zuanyan jiaocai*, or "studying teaching materials intensively," Chinese teachers call it) or, like Finland, by creating them ("field schools," lab schools are called in Finland).

But Japanese education officials also found ways to support the learning that teachers found most valuable, writing research lessons into school districts' schedules and even inviting leading teachers to help revise the national curriculum every ten years. As a result, just like the textbooks, the curriculum began to incorporate the new ideas.

The whole process was not unlike a great lesson. By trying out new ideas in real teaching experiments, noting what happened, and refining their craft in response—and (crucially) by doing all of this together, and frequently, with colleagues who were both fellow teachers and visiting subject-matter experts—they learned much faster than if they had tried to learn on their own. Working alone, a teacher might excel or innovate, or might not; the outcome depended mostly on the individual. Working together increased every single person's odds of improving. Through *jugyokenkyu*, teachers taught themselves how to teach.

To James Stigler, the American running the TIMSS study, *jugyokenkyu* jibed with what he'd learned about the country's culture generally. Japanese companies had gleaned a similar concept from William Edwards Deming: the idea of continuous improvement. Organizations, Deming argued, could improve only if they constantly studied their practices, always looking for little things they could do better. A dud in America, Deming became a sensation in Japan. The idea captured a commitment to craftsmanship that was already at the heart of the country's most prized traditions, from the careful lifelong study of the sushi chef, who spent decades mastering the particular flip of the hand required to make a perfect rice pillow, to the slow and steady apprenticeships in kabuki theater, where students spent decades mastering the special poses.

Akihiko's colleague Toshiakira Fujii used the analogy of his own pastime, *kendo*. A person could spend a lifetime slowly advancing through the *kendo* ranks. That "*do*" at the end of *kendo*, Fujii pointed out, could be appended as well to other careful crafts: *sado*, for the tea ceremony; *shodo*, for Japanese calligraphy; *karate-do*, for the martial art. Translated literally, it meant "the way" or "road"—a long way to go. Think of it, Fujii said, as "lifelong learning." Considering this tradition, Japanese teachers had done nothing particularly innovative when they created *jugyokenkyu*—except, perhaps, not calling it *jugyo-do* (*jugyo* means lesson).

Stigler saw the same attitude when he first pitched the Japanese government on the video study, one of dozens of optional components of the international test. As Stigler walked into the conference room to make his case, a colleague grabbed him with a warning. "He said, 'Oh, this is horrible. The Japanese have turned down every option.'" But when Stigler made his pitch, the official "looked up and said, 'Yes.' Just like that. And everybody's jaw dropped." Later, when Stigler asked the official why he'd said yes after turning so many other components down, he gave an answer no American official ever mentioned. "He said, 'because we want to watch the videos to see if we can get any ideas to see how to teach better' . . . No American had ever brought that up as a reason why they would do this study." Americans wanted answers, not improvement—a report filled with bar graphs and tables, not new teaching cases to study.

In 1999, when Stigler and the researcher James Hiebert published their findings in a book called *The Teaching Gap*, they made lesson study their triumphant conclusion. American teaching, their study had shown, was failing American children, denying them deep opportunities to learn. But the American approach to the problem largely missed the point.

At first, the business and political elites who led the US education reform movement had embraced many different approaches to improving schools. But by 1999, they had increasingly settled on just one: standards. It was the kind of argument that fit nicely into a PowerPoint checklist, a committee hearing, or a new bill. Documents soon laid out what students should know and be able to do in each grade (like "identify a main idea" and "distinguish between fact and opinion," in fourth-grade English; and "understand the concept of rate" and "add and subtract fractions with unlike denominators," in sixth-grade math). In just a year, the number of states with approved learning goals on the books would grow to forty-eight, and two years later, a diverse coalition including business and labor groups would support the No Child Left Behind law to make standards and accompanying annual tests a requirement—along with consequences when they weren't met. The country was moving toward the accountability idea that Eric Hanushek had articulated thirty years earlier.

Stigler and Hiebert supported this movement too. "Without clear goals, we cannot succeed, for we cannot know in which direction to move," they wrote in *The Teaching Gap*. Yet they suspected that simply setting standards and consequences for failure would not ensure that they were met. "It is equally important to recognize that standards and assessments, though necessary, are not enough." Reform's "next frontier," they wrote, was teaching—the way students and teachers worked together in school. "Standards set the course, and assessments provide the benchmarks, but it is teaching that must be improved to push us along the path to success."

The movement toward accountability ignored this vast middle piece of education, the part Hanushek had once called "the black box of the production process." This blind spot was the real reason efforts to scale TKOT had failed. Instead of incorporating the laboratory-style training process that Magdalene Lampert and Deborah Ball had devised for their students at MSU, the California and NCTM reformers described the changes they wanted without offering a plan to implement them.

"We have this idea that if you discover something quantitatively in a research study, and then you tell everybody about it, that'll improve teaching," Stigler says. "The truth is, with teaching, 10 percent of it is the technology or the idea or the innovation. Ninety percent of it is figuring out how to actually make it work to achieve our goals for students."

American ideas might have taken the Japanese 10 percent of the way there, but Japanese *jugyokenkyu* had done the rest. To change teaching, Americans needed to learn as much from the Japanese as the Japanese had learned from them.

One year after *The Teaching Gap* came out, Hyman Bass found himself standing at the back of a classroom at the Setagaya Elementary School with a group of American math teachers, watching a lesson unfold. With its carefully plotted beginning, middle, and end, the class reminded Hy of great theater. Then there was the way the teacher used manipulative tools, unlike anything he'd seen in the United States—so deliberately, with incredible precision. But he still felt some distance from the Japanese teachers.

Everyone else in the delegation did too—except one person. "The only American researcher who really connected deeply with the Japanese was Deborah," Hy says. "She noticed things and asked questions of them that were unlike what anybody else did."

What Deborah Ball noticed most of all was language. Translating what the teachers said after the lesson, Deborah's interpreter kept stumbling. The Japanese teachers would say something, and it wasn't that the interpreter couldn't hear them or that they weren't making sense. The problem was that the words the Japanese teachers kept using had no English equivalent; the language simply didn't exist.

It's okay, Deborah told him, entranced. Just translate literally. The *neriage* section of a lesson, in which many different ideas yielded to a consensus and a new academic concept, might not make sense to the interpreter—"knead and rise"—but it resonated with Deborah. There was a word, *bansho*, to describe the art of writing clearly on the chalkboard; another, *kikanjunshi*, to describe the part of the lesson in which the teacher walks between students' desks, looking at their work to determine which student should share and in what order. There was a word to describe the process of effectively using students' ideas to achieve a lesson's goal and another for the category of mistakes that, when shared with the whole class, offer the richest opportunities to learn (*neriage* and *tsumazuki*, respectively). There were key questions for posing the problem of the day (*shu-hatsumon*) and the practice of observing students (*mitori*) and the lesson opener (*donyu*). The words were another product of *jugyokenkyu*. To talk about teaching and all its components, teachers had invented new words to describe them.

There, in the middle of residential Tokyo, a city she'd never visited and probably would never see again, Deborah had the peculiar feeling of coming home. "I was like in heaven," she says.

"It would be as if, I don't know, you really like good food, and you're always eating McDonald's, and then suddenly, you're in this good restaurant." Or, she thought, as if after years painting alone, she had finally found the artist's colony.

On top of everything else, what Japan had was language. Of course Americans struggled to improve their teaching. When they tried to talk or even think about it, they suffered a fundamental handicap: they had no words.

AN EDUCATIONAL
START-UP

The man who invented an American language of teaching never visited Japan, never attended ed school, and, until recently, had never met Deborah Ball.

Instead of a traditional ed school like Michigan State, Doug Lemov came from the world of educational entrepreneurs. A new class of educators, the entrepreneurs emerged in the 1990s just as the reforms at Michigan State and California were winding down. Unlike Deborah and her cohort, Doug and his friends were just as likely to have degrees in business as in education. Instead of epistemology, child psychology, and philosophy, their obsessions were data-based decision making, start-ups, and "disruption." They were more likely to know the name of Eric Hanushek, the economist who invented the value-added teacher evaluation model, than Judy Lanier. They thought of themselves less as educators than as activists, members of a movement: *the movement*, some of them said. And they kept their distance from Deborah's world not only out of ignorance; the separation resulted from conscious—even righteous—design.

Their movement was born out of moral outrage. Doug Lemov's

involvement was ignited in 1994, during grad school at Indiana University. The son of a lawyer and a journalist from Bethesda, Maryland, the upscale suburb of Washington, DC, he had supplemented his studies (in English) with a side job tutoring members of the Indiana football team. Growing up, Doug was small, painfully shy, and a mediocre athlete. But toward the end of high school, the growth spurt he'd prayed for finally arrived, and in college, his six-foot-two frame won him a spot on the varsity soccer team. College athletes did not faze him, and he found that he was good at helping them study. Then, one day, the coaches presented him with a new pupil—a nose tackle named Alphonso, who, they told Doug, "needs more help than just study table."

Doug met with Alphonso and suggested that he start off by writing a brief autobiography introducing himself. Alphonso was not unlike Doug: sweet, gentlemanly, eager to please. But when he sat down to write, he struggled. His paragraph was virtually incomprehensible. Doug couldn't find a complete sentence in it. "More help" had been an understatement. Alphonso was practically illiterate—and he didn't even know it.

First, Doug was indignant at the university. Admiring the young man's considerable athletic talents, Indiana U, it seemed, had led him to think he had the skills to get through college. Doug felt this deceit was cruel and confronted the study-table official who'd given him the assignment. "I'm flattered that you think I'm the solution to Alphonso," he said. "But let me tell you, meeting with me three or four times a week isn't going to solve the issue here. He writes on the *fourth-grade* level."

"Actually," the staff member replied, "we tested him, and he writes on the third-grade level." Doug bristled. Shouldn't the coaches have considered that before persuading the university to take him? "That's the interesting thing," she said. "He's not a sponsored case."

The true deception, she explained, was perpetrated neither by the university nor the football team, but by his high school in the Bronx, which had promoted him year after year without complaint. By the time he graduated, he had good grades, flattering teacher recommendations, and not a clue as to how much he did not know. "Because he was not a troublemaker at a bad school, no one wanted to shit on his dream," Doug says. "Nobody wanted to tell him, I'm not going to pass you. They thought they were helping him by passing him along every year. And they killed his dream."

In 1971, writing about the birth of modern feminism in *New York Magazine*, the writer Jane O'Reilly described experiences like Doug's realization about Alphonso as "clicks"—the moments when an abstract social ill intersects with the daily minutiae of life and becomes personal:

> In Houston, Texas, a friend of mine stood and watched her husband step over a pile of toys on the stairs, put there to be carried up. "Why can't you get this stuff put away?" he mumbled. Click! "You have two hands," she said, turning away.
>
> Last summer I got a letter, from a man who wrote: "I do not agree with your last article, and I am canceling my wife's subscription." The next day I got a letter from his wife saying, "*I* am not cancelling *my* subscription." Click!
>
> . . .
>
> In New York last fall, my neighbors—named Jones—had a couple named Smith over for dinner. Mr. Smith kept telling his wife to get up and help Mrs. Jones. Click! Click! Two women radicalized at once.

They were clicks "of recognition," O'Reilly wrote, "the moment that brings a gleam to our eyes and means the revolution has begun."

Alphonso provided Doug's click moment. After encountering unequal educational outcomes firsthand, he couldn't get the injustice out of his head. He began to think less and less about graduate school and more and more about Alphonso. The last time Doug saw him, Alphonso was sitting in the computer lab, trying to write a paper. "He couldn't figure out how to scroll down on the screen, and the letters in his title weren't capitalized," Doug says. "I thought, he's going to fail out, he's going to go back to the Bronx, and he's going to have no idea what he did wrong."

What kind of country let children turn into young men without teaching them how to read? What kind of dysfunction led a public high school to pass a student who could not write a complete sentence? What had the civil rights movement and its *Brown v. Board of Education* decision accomplished if boys from the Bronx and their future tutors from Bethesda still got completely different educations?

Just as with feminism, Doug's click didn't happen in a vacuum; all over the country, other people were becoming, in O'Reilly's words, "clicking-things-into-place angry" after their own encounters with the injustice of the American public school system. There was Jay Altman, who realized that his rural California high school had shortchanged him, leaving him years behind most of his classmates at Williams College. There was John King, of East Flatbush, Brooklyn, who, comparing himself to the friends he grew up with, realized that he might never have graduated high school, much less gone on to Harvard, had an extraordinary New York City public school teacher not set him on a different path. And there was Wendy Kopp, who watched her Princeton roommate from the South Bronx struggle to keep up with her peers.

After meeting Alphonso, Doug had to call only a few friends before he found one boiling with the same frustration—a college classmate named Stacey Boyd. She was living in Boston, where she planned to foment an educational revolution. In just a few weeks, Doug had decided to move to Boston and join her. Together they would overturn educational inequity. They just needed to figure out how.

The approach they came up with reflected the spirit of the decade—and, in particular, two emerging theories that were then hardening into conventional wisdom. The first was Erik Hanushek's accountability idea. The economist's articles about the problem of throwing money at schools were eccentric, even radical, when they first appeared in the 1970s. But by the 1990s, Hanushek's ideas had become a bipartisan truism that stretched beyond education to all social programs. The roots of ignorance, unemployment, and other ills did not lie in a *lack* of government support, but an overabundance of it. By throwing money at poverty, the government had exacerbated it, giving the poor new reasons to be complacent rather than empowering them to change their stations. "The problem they were trying to solve," Irving Kristol put it, "was the problem they were creating."

In 1994, the year Doug met Alphonso, the Democratic president, Bill Clinton, vowed to "end welfare as we know it." Future antipoverty efforts, even Democrats agreed, would have to make support contingent on results. In other words, programs would have to attend not only to "inputs" like how much money the programs got and how many people they served, but also to results, or "outputs"—whether they showed quantifiable improvements.

In education, the assumption was that schools' dysfunction stemmed from an absence of accountability. Education had been a cornerstone of Lyndon Johnson's war on poverty, receiving billions of dollars in support for disadvantaged students like Alphonso by way of a new fund called Title I. ("Poverty has many roots," Johnson had explained, "but the taproot is ignorance.") In turn, between 1961 and 1991, real annual per-pupil spending nearly tripled, rising from $2,835 to $7,933 in constant dollars. But during roughly the same period, reading achievement as measured by the National Assessment of Educational Progress remained essentially flat. Just as welfare programs had allegedly created a permanent underclass by supporting the poor with no strings attached, federal spending had fostered a school system in which districts got increasingly large grants whether or not they successfully educated their students. The arrangement, according to the new conventional wisdom, conditioned schools to fail. They were like any monopoly; unchecked by the free market, they underperformed. Why did Alphonso's high school let him fail? According to the accountability advocates, the answer was simple. The school let Alphonso fail because failure carried no penalty.

The second influence on Doug and his friends was a new national obsession with the power of quantitative data. The metrics revolution elevated a budding class of nerdy "quants" (people like the statisticians hired by Oakland A's manager Billy Beane, as described in Michael Lewis's influential book *Moneyball*) above an old guard who followed intuition and business as usual, never guessing that within the piles of available performance data lurked a more effective approach. In education, the quants were people like Hanushek, outsiders who analyzed the new data pouring out of districts across the country and discovered that schools had no idea how to effectively spend their money.

These two influences—accountability and quantitative metrics—led to sweeping reforms in education, including the proliferation of standards, stakes, and tests that James Stigler observed. They came to take their purest manifestation in the charter school, a new category of school financed by the district, but under different management. Stacey Boyd, Doug's friend from college, wanted to start one in Boston. Targeted at poor students like Alphonso, living in heavily black and Hispanic neighborhoods, charter schools followed different rules. At traditional public schools, funding was tied only to attendance; schools stayed open as long as they had local children to teach. At charter schools, support was to flow only as long as student achievement met certain benchmarks. At the Academy of the Pacific Rim, or APR, the charter school founded by Stacey and Doug, students had to meet the targets or the school would shut down. Stacey took the promise a step further, vowing that if any student failed to pass the required tenth-grade state test, she would send the funds APR would have spent on the student to whatever school that student chose to attend instead—essentially a money-back guarantee.

Traditional public schools all reported to a single bureaucratic school district that ruled their operations with Byzantine obtuseness. Charter schools, on the other hand, could be like lean, efficient FedExes to the district's Postal Service—or, in the language of the decade, spirited dot-coms battling the mighty Microsoft.* They received government support, but they controlled their own affairs.

The best charters also obsessed over metrics. By studying everything they did and analyzing the results, they hoped to figure out what was really working and what wasn't, and then change their habits accordingly. In a newly competitive educational marketplace, they assumed that the "winner" would be the

---

*Some of the charter schools lived up to this promise, but many did not. Multiple studies of charter school performance have shown that the schools often perform just as poorly as the district-run schools they seek to outdo. And across the country, charter schools have been the victim of the same inefficiency and corruption challenges that plague neighborhood public schools.

school that pursued effective innovation, even if the result was vastly different from the way things had always been.

At APR, the first educational convention that Stacey and Doug discarded was architecture. The school occupied the second floor of the Most Precious Blood parochial school, a building constructed around a courtyard, like an inner-city DoubleTree. The setup did not include an athletic field; Most Precious Blood's only outdoor space was a parking lot. So athletics, including APR's daily Tai Chi lessons, took place on a landing. Staff meetings, in keeping with the latest management trends, were held standing up.

APR's founders also rejected almost everything associated with ed schools, including their ideas about teaching. Many of them, Doug included, hadn't gone to ed school. But those who had gave the rest an idea of what education professors advocated, and as far as they could tell, it was exactly the opposite of what their students needed. The broad label for the ed school approach to teaching, as they understood it, was *progressive.* The goals of this progressive pedagogy were laudable. In the hands of progressive teachers, classrooms were supposed to be little democracies, with children working with the teachers to create the rules; structures were supposed to be relatively loose, giving students a chance to express themselves and pursue their own interests; and instead of focusing on rote memorization, teachers were supposed to plan careful lessons guiding students through big concepts and ideas.*

---

*When similar characterizations were used to describe Deborah Ball and Magdalene Lampert's teaching—what other Michigan State educators named TKOT—the two women resisted them as false dichotomies. In good teaching, they maintained, structure was as important as freedom, fluency as important as concepts. But the teachers at APR had not heard of Deborah

But there was theory and then there was reality. The teachers who had worked at traditional public schools before coming to work with Stacey and Doug told horror stories about the attempted implementation of progressive pedagogy. Instead of inspiring creative learning and self-expression, the progressive ideas made chaotic urban schools more disorderly and struggling students more confused. Test scores were lower than ever. Scott McCue, an early APR teacher who came to the school after teaching at an alternative high school in New York City, described spending twenty minutes in a fifty-minute class period just getting students to pay attention. Progressive pedagogy sounded nice, but experience didn't support it.

Anyway, the entrepreneurs had more pressing concerns. Their students didn't need democracy; they needed the basics. At APR many of the students were poor, black, and years behind their more affluent peers. They needed to learn to read and write and add and subtract. None of the loftier goals—critical thinking, imagination, and creativity—could happen without a grasp of these fundamentals. How could a child study chemistry without knowing how to multiply? Or create a historical argument without being able to read?

APR students needed to learn something else too—the skill that undergirded all academic study, even simple number and letter fluency: discipline, the art of paying attention, obeying instructions, and following through. Disorder ruled in the

---

or Magdalene. Deborah and Magdalene also both rightly questioned what "progressive pedagogy" actually referred to. While some teachers took on the label proudly to describe a "child-centered" approach, there was no coherent school of pedagogical thought that could be called "progressive." Historically, progressive education described a political movement advocating certain educational goals, not a pedagogical approach to achieving them.

schools that Stacey and Doug sought to replace—the failing inner-city public schools, where fights broke out in the hallways, homework assignments were roundly ignored, and noise levels tested the limits of the human eardrum.

At APR, Doug and Stacey threw away the ideas about democracy and open-ended projects in favor of a pathological (some said authoritarian) focus on behavior. A supporter of the school, Linda Brown, noticed the germ of the habit when she telephoned Stacey Boyd on the school's inaugural first day, a sweltering July morning. (Hoping to pull struggling students ahead, the school launched with a summer boot camp.) "I called in the morning, and I said, 'Stacey, this is the day you've been waiting for!'" Brown says. "'The students have come, right?' And she said, 'Yes, yes, they have, but we had to send a few home.' I said, 'What are you *talking* about?' She said, 'They weren't in uniform.'" The offending children, Brown learned, had worn every piece of the required wardrobe (khaki pants, standard-issue polo shirts) except one: a belt. She pictured students trudging miles home in 100-degree heat. What kind of school was this, exactly?

But Stacey explained that what seemed punishing, even cruel, in fact represented a radical act of kindness. By being scrupulous about order, starting with the tiniest symbols, they could build a school where students obeyed more important codes of conduct, paving the way for the emotionally safe, academically challenging learning experiences that would be *truly* progressive. She cited the broken-windows theory—the argument, devised a decade earlier by two social scientists, James Q. Wilson and George L. Kelling, that catastrophic urban chaos, cascading from harmless drunks wandering the streets to violent crime, could be undermined by eliminating the tiniest signs of disorder. When a broken window is left unrepaired, "all the rest of the windows will soon be broken," Wilson and Kelling argued.

This is as true in nice neighborhoods as in run-down ones. Window-breaking does not necessarily occur on a large scale because some areas are inhabited by determined window-breakers whereas others are populated by window-lovers; rather, one unrepaired broken window is a signal that no one cares, and so breaking more windows costs nothing. (It has always been fun.)

Stacey had to make sure that students knew from day one that, at APR, breaking windows—or its school equivalent, not wearing a belt—cost something. Brown was convinced. "I realized . . . if you don't get that culture right at the beginning, you don't get another chance," she says.

The idea persuaded others too, less because of the philosophy than because of the response it engendered from the parents. Spencer Blasdale, another early APR teacher, and one of the few teachers there who had attended ed school, at Harvard, recalls hearing Stacey announce the zero-tolerance approach for the first time at a series of informational meetings for parents the year before APR opened. Every time, parents would push back on the idea. And every time, Stacey would hold her ground. "There's one case that I remember viscerally," Spencer says. "A mom said, you know, 'My daughter sort of swears sometimes. She's 13 years old, she's a teenager. If she swore under breath or something, you're really saying that you would call me at home to come to the school to get her?'" Stacey's reply: "Yup," she said, as Spencer recalls. "I will call you, you may not like it, and I think that's a service that we are doing."

"And every other parent in the room—they stood up and started clapping," Spencer says. Of all the pieces of APR's pitch to parents—from the plans to teach international finance in eleventh grade, to the Mandarin classes for every student (not to mention Tai Chi), to the glittering résumés of the founders (Stacey had just finished Harvard Business School; Doug came with his master's in English from Indiana; Spencer came from Princeton)—it was discipline that captivated parents most: a promise to keep their children safe. Once again, the hard data of experience trumped pretty dreams. And teachers saw immediate payoff in their results. Teaching at discipline-obsessed APR, Scott McCue now spent fifty-four of the fifty-five class minutes on content.

The staff at APR knew their zealous approach made a number of teachers uncomfortable. A student forced to apologize to the entire class for his misbehavior—wasn't that one step away from a dunce cap? But this discomfort with consequences was the conventional wisdom the entrepreneurs wanted to overturn— another romantic notion that experience did not support. Doug called it the "Hug 'Em to Harvard" principle—the idea that what underprivileged students needed most was warmth and kindness. The Hug-'Em-to-Harvards were "like, 'Oh, when those kids meet us, and they see how much we love them, then there won't be any behavior problems!' And you're like, how dare you think that when they meet you they won't show all the manifestations of the organizational dysfunction and scars of poverty," Doug says. "We were not going to be those fools." More than hugs, the faculty felt, the APR students needed limits.

Other charter schools were coming to the same conclusion. At Roxbury Prep, another Boston charter school, John King— the Harvard graduate from East Flatbush—debated with his cofounder Evan Rudall about how far to take their own radical orderliness. Like APR they had a strict dress code, but what about passing periods? John thought the kids should be allowed to talk as they moved from class to class. Evan disagreed. "Evan said, 'I'm telling you, if we don't do silent hallways, transitions are going to take forever, and it's going to be a total disaster for classes,'" John says.

To settle the debate, they decided to call Evan's wife—John's idea, because he knew she would sympathize with his softer approach. She did, and students were allowed to talk between classes. It took only two days of school for John to abandon ship. As Evan had predicted, moving between classes not only took up more time than they had allotted; it also created opportunities for misbehavior that spilled into classrooms, wasting valuable instructional time. By the time Jay Altman—who was in the process of opening his own school in New Orleans—visited Roxbury Prep a few years later, John had become the silent hallway czar. "He was radical about it," Jay says. "Every time, about two minutes before the bell would go off before classes, all year long, he or someone would get on the speakers and say, 'Teachers, the bell is about to ring. Please get in the hallway.'" According to John, the PA message came on only *as* the bell was ringing, and the request was for teachers to "join us in the hallway," but the result was the same. Without missing a beat, the teachers without a class that period appeared in the halls, ready to keep watch.

Soon enough, the entrepreneurs' approach—"countercultural," McCue called it—had solidified into a philosophy. It was the deliberate inverse of "Hug 'Em to Harvard": no excuses.*

---

*As with TKOT (the phrase describing the kind of teaching practiced by Deborah Ball and Magdalene Lampert), I borrow the "no excuses" label from some members of the group of people I've called the entrepreneurial education movement to describe their pedagogical approach. "No excuses" was popularized by Samuel Casey Carter in his book, *No Excuses: Lessons from 21 High-Performing High-Poverty Schools* (Washington, DC: Heritage Foundation, 2000). As with TKOT, the "no excuses" descriptor is not embraced by all

The second piece of the educational orthodoxy that Doug and the other no-excuses entrepreneurs rejected was isolation.

American teachers might work in school buildings with dozens of colleagues. But, as education scholars have noted, they operated essentially solo, like "lone rangers," as Deborah Ball's Spartan Village colleague Mindy Emerson put it. Sociologist Dan Lortie, who argued that American classrooms still operated like a one-room schoolhouse, described the approach as the "single cell of instruction" model. Despite growing faculties with greater numbers of specialists, individual teachers rarely interacted. Some education professors used the metaphor of the "egg-crate school," which carefully separated teachers, as if to keep them from touching.

The entrepreneurs hadn't read much of the academic theory, but they were zealous about their work nonetheless. Inexperience seemed to motivate them. Most of the teachers had just a few years of teaching under their belts (Doug, for his part, had taught English for three years at a private day school in Princeton, New Jersey, before grad school), yet they were responsible for running the school. Every day they faced a stream of difficult questions. "You know, the Tai Chi instructor didn't show up," says Spencer Blasdale. Or, "like, okay, what's the first report card going to look like? How are we going to do our first school dance? What are we going to do because this Tai Chi teacher's been absent three times?"

For Doug, the questions multiplied at the end of the first year, when Stacey decided to leave. "She was like, 'Guess what? You're

---

the entrepreneurial educators I write about. Notably, as I explain further in Chapter 7, Doug Lemov dislikes the term and does not use it to describe his own work.

principal!'" Doug says. "'It's your school. Go and get 'em!'" He was twenty-seven years old. One day, not long after that, a group of auditors approached him about an accounting problem he hadn't even known existed, which, if unaddressed, would jeopardize the school's future. "Every day there was something like that," Doug says. "We were so incredibly vulnerable. In part, because [we] were a tiny little organization with no infrastructure. In part, because there was no experience and no track record and no one knew anything to go back on. And none of us had any experience. And, in part, because none of the rules were written. It was terrifying." Running a charter school, he thought, was the ultimate crucible. Every mistake you made, you made in public, for all your staff and students to see.

Another group of people might have turned inward. But in their response, Doug and the rest of the APR teachers were distinctly more "Japanese." With no experience to fall back on, they tackled the problems together. Instead of regressing to the egg-crate tradition, the faculty at APR opened their doors—and learned from one another.

Indeed, the Academy of the Pacific Rim was "pacific" by definition. Its two founding board members had read James Stigler and Harold Stevenson's early research on Asian schools, and they had attended Asian schools themselves. They handed the charter over to Stacey, who had taught in Japan, with a mandate to blend the best of East and West.

As a result, Doug found himself leading study sessions on joint readings of *Teaching and Learning in Japan* and essays on Japanese management techniques. The TIMSS video study that introduced Stigler to lesson study had not yet been published, but the cultural approach underlying *jugyokenkyu* was embodied by the concept of *kaizen*—then popular among the Harvard Business School crowd—which described the "continuous improvement" of Toyota assembly lines. Imagining the educational equivalent of an efficient and responsive assembly line, Doug and his colleagues did not quite reinvent lesson study. But they came close, holding standing meetings on the minute details of the homework system and devising schedules to enable teachers to make regular visits to each other's classrooms. (In APR's case, it helped that so many of the teachers were young, unmarried, and childless; days started at 6:00 in the morning and didn't end until 7:00, 8:00, sometimes 9:00 at night.)

The school's culture of constant collaborative learning also stemmed from Doug himself. Though he outgrew his childhood smallness, Doug never shed the shyness. He was compulsively humble, painfully self-deprecating, and prolific on the subject of his own faults. In college, after a soccer game, he would spend the next two weeks fixating on the mistakes he'd made, even if his team won. When he did stumble on an idea that he knew was good, he always deferred responsibility to a colleague. "You can assume, because it was really smart, that it was not my idea," he'd say. Whenever he gave advice, he delivered it with a hint of a question mark. He was so self-effacing, so obsessed with his own shortcomings, that being around him could sometimes be physically uncomfortable. Colleagues couldn't talk to Doug for long without his casually declaring a failure at some deeply personal task, like raising his children or supporting his wife.

Doug thought there were two kinds of people in the world: the virtuosos, who could run or jump or write or act without thinking much about it; and the strivers, who studied the naturals' every move, perfecting their skills in an attempt to reach the higher level. Doug was sure he was a striver, a person for whom brilliance required imitation.

Doug responded to failure at APR by doing what he had always done: he looked for people who excelled at their work and studied what they did. His staff was his first and best source of ideas. Walking through the classrooms at APR, he learned how to become a better teacher. Sometimes the lessons were obvious, as with Molly Wood, whose peppy persona made her teaching techniques—an intriguing mix of extreme structure and warm emotional connection—easy to identify. Other times they were more mysterious, as with quiet, understated Kate Glendenning, who put her students into a kind of trance as they considered Shakespeare, never rushing into answering a student's question (the way Doug always did), but instead pausing a few seconds before crafting the most effective reply.

Doug studied them all, even bringing a video camera to Kate's class one day to enable further review. He also looked beyond APR, to the new movement of no-excuses charter school leaders in Boston and around the country. Together, the teachers and principals talked on the phone, huddled over coffee or at a party, and visited each other's schools, discussing everything from how to deal with troublesome parents to how to manage a school budget. "Any difficult decision, I would pick up the phone and call John [King] or Mike [Goldstein, of the Match charter schools] or Evan [Rudall] or Brett [Peiser] and say, what would you do in this situation, or what have you done in this situation? And we always would send teachers, groups of teachers—go spend a day at Roxbury Prep or [later] Boston Prep," says Spencer Blasdale, who became Doug's assistant principal when Stacey left.

Little comments often made the biggest difference. One day, watching Doug teach, a colleague gave him a simple suggestion. Trying to save time, Doug had given directions while he moved around the room, passing out papers. But the students weren't paying full attention. "When you want them to follow your directions," the colleague suggested, "stand still. If you're walking around passing out papers, it looks like the directions are no more important than all of the other things you're doing. Show that your directions matter. Stand still. They'll respond." Doug tried it, and he was floored. "I could see the difference right away."

The comments multiplied, and over time, everyone's confidence grew. Teaching presented a million problems, but by working together, watching each other and being watched, he and his colleagues could craft solutions. "The great thing about being in the crucible is that if you see something successful, you know right away," Doug says. "It's not working, and it's going to be a long hour! Or, 'Oh my God. It's working!' It was just a ton of very visible—like a laboratory—a ton of very visible feedback coming back to you. You're getting this, or you suck."

Not every member of the no-excuses movement was a congenital learner like Doug. But the ones who were—John King and Evan Rudall at Roxbury Prep; Jay Altman in New Orleans; Brett Peiser, a former teacher in Brooklyn who had started another Boston charter school; David Levin and Mike Feinberg, early Teach For America corps members who went on to found the KIPP charter schools in Houston and New York City; and (the rare early female founder) Dacia Toll, a Yale Law School graduate who had created Amistad Academy in New Haven, Connecticut, which later grew into the Achievement First network—became a community. Together they ensured that each school not only learned to solve its own problems, but also benefited from solutions invented by its compatriots.

After visiting the fifth-grade classroom of a teacher named Julie Jackson at the North Star Academy in Newark, New Jersey, Jay Altman decided to devote an entire professional development session back in New Orleans to reproducing her lesson. "Ms. Jackson's Mythical Math Class," he called the workshop. "I had everyone go through the experience of her class and used all these techniques I'd learned from the visit. One of them was oral warm-up in math, like language class." He brought his staff to their feet and peppered the room with questions, just as Julie Jackson had done with her fifth-graders. "Like, 'Who can point out a pair of parallel lines in this room? Okay, three hundred times thirty plus ten times five equals what?' And then, if a kid answered, say, 'Okay, who agrees with that answer? Who disagrees? Why or why not?'" In one short exercise, she'd managed to get her students thinking, talking, practicing fluency, using math vocabulary, and giving herself lots of insights into what they did and didn't understand. Altman wanted all that for his students too.

Another trip, organized by Linda Brown, the Boston charter school advocate who had been at first perplexed and then impressed by APR's belt policy, offered a tour of innovative schools in New York City. "We rented a bus that held 44 people, and we took the Massachusetts charter schools that had opened," Brown says. It was 1996, the second year of charter schools in the state; only twenty-two schools had opened so far. "We filled the spaces in about 25 minutes." The trips eventually became a formal training program for no-excuses principals: the Building Excellent Schools fellowship.

Reading Po Bronson's account of life in Silicon Valley during the dot-com boom (*The Nudist on the Late Shift*), one APR teacher, Chi Tschang, saw himself and his colleagues in the descriptions of the scrappy Hotmail programmers who slept under their desks. Later, after Chi introduced himself to Bronson by e-mail, the author visited and wrote about APR. An "educational 'start-up,'" Bronson called it.

As no-excuses charter schools proliferated, their students prospered. All the students in APR's first graduating class passed the state exams, just as Stacey had promised (or their money back!), and all went on to four-year colleges. At Roxbury Prep, a middle school, students consistently led the state, fancy Boston suburbs included, in math and science proficiency. Jay Altman's New Orleans Charter Middle School became the highest-performing nonselective middle school in the city. North Star, KIPP, and Amistad followed the same pattern.

Observers interpreted the success in the same accountability framework that had generated charter schools in the first place. The no-excuses schools must have done better because they were more accountable to results—and therefore, in the language of the day, "results-driven." Free of bureaucratic red tape (such as the rules about teaching hours and substitutes that eventually doomed Jessie Fry's efforts at Spartan Village), and finally given the incentive to succeed, they produced the outputs demanded of them. "Had we tried to invent North Star at the federal government," joked then-governor George W. Bush on a visit to the school in 2000, "they'd still be in committee hearings."

Doug Lemov believed in accountability too. Indeed, he believed in it so much that, three years after APR opened, he decided to leave for business school at Harvard, where he hoped to learn skills to improve school accountability. While many charter schools served children well, others, Doug knew, stayed in business even though they posted less sparkling results—the opposite of charter laws' intent. At business school, he thought, he could figure out how to make accountability work better for all schools, not just successful charters.

Eventually, Doug put the idea into practice at a new dream job, managing the accountability systems for charter schools across New York State. Later, he went off to start a company of his own, building diagnostic tests to help schools meet their goals. At Harvard he'd become especially bullish about data. Treated carefully, he learned, data could both paint an accurate picture of which companies (or schools) were performing and which weren't—and give them the tools to get better. The diagnostic tests were an example. Schools that Doug worked with could use them to track their students' progress toward state standards throughout the year, recording each child's advancement in order to spot lapses: Why does Kayla understand two-dimensional figures and time, but not money? Why is Destiny doing well with congruence but not the calendar? Scrutinizing data could help teachers make decisions. Ahzheona, with her 50 percent scores in a certain category, probably needed a day of tutoring; Jasmine, who scored below 50 percent across the board, needed tutoring *every* day; and Kendra and Amirah, with the class's highest marks across all the standards, were ready for a new challenge.

Doug's work at both jobs earned him praise. New York's charter school standards were heralded as the best in the country, and the diagnostic testing company, called School Performance, won him the acclaim of the US Department of Education, which asked him to speak about the approach at an education summit in 2006.

By the time he gave the presentation, though, he was already beginning to see the limits of accountability. The year before, he'd worked with a school in Syracuse that presented a conundrum. Walking through the hallways and meeting with teachers and administrators, Doug found a school drenched in just the kind of great expectations he had practiced at APR. The school used Doug's diagnostic tests, and the principal was so obsessed with goal setting that she had hung a banner in the entrance listing her top three goals for everyone to see:

1. Increase parental involvement to 100%

2. Intentional practice for goal-setting

3. Increase achievement in reading, math

Doug could see that everyone in the building shared the principal's goals. The teachers were not lazy monopolists, enjoying tenure, raking in attendance checks from the district, and promoting kids who hadn't earned it. Instead, they sat down on the floor, holding books right in front of the children's faces, practically begging them to succeed.

But as he spent more time in its classrooms, Doug saw that the school's high hopes, however staunchly held, failed to materialize in practice. This was not a Hollywood-style urban jungle, the kind of brutal failure Doug had seen where students called their teachers motherfuckers and instructors made basic factual mistakes. (At one school, a teacher had solemnly lectured about the "farmers" of the Constitution.) Here, the failure was much more insidious and also, Doug suspected, much more common.

Students obeyed basic instructions, and teachers' lesson plans had beginnings, middles, and ends. But it was as if the two sides had reached a truce: the students would create minimal chaos, provided the teacher wouldn't demand too much of their concentration. It was a lose-lose compromise. Class discussions dragged grudgingly forward. The same three students always raised their hands. And the same ones launched subtle protests against serious learning. In one class that Doug observed, the teacher spent several minutes debating a student about why he didn't have a pencil. Another divided her students into two groups to practice multiplication together, only to watch them turn to the more interesting work of chatting. A single quiet student soldiered on with the problems, alone. The teacher looked the other way, and Doug couldn't watch the rest. He walked out the door.

Teaching did not have to feel that way, like suffocating slowly. And high expectations had to be more than a poster hanging from the ceiling or a law signed in Washington, DC. To guarantee that real learning happened, something had to change in the actual *classroom.*

The problem did not seem to be a lack of models. Following Doug's old strategy of watching better teachers at work, the school had already taken a group field trip to one of the crown jewels of the no-excuses world: KIPP Academy in New York City. Created by David Levin and Mike Feinberg, two early Teach For America corps members, KIPP was a perfect model of both the zero-tolerance discipline approach and the sermonizing school-as-pep-talk culture.

Yet when Doug asked the Syracuse teachers about the trip, he found that the visit had not proved instructive. The teachers had seen plenty of things—the arrangement of the reading rugs, the colors of the uniforms. But like the visitors who watched Magdalene Lampert and Deborah Ball teach at Spartan Village, they had not seen the things they needed to learn. "I just remember thinking, 'Holy shit. *That's* what you took away?' The things they took away were so random, and if you ranked the most important things about a high-performing school from 1 to 100, they had seen number 63, number 84, and number 47. As opposed to numbers 1, 2, and 3."

But what were 1, 2, and 3? Doug always told client schools that his data reports were only the beginning. "This tool is only as good as what people do with it," he told the audience at the national summit. "Empower them to take real action." But what actions should teachers take?

Doug understood the Syracuse teachers' struggle, going to KIPP and not knowing what to focus on. He could think of plenty of great teachers he'd seen since he started working in urban schools. But describing the things that made them great was like trying to describe a dream. He could explain how their teaching made him feel: good or bad, pained or giddy. But he could not explain exactly what happened or why or how to make the bad moments better.

He thought about soccer, the sport he'd played through college and beyond. If his teammates wanted him to do better, they didn't just say, "Improve." or "Be more like Beckham!" They broke that "it" factor down, telling him to "mark tighter" or "close the space." Maybe the reason he struggled to talk and even to think about teaching was that the right words didn't exist—or at least, they hadn't been invented. Not yet anyway.

6

LEMOV'S TAXONOMY

Driving home from Syracuse with his colleague Karen
Cichon, a former Catholic-school teacher who now
worked with him at School Performance, Doug Lemov
couldn't stop thinking about the soccer metaphor. As a teacher,
he had always been an evangelist for the power of clear language
to help students understand exactly what you wanted them to
do. He often crusaded against what he called "the fundamental
ambiguity of 'shh,'" one of the most widely used teacher phrases
in the American school and also, tellingly, one of the least specific. "Are you asking the kids not to talk, or are you asking the
kids to talk more quietly?" he would ask teachers. The same lesson applied to teachers. Learning how to teach, they needed specific instructions as much as their students did.

But where could the words come from? Doug thought of a
recent visit he'd made to a classroom at Roxbury Prep with one
of the school's administrators, Josh Phillips. At a certain point,
Josh pulled Doug into the hall. "Did you see that?" he said. "The
teacher told the kids to put their hands down." It had been a
counterintuitive move. Presented with eager hands, most teach-

ers would naturally reward their enthusiasm by letting the children speak. But this teacher decided the questions had become redundant, and she moved on. "That's how we do it here," Josh told Doug.

A decade of work had come down to "how we do it here," a way of doing school so detailed and intricate it even included an opinion on when to stop taking students' questions during a lesson. Learning together, the no-excuses leaders had taken a blank canvas and turned it into a system of thought and practice. What Doug needed was a way to communicate that vision, to foreground all the little things that made up the no-excuses way so that any visitor would be sure to see them. He needed better words.

As Karen drove them down the highway back to Albany, Doug explained his idea from the passenger seat. They needed to create a "common vocabulary" to describe the elements of good teaching. He wanted the Syracuse principal to be able to sit in the back of a classroom, take notes, and, just as the bell rang, pass the teacher a Post-it: "Nice job closing the space. Next time, mark tighter." Or whatever.

Whatever.

Sitting at the wheel of her Jeep, Karen thought it over, rewinding through her memory of everything they'd just seen at the school. Suddenly, she had one. It was a small thing she'd seen a few teachers do that always drove her crazy—maybe because, when she taught, she'd often succumbed to the same temptation. Frustrated with bad behavior, teachers often fixated on it, complaining so much about what students were doing wrong that they forgot to explain how to behave right.

Suppose a boy named Daniel tossed a pencil up and down until, whoops! the pencil parachuted over to the other side of the room. The sensible teacher would want Daniel to quit playing with that stupid pencil. Then she would want him to put it in the little groove on his desk and not touch it again. Then she would want the class to return immediately to the matter at hand. Given these goals, the sensible teacher might say something calm like, "Daniel, put that pencil in the pencil holder and look at me."

But the frustrated teacher is not usually sensible. Watching that pencil sail across the room, and maybe imagining it spiking Lawrenesha in the eyeball or skewering Dante the goldfish, the words flying out of the frustrated teacher's mouth, more likely, would be something like, "*Daniel!* I'm going to glue that pencil to your *fingers!*" Not only would these words fail to describe the correct behavior; they would draw unnecessary attention to the misbehavior. Any student who hadn't noticed that flying pencil would know all about it now, and the power in the room would shift from the diligent students to the dunce.

More examples emerged. "David," Doug said, taking on a teacher voice, "I asked you to sit up, and I still don't see several of you sitting up. Pause." He went back to his regular voice. "Okay, so what [I] just did was make it explicit that the kids didn't do what [I] asked them to do, and there wasn't a consequence for it. You almost couldn't do anything *less productive* in your classroom."

If a principal caught a teacher making this mistake, Doug and Karen thought, he should be able to send her a one-phrase reminder. Maybe they could call it "What to Do," to represent the goal of responding to misbehavior by pointing out exactly what to do instead, rather than giving attention to the failure. "John," the teacher might say, "that's the *third time* you're out of your seat." Okay, the principal could write, but *What to Do*? Or, "Andrea, why do you have to go to the bathroom so much? Why didn't you go at lunchtime?" Another *What to Do*.

Karen and Doug thought about problems beyond behavior

too. At the time, everyone had "high expectations." There wasn't a teacher to be found who would admit to having *low* expectations. Yet in Syracuse, and in other schools across upstate New York, they'd seen a thousand small ways that teachers unwittingly showcased that soft bigotry. Like, when a teacher asked a question and all hands in the room went up but three, and the teacher was happy because that was pretty good. But she never followed up with those three, and the ones who got the question right—she never asked them to take a step further and try to solve a slightly harder question.

Or what about when a student answered a question with *almost* the right answer, but not quite, and that was good enough? Or when a teacher asked a specific student—say, Benjamin—for an answer, and the student shrugged? "I-o-no," Benjamin would say, looking somewhere else. And because it seemed impossible to pull anything more out of him, especially under the time constraints and considering the fact that he was one of only thirty students in the packed, maybe also hot room, the teacher would move on. And Benjamin would get away without saying another word.

Karen and Doug came up with more categories to go along with What to Do. "100 Percent" would remind the teacher to make sure that every single student in the room was engaged, following along, and understood. "Right Is Right" would encourage a teacher to insist on getting the precise correct answer from the student, not a close-enough one. "Stretch It" would demand that teachers press students who easily provide the correct answer, challenging them to take the problem a step further.

Doug, who'd been writing their ideas furiously in his notebook, looked up at the dashboard. MILES TO EMPTY, the light read: 0. They'd been so engrossed in creating their new language, they hadn't realized they'd run out of gas.

A week later, Doug and Karen returned to the road. This time their destination was an elementary school in Brooklyn. Taking notes in the backs of classrooms, they once again tried to think of constructive feedback, concrete "real action" that they could tell the teachers to help them improve. Except this time, they actually had some words. It was like finally visiting the optometrist after a lifetime of nearsightedness: Fuzzy lines suddenly clicked into focus revealing clear, discernible letters. The trees had leaves.

In the first classroom a teacher was running an exercise in proofreading. To practice symbols like delete, insert, and new paragraph, students walked one by one up to an overhead projector and filled in the correct signs. One student came up and announced that a word needed to be removed. But she could not remember the name of the symbol, that loopy thing. "It's okay," the teacher said. "You can say loopy thing. I'll know what you mean."

"Right Is Right," Karen wrote.

Later the teacher moved on to a vocabulary lesson. She gave the students a word from their list and then asked them to use the word in a sentence. The first word was *enjoy*. A student said, "I enjoy my weekend."

"Can you add on that?" the teacher said.

"I enjoy my weekend by going to my cousin's house," the student said.

"Well," the teacher urged, "can you describe that boy [his cousin]?"

Karen and Doug took notes. The teacher was clearly trying to draw the student out, to push him to describe the cousin in a way that would demonstrate that the student understood the meaning of *enjoy*. "Stretch It," Karen wrote in her notebook; this time, she'd found a good example.

The next word was *poison*. "One day when my uncle came," a student offered, "I made a poison." The teacher nodded. "Okay," she said. "Now, next word."

Karen wrote this down in her notebook too—as a bad example of "Stretch It." Without any context clues explaining why the student had made poison when his uncle came, he hadn't demonstrated that he understood the word's meaning. Not only that; in the process, he'd gotten the whole class thinking about his uncle, rather than the meaning of the word *poison*—and the teacher had done nothing to steer back their focus.

Later, Karen took account of the lesson in her notebook: "Think of all of the things going on there," she wrote. "What are the important words to learn? In the sentence they're using, is that the best way to decide: is that the right word to use or not? If a sentence comes up that takes them off task—well, now there's 18 kids that really want to hear about the uncle making poison, as opposed to deciding what is the word, what does it mean, on we go. There's a whole lot that you could analyze just based on what was a quick homework review."

The simple vocabulary that Doug and Karen were developing—only a handful of terms so far, representing a handful of techniques—helped them say so much more.

By 2010, Doug had traveled to dozens more schools, this time not to solve problems, but to find solutions, more techniques to name. He always began a school visit by asking the principal for a report on the teachers who helped students the most. Then he went into their classrooms, bringing a videographer with him— the first videographer was basically a wedding photographer, whom Doug had met through a friend—so that afterward, he could study the tape more carefully, rewinding the key parts like an NFL coach reviewing the opposing team's plays. Soon, he'd brought the wedding guy on full-time. For Doug, too, the project had grown from a side interest to a nearly full-time job.

A few years earlier, Doug had left his data business to start two new charter schools—one in Rochester and another one in Troy, New York, just outside Albany. The schools were part of the new Uncommon Schools charter network, a collaboration that brought Doug together with some of his old friends: John King and Evan Rudall of Roxbury Prep in Boston; Norman Atkins of North Star in Newark, New Jersey; Brett Peiser of Boston Collegiate, who was now opening schools under the Uncommon banner in Brooklyn. Uncommon had institutionalized the group's informal community. Now, rather than just calling each other up when they had a question, Doug, John, Evan, Norman, and Brett held regular "managing director" conference calls to chart strategy. And instead of sharing ideas and curricula and worksheets and tests haphazardly, they shared them by design.

The taxonomy project emerged in the same way—a weird side project of Doug's that gradually became something bigger. One reason Doug and his cohorts built Uncommon was to help all their schools expand. After achieving isolated successes, they were under pressure from funders, parents, and themselves to create more high-performing charter schools. But growth had introduced a million new problems; chief among them was talent. They had all been in the practice of finding great teachers the same way corporate head hunters find skilled employees: they scouted out the best talent at other schools and recruited those teachers away by offering a better work environment and, when necessary, a nicer salary.

Now, as the group opened more schools, and other charters did the same (Achievement First, KIPP, and other no-excuses schools were becoming franchised networks at exactly the same time), the competition for great teachers was growing fierce.

Uncommon decided to change its approach. Rather than buy talent, the network would try to build it. The "build it/buy it" epiphany gave Doug the same illuminating sense he had felt in Syracuse when he realized the limits of data and accountability. Attracting the best teachers through incentives got the charters only so far. To scale up, they needed a way of helping any average teacher get better. They needed a kind of playbook, an understanding of what made the best teachers great so that they could help the merely ordinary get even better. They needed Doug's taxonomy.

That was what teachers had started calling his vocabulary project: the Doug Lemov taxonomy, an organized breakdown of all the little details that helped great teachers excel. Soon, the taxonomy had become part of Doug's official job. Instead of expanding his upstate New York branch of Uncommon at the same pace as the others, he would focus half of his time on building his taxonomy and recruiting a small team of video "analysts" to help him do it. Charter school supporters on the outside might conclude that the key driver was accountability, but inside Uncommon, Doug and the others knew that training was just as important.

As Doug built the taxonomy, he took advantage of the growing Uncommon network, which gave him a wide new pool of teachers to study. Soon his list of techniques had expanded to forty-nine. Some, like "Right Is Right," covered academic standards. But the techniques that got the most attention covered discipline and attention, the vital core of no-excuses culture.

At its heart, the no-excuses idea actually represented an end, not the means. Doug and Karen had called one of the first techniques "100 Percent." It described a goal—a classroom where 100 percent of students meet 100 percent of the expectations 100 percent of the time—rather than the means of achieving it.

How did the best teachers get all those eyes on them, or all those brains thinking through the problem?

To the untrained eye, the key to obedience seemed to be sheer personality. Observers often spoke of how great teachers worked "magic," as if they turned a hat into a rabbit. In a way, they had. Where previously had sat defiant, misbehaving children, voilà!: eager, attentive, curious scholars. These virtuoso teachers had "it," whatever "it" was. But when Doug studied these teachers more closely, he saw that the students had not actually transformed— not completely anyway. Presented with the most charismatic, engaging teachers, some students would still deviate—refusing to pay attention, for instance—or they would forget to follow a rule.

The difference lay in what happened just after a student strayed. What did the teacher do *then*? The more Doug studied his videotape, the more intricate the answer seemed to be. Just as students seemed to find a million different ways to misbehave or make a mistake, there was also no one way for a teacher to respond, no secret formula. But there did seem to be a series of principles that all the "it" teachers followed, consciously or not, and the principles seemed to lead toward certain important moves, a sliding scale of responses to select and deploy in each particular moment.

One of the first teachers to impart this lesson to Doug was Colleen Driggs, a Teach For America alumna who taught at his school in Rochester. Colleen had "it," that enchanting quality that transformed children into students. But one day, watching a videotape of her teaching a vocabulary lesson, Doug noticed something he hadn't seen before. Just beneath the surface of her calm, cool teaching—she was especially good at getting students to talk not only to her, but to each other—lay a series of practically invisible hand gestures. Midsentence, she would point two fingers at her eyes, bat down an imaginary fly with two quick swipes, or, with no explanation, briefly clasp her hands before her, as if in prayer. During one five-minute video clip, a discussion of the meaning of the word *scarce*, Doug counted fifteen such gestures, one every twenty seconds.

Watching again, he could see that the gestures clearly meant something, both to Colleen and to her students. Two fingers to her eyes—that meant "track the speaker," code for paying attention to the person talking, usually another student. The fly swat, applied to a raised hand, meant "I'm not taking questions right now." And the prayer sign reminded students to get into the attentive position that no-excuses schools called SLANT or STAR, a back-straight pose tied off with primly clasped hands.*

Colleen had created the gestures, she explained, so that she could subtly correct students' misbehavior without interrupting the flow of her lesson. At the beginning of each year, she taught the three gestures explicitly. For the first few weeks, every time she used one, she would say its name too. But pretty soon, she could pull off performances like the one Doug had witnessed. When she said, "The food in Mrs. Driggs' refrigerator is *scarce* because the inconsiderate guests came over and ate almost all of it," the only person who noticed that she'd also gripped her hands in prayer just between "scarce" and "because" was the student who had lapsed from SLANT. The practically invisible corrections explained her "magical" command of the classroom. By nipping interruptions in the bud, she kept everyone in the room on task.

* Although the wording varies slightly at each school, in general, SLANT stands for "Sit up, Listen, Ask questions, Nod, and Track the speaker with your eyes." STAR stands for "Sit up, Track the speaker, Ask and answer questions, and Respect those around you."

The practice became one of the core principles of the "100 Per-cent" technique. What did "it" teachers do when confronted by student misbehavior? They used "the least invasive form of inter-vention," Doug wrote in the taxonomy.

He found another example in a video of another Rochester Prep teacher, named Patrick Pastore. Asking a class of sixth-graders for attention, Patrick counted down how many pairs of eyes he needed, until the number was just one. The last student was a boy named Dwayne. But Patrick had never said the boy's name. Instead, he'd just said, "We need one more set of eyes." The move echoed Colleen Driggs's technique. Presented with a child refus-ing to follow directions, Patrick corrected him—but in a way that was almost invisible. The alternative, of course, would have been to call his name. *Dwayne*, Patrick could have said, hands on his hips. *We're all waiting.* But imagine, Doug thought, what would have happened then.

"Everyone's looking at Dwayne, and then Dwayne has a choice," Doug explained to a group of teachers later, giving a workshop on the taxonomy in Boston. "Am I going to have everyone see me bend and do what Patrick asked me to do or am I going to [act] out, even at great cost to myself, to save my honor?" A power struggle would ensue, and, in all likelihood, the situation would escalate, with Dwayne resisting harder, forcing Patrick to push back equally hard. They might spend two minutes just resolving the fight. Or they might never resolve it.

In the second it took to notice that Dwayne wasn't paying attention, Patrick seemed to have made all these calculations and decided to try his hardest to avoid a showdown. Using the least invasive form of intervention lightened a teacher's job, but it also lightened the student's. Compliance came at a much lower cost.

Too often, Doug knew, teachers made another choice, and the consequences multiplied. "The death spiral," he called it. "Let's

say I'm teaching, and Anne is slouching," Doug said at the workshop in Boston, motioning to a teacher named Anne. "I could
stop and say, 'Just a minute, class. Anne, I really need you to sit
up.'" He switched perspectives. When he made that move with
Anne, what was likely to go through the minds of the rest of the
class? "The kids who were least engaged are least likely to get
back on task with me," he said, answering his own question. "I
stop my lesson to correct one student, and when I correct that
student, three more kids get off task, and then I have to run over
here, and I have to correct another student, and then three more
kids over here get off task. And then I never catch up. I never win.
It's the death spiral."

But what about the cases when it simply wasn't possible to
correct a student without naming him? Colleen Driggs could
point to her eyes because the student who had failed to watch
the speaker was watching her. Same with the student who lapsed
from SLANT and the ones with their hands up at the wrong
time. But what if the child was staring into space? What if the
hand gesture or the anonymous hint ("We need one more set of
eyes") didn't work?

Doug grouped possible responses into six accelerating options,
each one slightly more invasive than the last. Just one step above
"nonverbal intervention," a nearly invisible hand gesture like
the ones Colleen Driggs used, was "positive group correction."
By *positive* Doug meant constructive—describing the desired
behavior, rather than the problem. "We're following along in our
books," a teacher could say, posing the statement like self-evident
narration, even if it also contained a hint of aspiration, serving to
remind the boy in the back that he shouldn't be looking out the
window. To make the point slightly more clear, a teacher could
shift to second person: "You should be following along." Level
three, "anonymous individual correction," was Patrick's move.

"We need two people," a teacher could say. Often, "it" teachers even fudged numbers, optimistically declaring they needed two when really the number was four or five, a purposeful misstatement designed to create the illusion that the order under request was in fact happening now. Act as if it is already so, and before you know it, it will be.

Level four approximated anonymity as much as possible without actually preserving it. "Private individual correction," Doug called it, after watching several "it" teachers casually place themselves next to a misbehaving child (oh, did I end up here? what a coincidence!), kneel down, and whisper a reminder. The best executions failed to distract anyone except the student who was not paying attention in the first place. The teacher did this by somehow making an action that was both purposeful and antagonistic appear exactly the opposite, a friendly accident.

One ingenious Rochester Prep teacher, Jaimie Brillante, began with a diversion: she gave the whole class a quick, silent task: "Copy it down, please." Then, with the students' faces pointed to their papers, she walked casually in the direction of a girl on the right who hadn't been paying attention. But instead of marching straight over to her, she meandered, picking up two tissues from the classroom Kleenex box, dropping them warmly on the desk of a girl in her path, and peering curiously over the shoulder of another girl. When she took a few more steps over to the one who was her real destination all along, nobody noticed, and they didn't eavesdrop on her stage-whispered correction either.

The whole move required strategic finesse, especially considering that it was laced within a lesson that Jaimie never stopped teaching. It also depended on the ordinariness of Jaimie's happening to weave from one corner of the classroom to another. She could walk around like that without attracting attention because she walked around all the time, not just when someone misbehaved.

Doug labeled the next intervention, level five, "lightning-quick public correction." This, too, was best conducted surgically. "Andrew, I need you with me, just like Jeremy and Anne and David. Now we're looking sharp!" Doug modeled at the workshop. "So I corrected Andrew publicly," he explained, "but I did a couple of things. One, I instantly diverted the gaze from him to someone else or something else, and, when possible, that something else is much more positive. So if I said, 'Andrew, I need you with me,' then you're all going to divert your gazes to Andrew, and we're in that situation where I have to win, it's all public, and then I can't afford to lose." Instead, he let Andrew take the stage for half a second before quickly moving on to Jeremy, Anne, and David and the idea that "we" (read: *everyone*, even Andrew) were now "looking sharp."

The sixth and final level was "consequence," the most visible response. But even a consequence did not need to look the way one might picture it, a tense exercise of power that grabbed everyone's attention. (How many times had a teacher handed out a detention only to find the room taken over by a chorus of "ooooh!" solving one problem but creating another?) He referred the Boston teachers back to a video he'd shown earlier, a cheerful sequence in which a kindergarten teacher, George Davis of the Leadership Prep school in Brooklyn, declared that "one of our friends is not ready yet" and asked his students to try composing themselves in the SLANT position one more time. Making the students get to SLANT again, Doug pointed out, was a consequence—physical work doled out because of a small behavioral lapse. "It" teachers did sometimes resort to detention or that easiest of Hail Marys—"Dean's office, now!"— but they usually reserved these for the most severe cases, and even then, they kept their cool, working to keep interruptions to a minimum.

The six levels of behavioral intervention represented just one subprinciple of one technique among Doug's ultimate list of forty-nine, the "Taxonomy of Effective Teaching Practices." In addition, there were Technique No. 43, "Positive Framing" ("Narrate the world you want your students to see even while you are relentlessly improving it"), with its six rules (including one, "Assume the Best," describing how the best teachers acted as if students misbehaved out of ignorance, rather than willful defiance, unless proven otherwise); Technique No. 26, "Everybody Writes" (in which a teacher follows up a question by asking every student in the class to write down her thoughts on paper); and Technique No. 44, "Precise Praise" (reflecting Doug's conclusion that successful teachers distinguish praise, which includes a positive judgment, from acknowledgment, which merely describes an expectation met, and offering two other "rules of thumb" for giving good praise, including the suggestion to "praise loud; fix soft" and to ensure that all praise is genuine—not a means to another end, like pointing out one student's success in order to chide another on her failure).

But did the taxonomy capture the magic of teaching as well as the science? Doug's experience with Bob Zimmerli suggested it could. Bob was a teacher Doug had first met in 2005, when he interviewed for a position on the founding team at Rochester Prep by teaching a sample lesson on place value. "It was like seeing the truth," Doug says. "Bob just walked in with a pencil, and it was like a bolt of lightning came down." Doug knew that the students, on loan from a school he worked with, were not the most enthusiastic bunch. But in Bob's hands, they turned into new people, individuals who took an interest not just in school but in math. Doug immediately asked him to teach a second sample. He had just started building the taxonomy, and he needed to capture Bob on videotape. "I knew that if you could bottle what he'd done, you would have something incredible."

Five years later, the tape of the second sample lesson had become a classic in the taxonomy canon. The video opens at the start of class, with Bob standing in front of another group of students he has never met. As class begins, the children—fifth-graders, all of them black, mostly boys—are looking everywhere but at Bob, who stands at the board. One is caught playing with a pair of headphones; another pages slowly through a giant three-ring binder. "Okay, guys," Bob says, "before I get started today, here's what I need from you." He's dressed in a neat suit and tie, with the thin, athletic build of a cyclist. "I need that piece of paper turned over and a pencil out." Almost no one is following the directions, but Bob persists. "So if there's anything else on your desk right now, please put that inside your desk." He motions a quick underhand pitch, demonstrating what he wants the students to do. "Just like you're doing, thank you very much," he says, pointing to a student in the front who has put her papers away. Another desk emerges neat; Bob zeroes in. "Thank you, sir." "I appreciate it," he says, pointing to another student. By the time he points to one last student—"Nice . . . *nice*"—the headphones are gone, the binder has clicked shut, and everyone is paying attention.

Bob Zimmerli might have been the perfect case of the unexplainable "it" teacher. A preacher on the side, he possessed a charm that seemed downright ethereal. But watching the video in the context of the taxonomy research, Doug saw the lesson with new eyes. "Imagine," Doug told the teachers in Boston, after showing the clip, "if his first direction had been 'please get your things out for class.'" Instead, he'd deployed a perfect version of one of the first techniques Doug and Karen Cichon had named: "What to Do," which had now become Technique No. 37, an extension of the principle behind "Assume the Best." More often than defiance, Doug had noticed that misunderstanding lay behind students' failure to follow directions. "It" teachers got students to do something by being brutally specific about exactly what they wanted. Bob had also deployed rule number four of the "Positive Framing" technique: "Build momentum, and narrate the positive." Instead of focusing on the binder or the headphones, he'd pointed out the students who *did* listen. "It's this positive wave," Doug said. "You can almost see it going across the classroom from right to left."

He played the clip one more time, directing the group's attention to the boy with the binder. When the video starts, his head is down as he pages slowly through his papers. Ten seconds in, he looks to his left, where another boy has the paper and pencil and is staring at the teacher. For the first time, he looks up at Bob and stops paging. "He's like, 'OK, what's this?'" Doug narrated. "'I guess I'm going to go with it.'" Thirty seconds later, his binder is closed, and he's pushing it inside his desk, underhand—just like Bob showed him.

Not only did the taxonomy explain Bob's success; Bob himself said he learned something from it. His testimonial was one of dozens. Doug had been sharing his ideas since the beginning, typing the taxonomy into increasingly dense Word documents and e-mailing them to colleagues across the country with video files to match. Every time he shared the list with a new person, he learned something new, and he built the new ideas back into the document.

The effects accelerated as he started collecting more video. When he and the new team of data analysts hired to help sift through the growing volume of classroom tape went through the new videos, they not only found new ideas; they also found evidence that the original techniques were spreading. Having watched Bob Zimmerli "narrate the positive," other teachers tried the same thing themselves. And often they improved the techniques in the process. Sometimes the new footage even outshined the originals.

An early star, a teacher at the all-boys Brighter Choices charter school in Albany named Darryl Williams, had shown Doug the first case he'd ever seen of Technique No. 39, "Do It Again," in which teachers deploy the most minor form of a consequence, teaching students to perform simple routines by asking them to repeat them until they can do them well. But as the DVD clip of Darryl made its way around the country, more teachers picked up on the idea, and soon their interpretations took the idea to new heights.

The new elaborations made Darryl's execution look commonplace, even weak—his delivery too slow, the routine too insipid, his students needlessly morose. The new videos showed how to keep the power of the exercise without sacrificing time or pep. "Saying, 'Oooh, let's line up again and prove why we're the best reading group in the school,'" Doug wrote in the taxonomy, "is often better [than] saying 'Class, that was very sloppy. We're going to do it again until we get it exactly right,' even if the purpose is to *Do It Again* until you get it exactly right." "Do It Again" also seemed to work just as well when teachers called for a video game–style redo right in the middle of a routine, rather than waiting until the end. Indeed, interrupting at the first sign of a slip was less dismal and took up less time. The taxonomy became a kind of recursive process. Doug and the analysts sent a technique out into the world, and then the world sent it back: the same idea, refined.

Perhaps the best evidence of the taxonomy's success was Doug himself. He'd considered himself a weak teacher since his first job, teaching English in Princeton, New Jersey, where his lovingly crafted lessons always seemed to fizzle, leaving him to count the remaining minutes. Now, teaching fellow teachers, it was like he had left his old persona back in Princeton and wrapped himself in new skin.

He called on his students cold ("Cold Call," Technique No. 22), without making anyone feel pressured, creating the feeling of a natural, spontaneous conversation while still carefully keeping track of time and steering the learning in one purposeful direction. When he posed a particularly difficult question ("Number one, what does [this teacher] add to our understanding of non-verbal intervention? And then two, can you find evidence of the other principles of 100 Percent?"), he made sure to give each participant time to write down her thoughts on a carefully prepared worksheet. And he built in jokes, getting the whole room to laugh just when the proximity of lunch might have stolen attention from the collective enterprise. The result was the truest measure of the master teacher. Sitting in a Lemov taxonomy workshop, a participant experienced that most satisfying buzz, the revelatory aha! feeling that comes from thinking deeply—the unmistakable pleasure of learning.

The taxonomy was not *jugyokenkyu*, exactly, but it was a twenty-first-century American hybrid. Instead of devising a language organically, as an accidental by-product of postlesson discussions, Doug and his team built the new words deliberately, during structured "cutting log" meetings where analysts sat around a conference table, watching videos together and making notes. And instead of building time into the school calendar for city- or even statewide lesson observations, they sent around video files and an accompanying Word document (and later, DVDs and a book).

Yet, in more important ways, the taxonomy and the crucible that wrought it were just Japanese lesson study in a slightly different form. They produced the same effects. For one, American teachers began to develop followings. Bob Zimmerli, Colleen Driggs, Darryl Williams—they became the American equivalents of Takeshi Matsuyama, Akihiko Takahashi, and Toshiakira Fujii. If the collaborative development of the taxonomy was the entrepreneurs' version of lesson study, then the no-excuses schools were their laboratories, the equivalent of the *fuzoku* schools where Akihiko had learned and taught. And their ranks were growing. According to Linda Brown, the Boston charter school supporter who went on to train charter school principals, by the time Doug wrote the taxonomy, the number of no-excuses schools had grown from about fifteen to more than a hundred.*

The biggest difference between the American and Japanese teaching laboratories was not how they studied teaching, but what kind of teaching they described. Both Doug and Akihiko disavowed the usefulness of "shh," but for different reasons. Whereas Akihiko thought that children needed structured opportunities to talk in order to learn, for Doug, learning first required the foundational ability to be quiet and listen. He just didn't think "shh"—with its fundamental ambiguity (should students stop talking or just talk more quietly?)—was a good way to get them there. And so, whereas in Japan school was interrupted by a chaotic burst of screams as children took their hourly break, at no-excuses schools students walked between lessons in a determined (and not necessarily unhappy) silence.

---

*That was a tiny fraction of the number of charter schools in the United States—just over six thousand by 2013. (National Association of Public Charter Schools, http://dashboard.publiccharters.org/dashboard/schools/year/2013.)

Indeed, had James Stigler and his TIMSS colleagues taken their video cameras into the no-excuses movement's classrooms, they would have found teaching that looked not Japanese, but classically American. Doug and his colleagues had advanced far beyond the chaos of the average urban school, creating schools where studying was possible and achievement was valued—no small feat. They had even eliminated the tyranny of the unannounced PA interruption. But in many other respects, their classrooms looked no different from any other in the United States. Like their fellow Americans, the no-excuses teachers used the "I, We, You" structure (*I* explain, *we* try an example, and then *you* practice) for most if not all of their lessons, asked questions designed mainly to generate simple answers rather than to "explain how or why," and devoted most of their students' work time to practice, rather than the equally common Japanese activity, "invent/think." It was no wonder that they valued quiet, "eyes on me"–style attention so highly; for them, as for so many American teachers, attention held the keys to learning.

Ironically, this orthodoxy followed, in part, from a move that had originally seemed countercultural: the entrepreneurs' rejection of ed schools. They had spurned the schools for understandable—indeed, *data-based*—reasons. Many ed school professors' ideas about teaching—abstract advocacy for classrooms where order was less important than creativity and students' voices could always be heard—really did not work in practice. The sad truth was underlined in study after study showing that ed schools failed to help their teachers teach well.

Yet by disregarding ed schools, Doug and his colleagues also unwittingly distanced themselves from the ed school professors who *were* producing innovative ideas—people like Magdalene Lampert and Deborah Ball and their colleagues doing similar work in history, English, and science. (People who, incidentally, had made the same observation about the tendency of lovely teaching ideas, like the new California math framework, to wilt in practice.) As a result, the American *jugyokenkyu* that was the Lemov taxonomy had all the features of its Japanese counterpart except one: American ideas.

While Akihiko and his colleagues combed through the standards of the National Council of Teachers of Mathematics, devoured descriptions of Magdalene Lampert's lessons, and closely studied videos of Deborah Ball's teaching—all the way from Tokyo—Doug and the no-excuses educators unknowingly ignored their own country's best teaching innovations. As a result, when Doug built the vocabulary that Deborah longed for, he built it to describe a sort of teaching that she didn't do. Inspired by Japan, Doug created the structure that the United States had never had—a system focused on helping teachers learn—but with none of the ideas (originally American) that the Japanese filled it with.

For any other group, that strange state of affairs might have continued for years. But if anything matched the strength of the entrepreneurs' allergy to the educational status quo, it was their itch to improve. If Doug's generation had built the start-ups to disrupt the old monopoly, they had also built a machine designed to take new ideas and improve them—even if that meant attacking the core of the no-excuses approach.

THE DISCIPLINE OF
DISCIPLINE

When Rousseau Mieze joined the education reform movement, he was a true believer. The son of Haitian immigrants—his mother cleaned houses, his father drove a cab—he knew firsthand how the right school could change your life. With his parents always working, it was his teachers who first fed him sushi, his teachers who showed him how to fly through two hours talking about history and philosophy and humans' place in the universe, and his teachers who helped him return a proper handshake without laughing. Teachers acquainted Rousseau with the best tool he had: his intellect. And then his intellect took him to Williams College, the most academically stimulating place he'd ever been.

He wanted to give other kids the same gift, and he counted himself lucky that when he started college, in 2004, an ecosystem of schools already existed to do just that. Instead of interning with professors or catching up on sleep or whatever it was that other people did during breaks at Williams, Rousseau spent his time apprenticed to the movement. One summer he worked in the dean's office at a Boston charter school. The next he went to Rochester Prep and shadowed some of the Lemov taxonomy's biggest stars—Patrick Pastore, Colleen Driggs, Bob Zimmerli. To Rousseau they were heroes in the flesh.

Rousseau would defend charter schools to anyone, and by that time, he sometimes had to. By the mid-2000s, the no-excuses movement's growth had generated a considerable amount of attention and then, in turn, a backlash. Preparing for his first job, at a charter school in Rhode Island, Rousseau found himself confronted by another first-year teacher who wondered out loud whether the "no excuses" style amounted to "brainwashing." All those single-file lines and mandatory chants seemed like prison, some said. The teacher wondered if they squashed independent thought. "Nah, man," Rousseau told him, running through the key arguments, which boiled down to: Look at everything the students *learn*!

And yet, by his second year teaching, Rousseau found himself wondering what, exactly, the students were learning. That year, he was working at a charter school in Harlem where, on the surface, the teachers seemed to be doing everything right. The Lemov taxonomy was omnipresent—teachers quoted from it like the Bible. But something about the school made Rousseau feel uncomfortable. It had to do with the way teachers talked to students. They commanded them to follow rules, but they didn't offer them any rationale. Sometimes they even seemed to mock them. The kids, in turn, were great—funny, smart, sweet, like all the kids he'd ever met. But too often, they marched into class either defiant or sullen. Lifeless. Not happy. "We weren't treating kids like they were people," he says.

This was not what the taxonomy advised. "While you should expect students to do something when you ask them to, it's not really about you in the end," Doug Lemov wrote in a part of the taxonomy he called "purpose, not power." "Command obedience not because you can or because it feels good but because it serves your students." Yet somehow, the teachers seemed to be divining exactly the opposite lesson. If the point of no excuses was to teach discipline—the habits required to live a happy, productive life—then why did these children keep acting out? The teachers had only the best intentions. So did Doug Lemov. But what were all these taxonomy techniques actually teaching?

Sometime during that year, another educator sent Rousseau a chilling report about a KIPP charter school in Fresno, California. In a sixty-three-page investigation, the Fresno Unified School District described dozens of cases of what it called "inappropriate" student discipline, most of it meted out by the school's principal, a young man in his thirties named Chi Tschang. The accusations were extreme—stories of punishing disobedient children by putting them outside in the cold, locking an entire class in a two-stall bathroom, and putting a trash can on a student's head—and Chi and his teachers (as well as some of their students) argued that many were also false or misleading, given the school's ongoing feud with the school district. Even so, the overall picture was shocking.

Many dismissed the school and its principal as bad apples—an isolated case of good intentions gone wrong. That was the position that KIPP implied, declining to make a public statement backing Chi after he resigned. But others hinted at a broader takeaway message. One educator who was friendly with Chi and Rousseau—a KIPP principal in Newark, New Jersey, named Drew Martin—wrote out his thoughts in a weekly staff memo. The memo urged Drew's teachers to read the Fresno report and reflect on a single question, highlighted in a gray box: What does good discipline look like?

Chi Tschang may have been extreme, but he had drawn on a specific tradition, and the tradition deserved scrutiny too. The question Drew Martin wanted teachers to consider was not whether Chi had taken the idea of no excuses too far, but what the no-excuses approach taught in the first place. For all the infelicities described in the report, Drew knew that Chi was more typical than most people were comfortable acknowledging.

Rousseau knew this perhaps better than anyone. As one of the first graduates of the Academy of the Pacific Rim charter school, in 2004, discipline had turned his life around. Chi Tschang had been his history teacher at APR, and the person who had had the biggest influence on both of them was another young principal, named Doug Lemov.

Back then, students at the Academy of the Pacific Rim could agree about one thing: they absolutely hated school. "Nothing about school was fun," Rousseau says. Instead, APR was a parade of rules that dragged everyone down—"like a whipping and ball and chain," one student told a researcher at the time. Every chair had to be pushed perfectly in, every shirt tucked, every instruction followed, every tooth unsucked and eyeball unrolled. Either that, or you'd find yourself sitting in the dean's office with Mr. Lemov, explaining how you planned to act differently next time. When students did come to love APR—and many of them did, fiercely—their affection was always bracketed: "love-hate," said one of the school's star students and strong admirers, Millisent Fury Hopkins.

Rousseau's first memory of APR was from the second day of school, which was also the first time he got suspended. The class was working on an activity called Math Minutes, in which students competed to see how many math problems they could solve in a minute. "So I got through them, I finished, I did it, and I celebrated," Rousseau says. "I was like, '*Yessss!!* I got 100 on my Math Minute!'" The next thing he knew, he was being sent to the office. From there, he was sent home early for disrupting class.

"I was terrified," he says. Rousseau was a talker, yes, and a class clown, but he was not a bad kid. *"Please don't do this!"* he pleaded. But he had called out, disrupting his class, so they sent him home. The pattern was set. Practically every day, a teacher would send Rousseau out of class. Sometimes it happened three or four times. Most of his offenses were like that first Math Minutes celebration. No matter how hard he tried, he always seemed to find himself talking when he was supposed to be quiet, making a comment when he hadn't been called on, joking around when he should have been working. Suspensions piled up. Sometimes he got suspended three times in one week.

The flip side of Stacey Boyd's "broken windows" theory of discipline—squashing the littlest signs of disorder before they exploded into chaos—was that students spent a lot of time inside the dean's office. According to the school's annual report, in the 2002–03 school year, when Rousseau was a junior, 38 percent of students received at least one out-of-school suspension. That was down from 58 percent the year before. The combined suspension and expulsion rate in the traditional Boston Public Schools, meanwhile, was estimated at 6 percent for all students and 8 percent for black students.

Punishments at APR could be embarrassing. An untucked shirt yielded "shirt tuck-in exercises"—a calisthenics routine performed in view of the whole school. "You know, we touch our toes, we reach for the sky, we jump, and then we have to tuck our shirt back in," says Kevin Thai, a member of the school's first graduating class. With every jump, the offending shirt untucked itself again, requiring another round of calisthenics. The smallest infractions could produce the most extreme reactions. Once, in sixth grade, Chimel Idiokitas, a friend of Rousseau's, spent an entire day in the office just for dropping his pencil. Another student was joking, accusing Chimel of hitting her with his pencil, and "at that exact time, I dropped my pencil. And my teacher just assumed I did that on purpose." One time, Kevin even got in trouble for the color of his gym pants. They were supposed to be navy blue, but Kevin's were king's blue.

The students weren't always clear on the reasons for such draconian discipline. "They want you to come in like a robot. Like, just follow and follow and follow," another student told a researcher at the time. "It's really fake," said another. "It doesn't really mean anything in the real world . . . I think some of it is just a lot of pointless rules." (On the other hand, if it weren't for APR, Kevin Thai would never have known that "king's blue" is a color, not to mention have been awarded a full scholarship to college.)

All of Rousseau's friends complained. That was how APR kids bonded. They followed instructions in the manner that researchers Jere Brophy and Mary McCaslin term "grudging compliance." But while the school could be strict, the teachers also worked hard to build in time for fun. Chimel Idiokitas couldn't understand why he spent that one day in the office instead of in class, but he loved the plays APR teachers helped students put on, the field trips they took them on (including one to China), the raps they let him and Rousseau and their friends perform in the lunchroom. Even the shirt-tucking exercises, a creation of Doug Lemov's, were led in the spirit of laughter—an ironic send-up of the school's strictness, in which offending students were the "shirt tuck-in team," Doug played the role of overzealous coach, and a longtime repeat untucker was appointed team captain. Kevin Thai felt embarrassed, but many other students laughed as their principal jumped around wildly, making a deliberate fool of himself.

Rousseau defended the school, even back then. He might have been terrible at following the rules, but he believed in them. His teachers were trying to get him to college, and the rules were there to make that happen, so he did his best to find the value in them. The teachers were tough, but they cared deeply about the students. During a bad period when Kevin Thai was fighting with his parents, Chi Tschang mediated a session at school that helped them reconcile. Another time, Chi stayed at school until 11:00 at night just to make sure he replied to an e-mail Kevin had written him. Later, when Kevin became a teacher, he often thought of an APR teacher, Alexander Phillips, and tried to model his own devotion to his students on Mr. Phillips's example.

But for all that APR gave them, there were some legacies Rousseau would have preferred not to carry. Just as Kevin Thai had looked up to Alexander Phillips, Rousseau looked up to Chi Tschang as a model later, when he became a teacher himself. "If I'm a good history teacher, I should be as prepared as he was," he would think. But Chi also "became the embodiment of my low self-esteem," Rousseau says. In high school, Chi had always been the one to remind the students of what they needed to do to succeed—and what would happen if they didn't: the colleges they wouldn't get into, the dreams they wouldn't fulfill. So in college, whenever Rousseau questioned himself, he found himself thinking of Chi. "I would always hear Chi's voice, even while I was a freshman at Williams, telling me that I didn't belong there and that I didn't work hard, that I didn't deserve to be there."

As a teacher, Rousseau thought of that legacy too. Just like Chi, he often stood in front of groups of students, knowing the grim odds against them and feeling compelled to let them know too: "This is where you're going to end up if you don't get it together." But he couldn't help wondering what effect his words would have on his own students, years later.

Fear represented a fundamental irony of no excuses. The point of all those rules and consequences was to teach the students the discipline they needed to succeed. But in practice, the same consequences that seemed necessary to help students succeed could also make them more anxious, even angry. Researchers studying school discipline found that punishment often produced "resentment, retaliation, and/or emotions that are counterproductive to learning." At APR, sometimes the punishments could even push students out the door. Many of Rousseau's friends came to appreciate APR later, and even love it (the most notorious complainer, Jonathan Correia, wound up joining the school's board). But Rousseau knew that for all the students APR helped, there were others the school lost.

The first year, Doug Lemov and Stacey Boyd had started out with a class of fifty-five or so seventh-graders. But by the time that class made it to senior year, only eleven students remained. And three of them had only joined later on, in ninth grade. In Rousseau's year, the winnowing went from about a hundred kids who had started together in sixth grade to thirty-four in ninth. About thirty graduated together as seniors. (By comparison, the percentage of ninth-graders who entered Boston's public high schools in 2000 but didn't make it to graduation was 21.6.)

Much of the attrition was innocent. Even in the beginning, APR never asked students to leave (a badge of honor that some other charter schools—and many noncharter schools, for that matter—could not claim). Some of the students who didn't make it to graduation, meanwhile, were like Rousseau's friend Chimel Idiokitas, who left after middle school when he got into the prestigious Boston Latin Academy, an exam school. And over time, as APR found ways to support more of its students, the leakages declined.

Yet even with the best intentions, APR—like many schools serving high-risk communities—still lost some of the students the school most wanted to help. Some left because, fed up with either the discipline or the long school day or both, they sought another option. According to their old classmates, the students who left because they grew tired of APR's discipline tended to be the ones with the least support at home. "They were making their own decisions," Chimel says. "There wasn't a parent telling them that they had to stay because it would pay off." Without that push, "they couldn't cut it," Kevin says. So they left.*

What wasn't clear was whether the paradoxical effects of no excuses—life-changing for some, crushing for others, and sometimes, as with Rousseau and Chi Tschang, both at the very same time—needed to be that way. Did the teacher who inspired Rousseau also have to gut his self-esteem? Or was there another way?

For Drew Martin, there were many moments of truth—"stop-everything moments," one of his teachers, Ranjana Reddy, called them. The Chi Tschang report, which Drew had written up in his weekly staff memo on February 22, 2009, was one of the big ones. Another came just two weeks later, when Drew fielded reports of bad behavior on the No Limits bus.

His school, Rise Academy, a middle school that is part of the KIPP network in Newark, New Jersey, had four bus routes, all named after the school's values: No Limits, No Shortcuts, No Excuses, and Opportunity. The buses all had strict rules. Since the bus was a place where disruptive behavior could put children

---

*There is some evidence to support concerns that charter schools serve selective student populations, even though they are supposed to be open to all children. My own reporting has found evidence that some charter schools take actions that tailor the populations they serve, including discouraging applicants and "counseling out" students who are already enrolled. But I have also found cases of schools, including APR and Rise Academy (described later in this chapter), that actively oppose these selective policies.

in real danger, Rise banned every behavior that might distract the driver. Moving around was prohibited, and so was talking. Transgressors, meanwhile, faced steep consequences. Talk once, and your parents got called; talk twice, suspension. Get up from your seat? Don't even think about it. Automatic suspension.

For two years, the rules had paid off. Students got to and from school safely and obediently. But now, halfway through the school's third year, something had evidently shifted. Students were not only getting up out of their seats; they were pushing each other midtransit. Alarmed, Drew and the other school leaders temporarily suspended the entire No Limits route. Then, on Friday afternoon, just as they were preparing for an emergency parent meeting the next week to figure out what to do with No Limits, the Opportunity bus surprised them by returning to school midway through its route, still half full of children. The driver provided another unsettling report. "It turns out," Drew wrote in his weekly staff memo that weekend, "there were 3 fights on the bus that afternoon and, according to the kids, this has been going on for quite some time."

Drew's response was a bit overblown. What he called "fights" were really more like arguments, with some pushing. And, outside of the bus, a healthy majority of students at Rise were still happy, hardworking, and successful. Yet Drew could still remember Rise's first bus rides—hushed, punctilious affairs, with picture-perfect, adorable students in brightly colored backpacks riding silently to school. It pained him to watch as those same students—a few years older, sure, and unavoidably unrulier as they entered adolescence, but the same children!—now openly flaunted everything they'd been taught. "Two years ago," Drew wrote, "if I had seen a paragraph like the one written above I would have been apoplectic and completely inconsolable." The students not only talked; they fought. Official student monitors not only failed to report incidents; they actively lied about what went on.

Like the rest of the no-excuses schools, Rise was built on the proposition that behavior—or *culture*, as some of them put it—came first. Alumni of Teach For America, many of the no-excuses teachers got their starts in urban schools where learning was subordinated to mayhem. Their first pressing order of business was to change what school felt like. Plus, as Drew and the others saw it, interpersonal skills were as important as any academic subject, maybe even constituting their own subject: the discipline of discipline. Just as in math, reading, science, and history, in discipline the measure of success was simple. Had the students learned?

The bus episodes suggested that the answer was no. Like Deborah Ball's fifth-graders, who mastered long division one day only to have to relearn it from scratch the next, the students at Rise *appeared* to learn—and then, somehow, by seventh grade, they forgot. They took all that order their teachers had given them, and they turned it back into chaos.

The failure reminded Drew of a book he'd read a few years earlier: *A Short History of Progress*. The author, Ronald Wright, describes a phenomenon he calls the progress trap, in which societies, pursuing what they think is progress, instead create the machinery of their own demise. Weapons, for instance, initially solve a short-term problem—easier hunting and readier access to food. But they also create a long-term menace, threatening human survival. Nuclear power begets nuclear war, and the expansion of energy yields to environmental devastation. "A seductive trail of successes," says Wright, "may end in a trap."

Perhaps the logic of no excuses was a progress trap too. Silent hallways were the best example. "When you go and you see that," Drew says, "you're impressed. Maybe that's because you've been to a traditional public school, where the kids are off the hook, and therefore, 'Wow. This shows that we're in control.'" Plus, the hallways solved an obvious short-term need: getting students between classes quickly, calmly, and without disruption, so that teachers could maximize their time on academics.

The approach built on some of the early ideas that defined the movement—like broken windows theory. Eliminate short-term disorder, the thinking went, and teachers could create long-term gains. "The way the thinking goes, if you give an instruction, and it's not followed," Ranjana Reddy says, "every child in that room learns the lifelong lesson that instructions don't have to be followed." The entrepreneurs *had* to respond to even the smallest infractions; it was the most important thing they could do to help.

But there was evidence that the thinking, however logical in theory, was flawed in practice. The most frightening data came from noncharter public schools, where, during the 1990s (the same time period during which the no-excuses movement arose), a parallel approach to discipline called "zero tolerance" gained increasing popularity. Like the broken windows theory, zero tolerance made powerful intuitive sense. Yet, a decade and a half later, a growing body of evidence suggested that, in practice, the policies did not pan out. One seemingly obvious idea had to do with the calculation—supported by the experience of educators in classrooms all across the country—that removing a few very disruptive students from a school would create a better space for the many remaining students to learn. In fact, as the American Psychological Association reported in a 2008 summary of the research, "data on a number of indicators of school climate have shown the opposite effect." Schools with higher suspension and expulsion rates actually had *worse* school climates and spent more time on discipline.

The policies disproportionately targeted nonwhite students, even though studies suggested they were not disproportionately disruptive. And increasingly severe consequences for misbehavior led schools to refer more students to the juvenile justice system—a phenomenon known as the "school-to-prison pipeline." There was also evidence, the APA report said, that "zero tolerance policies may create, enhance, or accelerate negative mental health outcomes for youth by creating increases in student alienation, anxiety, rejection, and breaking of healthy adult bonds."

At the best charter schools, educators poured their energies into building strong relationships with students as zealously as they meted out consequences for misbehavior. From the beginning, they aimed at getting students not just to *comply* with rules, but to decide to act morally all on their own. At the first KIPP school in Newark, teachers talked with students explicitly about these levels of moral development, as the psychologist Lawrence Kohlberg called them, even writing them on the steps of the school's staircase to underscore the point. Yet at those same schools, no excuses could take on a life of its own. If, as Ranjana Reddy understood early on, the best way to serve children was to respond to even the littlest sign of disorder, then shows of extreme, even macho, toughness should be celebrated. Indeed, for better or worse, stories about educators' most outrageous efforts—like the tale, chronicled in Jay Mathews's history of KIPP (*Work Hard. Be Nice.*) of how KIPP cofounder Mike Feinberg once traveled to a student's house to uninstall her television—became legends.

The stories arguably did some good. In Mathews's book, Feinberg says that while he wasn't sure if taking out the TV set was the right thing to do, he did think it "sent the message to students that he would go to crazy lengths to make sure they had the time and opportunity to get a good education." But the stories could also create a perverse pressure to prove one's dedication through crazy acts. One educator, after being told that she was described as a loving, sensitive, and understanding teacher, felt compelled to share a tale that seemed purposefully shocking—of a time she'd compared her students' failure to pick up a single cereal piece to the September 11 tragedy.

The extreme efforts impressed observers and produced visibly obedient children. And yet, Drew says, "some of the things that I think sometimes look the greatest are not always necessarily the greatest practices." What mattered wasn't what a visitor saw; it was what all that control did to children in the long run. In Rise's case, the kids who grew up with silent hallways were now unable to sit through a bus ride. "If that's progress," Drew says, "we're all completely screwed. We're running ourselves off the cliff." To produce a different outcome for the students at Rise, they were going to have to find a different way to teach discipline. They just had to figure out what that way was.

As it turned out, Rise's teachers already had another tool. They'd been building it for years without quite knowing they were doing it. The approach evolved from their frustration, early on, with the limits of a longtime KIPP tradition, the Bench.

The Bench was like a glorified time out, punishing misbehavior with social isolation. A student on the Bench wore a different colored T-shirt and was barred from talking to peers. The KIPP twist was that students on the Bench did not actually miss class; instead, they sat either at the edge of the room or in a normal seat, separated only by the color of their shirt and the prohibition on talking (although talking for the purpose of class was often permitted).

The Bench was effective as a deterrent. From a fifth-grader's point of view, it was "the worst thing you could ever get on," according to Malik, a Rise seventh-grader. "I see fifth-graders that be walking through this hall like they're scared," he said. "They're scared to even look at me." They didn't want to do anything that would land them on the Bench. (Interestingly, from an adult's point of view, the fifth-graders could not have looked happier: walking through the hallways, they grinned and held each other's hands; later, in class, they threw their hands into the air to answer a teacher's question with gleeful gusto.) But the Bench also had a perverse side effect. The students who had the hardest time interacting with each other were also, naturally, the ones most likely to get on the Bench. Some of them would stay on "for weeks and weeks and weeks," says Ranjana Reddy, the former Rise teacher. As a result, "our biggest behavioral problem kids would have no practice interacting with other kids socially."

The irony wasn't lost on the teachers. So as the students got older, Ranjana and the other teachers decided to modify the Bench. Soon, seventh- and eighth-graders—the "upper school" at Rise—had a new Bench alternative. Choices, the teachers called it. Choices traded the Bench's immediate social isolation for the relatively less disruptive consequences of detention and silent lunch. (Instead of eating in the cafeteria, silent-lunch participants ate in a classroom with other misbehavers.) Choices added a new requirement too. To get off of it, students had to deliver a public apology to the class in which their original offense occurred— and the class had to accept.

The goal was to switch the way the school taught its disciplinary lessons. The Bench presumed that students would learn from the consequence of their actions; the punishment of social isolation would be enough to teach them never to misbehave in the same way again. And maybe that worked with fifth-graders. But for seventh- and eighth-graders, the teachers suspected, a punishment wouldn't be enough to teach better behavior. Some kind of reflection was also necessary. With Choices, Ranjana says, "the theory here is that the learning happens at the end of that piece—that there is a conversation when the person gives their apology later, and people are allowed to ask them questions when they give their apology." The resulting dialogues forced students to make sense of their mistakes, to think them through.

As Rise's teachers facilitated more and more of these public apologies, they also started to lead spontaneous conversations about behavior. "Culture conversations," they called them. Like Choices, culture conversations had their origins in more choreographed routines, in which teachers would introduce the reasons behind the school's rules by reading a book or showing a clip from a movie that illustrated the idea they wanted students to learn. But over time, the conversations about behavior started to happen right in the middle of class. Some conversations were modest, small-group affairs. Watching two students deliberately leave out another as they picked partners for a science lab, for instance, a teacher named Shannon Grande turned the moment into a chance to discuss the pitfalls of cliques. Later, in the same lesson, Shannon responded to a meltdown of a student named Destiny—"You need to be in LINES and QUIET!" she had screamed before storming out of the room—by asking the whole class to pause and discuss how to respond when Destiny returned.

Shannon didn't know about Deborah Ball and Magdalene Lampert's TKOT, but the culture conversation approach bore similarities to it. Just as with TKOT, they didn't forsake lectures, which were still crucial for clarifying important concepts and introducing new ideas; they simply supplemented them with responses to students' in-the-moment misunderstandings. And just as in TKOT, the culture conversations didn't just happen over the course of a single lesson. They sometimes stretched over weeks and months as students helped each other think through their behavior decisions—the source of which they came to think of not as "discipline," but as social and emotional growth.

In Shannon's classroom, for example, a seventh-grader named Jamal often failed to control his anger. Even the littlest comment could set him off. Your shirt's not tucked in, another student would tell him, and he would scream, slam his books on the floor, and shut down. "Ohh, why do you always have to say this to me?" he'd say. And, "I hate this place!" Sometimes, he would break out and cry during the middle of class with no explanation. At one point, he even got into a fight with one of the grade's best students, usually a paragon of perfect behavior. Frustrated, the girl lashed back, telling him that he was dirty, that he smelled. Shannon couldn't believe it. "I pulled the girl, and she was like, 'Well, he brings it on! He gets angry and then what am I supposed to say?'" Perhaps, Shannon suggested, don't tell him he smells. "And she's like, 'Well, he does!'"

That was true. Shannon knew that Jamal's hygiene was an issue. His home was a chaotic place. Just the week before, the power had gone off. The week before that, the water was shut off. At another point, part of the roof caved in. Often, with their mother gone, Jamal and his brothers would be on their own to cook dinner. He and one of his brothers didn't have regular access to showers until the staff at Rise arranged a private bathroom they could use before school.

Faced with the girl's legitimate statement—yes, Jamal did sometimes smell—Shannon decided to give the girl more context to shape the idea into something more constructive. One day, in between classes, she took that girl and three other high performers in Jamal's advisory (Rise's version of homeroom) aside. "I said, I'm going to have a very mature conversation with you right now," she says. Jamal, Shannon explained, "struggles just to get here everyday. I was like, 'you wake up in the morning and you've got somebody that's getting you out of the door, giving you breakfast, making sure your clothes are clean, making sure you're getting here on time. He doesn't have that.'" His anger wasn't acceptable, but it was understandable. And what he needed was not more reasons to feel attacked, but support—and examples of ways to react differently. Shannon concluded with a plea. "I was like, 'So I need you to keep this quiet, but I also need you to use your power and influence in the advisory to start making a change.'"

The girls were taken aback. "I didn't know that," Jamal's original combatant said. Then she asked her a question that Shannon hadn't anticipated. "She's like, 'Well, can we talk to him?'" At first, Shannon balked. She'd hoped the girls could just lead by example, responding to Jamal's outbursts with more equanimity. She certainly didn't want to create a situation that would make him even *more* vulnerable. But after thinking for a minute, she decided to let them try. The risk in drawing more attention to a behavior problem was obvious. As with Destiny, the original trigger for Jamal's meltdowns was often other students. Giving the students an opportunity to share their feelings could exacerbate the teasing, making Jamal feel worse. But Shannon also knew that middle school was a cauldron of social relationships, whether teachers paid attention to them or not. When Destiny stormed out of science class, she was gone for the moment, but soon enough she had to return, and when she did, the students had to figure out how to treat her. Similarly, Jamal and these girls saw each other every day. They went to class, lunch, and recess together. They were all on Facebook. If they didn't talk now, in the safety of a conversation that Shannon could moderate, they would talk someplace else.

Plus, just as Deborah Ball and Magdalene Lampert had found with TKOT, the upside of a conflict—the behavioral equivalent of a mathematical mistake—was a chance to learn. Opening up Jamal's behavior problem for collective examination might help him think about it differently. The group might do it better than Shannon could on her own. "Social problem solving," researchers called similar approaches.

Still, when the conversation began, Shannon was nervous. And the girls launched it with a bomb. "When you get angry, we get angry back," they said. "What do you expect us to say?" But to Shannon's amazement, Jamal responded not by lashing out, but by talking calmly. Soon enough, all of them—Jamal and the girls—were asking Shannon to let them finish the conversation in private. She decided to let them go for it. All of the students were in her advisory, and by that point, she was not only holding culture conversations with them, but letting students lead them.

Whatever they said, over the next month their advisory transformed. When Jamal had an outburst, instead of lashing back at him the other students would lead him in a conversation on what he was doing to change: journaling or deep breathing or taking a minute in the hall. The most powerful strategy of all seemed to be not any single technique, but the conversations themselves. "Even when he has a rough day, we talk about it in advisory, and he gets it out, and he moves on," Shannon says.

For his part, Jamal began to see school differently. Early on, with all its crazy rules, Rise had felt like the rest of his life: a series of personal attacks all devised to break him down. But as Shannon Grande and his classmates worked with him, Rise started to feel different, even safe. The new feeling transformed him. "Rise was my turning point," he said that year. The change wasn't academic, but much more abstract. What Rise gave him, Jamal said, was "a different view on life." Before coming to the school, he was an expert at negative thinking. He felt alone, and he thought a lot about death. At Rise, he learned to imagine success as clearly as he could imagine failure. One morning, he even woke up remembering a dream he'd never had before. "I was living by myself, but with my family, in this big house, and it was peaceful. No yelling, no arguing. Nobody saying somebody stole this. Nobody dying. Just one peaceful area." Before, he said, "I was expecting to die." But "at Rise, it gave me a new future. It gave me hope."

Educators often talk about discipline as a choice between rules and autonomy, systems and freedom, "tight" and "loose"—as if they have only two choices: either build elaborate behavior systems like the Bench or let students roam free. At Rise, changing the way the school exerted control by no means meant letting go of it. In fact, it was the opposite. Just as Ruth Heaton and Sylvia Rundquist had found at the Spartan Village school, giving students more independence meant the teachers had to do *more* work, building more intricate systems with more deliberate supports—the stuff teachers call "scaffolding." They weren't less strict. They just changed the point of intervention. Instead of building a million rules to prevent misbehavior from happening in the first place, they loosened up at the start—only to erect ever more elaborate responses when, inevitably, students crossed a line.

In addition to culture conversations, teachers increasingly sought outside help. As Paul Tough explains in *How Children Succeed*, a combination of research in economics, psychology, and neuroscience has shown that the students targeted by charter schools—the children of families suffering from multigenerational poverty and a history of racism—face more challenges than their more affluent white peers face. Even the best teachers often needed the help of psychologists and other professionals for students who continued to struggle.

Sometimes teachers used more specialized approaches. "Does it make sense for one fifth-grader to bring up a concern about another fifth-grader in front of thirty kids?" says Mariel Elguero, one of the school's founding teachers, who became dean of instruction. "Maybe in some contexts, yes, and maybe in some contexts, no. Maybe what would actually make sense is if we got those two kids together and they sat in the corner by themselves, and we gave them tools, and they figured it out."

The more complex approach did not solve all behavior problems, not even close. Although Rise was religious in its refusal never to ask a student to leave (a policy the school did not share with all other charter schools, or all district schools for that matter), every teacher could still rattle off a list of the students who made the decision themselves, resisting Rise's considerable efforts to change their minds: Aisha, who twice had to be taken from the school in an ambulance and once threatened to kill both of her parents in the school's main office; Deon, who missed two months of school one year and failed all of his classes; Abdul, the best basketball player ever to attend Rise, but a struggling student whose mother refused to let him repeat a grade. Some days, even after Jamal's turning point, it was hard not to worry that he would fall down the same path. "We have a lot, *a lot* of kids that it doesn't work for," Drew says. "We don't have an answer. We just hold on as long as we possibly can."

At the Academy of the Pacific Rim, *culture conversation* was not a term teachers used, and neither was *TKOT*. But the moments that Rousseau remembered best from school bore striking similarities to those conversations at Rise. Each punishment came with the requirement that the offending student reflect on the mistake made. As a result, students spent almost as much time talking about their behavior mistakes as they did complaining about all the school's rules.

Sometimes the reflection took the form of a public apology like the ones Rise students had to make to get off of Choices. For more serious offenses, APR required students to write out their apologies in an essay. The process was "what I think suspension should be," says Kevin Thai. "Every time, they sat me down, they talked to me, they figured out what was wrong, and tried to [help me] learn from that experience." They didn't "just throw [me] into a box and say go home."

Rousseau went through a similar routine with Doug Lemov every time he was sent to the dean's office. Looking back, these were the moments he appreciated the most, the minutes between the delinquency and the consequence, when the two of them sat down and talked—not just about what had happened, but about why. Usually, Doug began by listening. What was Rousseau struggling with? What had made him call out? Why hadn't he turned in his homework? Then they talked about his response— why calling out was unproductive for the whole group, or why disrespecting the teacher prevented Rousseau from working well with him or her.

Doug himself had gone through an evolution parallel to Drew Martin's at Rise, enhancing these more purposeful moments over time. That was the beauty of the crucible. "We were rebuilding that machine weekly, monthly, yearly," he says. The school Rousseau and his friends arrived at, in APR's first year of existence, was not the same school they graduated from. Just like Drew, Doug questioned almost everything he did. And one of the practices he thought about most—*changed* the most—was discipline.

So did many no-excuses educators. The evolution at Rise tracked similar changes at dozens of other schools. At the first KIPP replication school, in the South Bronx, the network's cofounder, David Levin, never used the Bench at all. The original KIPP school, in Houston, replaced its rigid rules with a more invisible (and more intricate) structure that gave students the space to make more mistakes. And across the network, officials added research-based substance to their intuitive early ideas about culture, creating a character curriculum that helped give teachers like Shannon Grande words and ideas to flesh out their culture conversations.

The simple way to understand the change over time was that educators collectively decided to stop crossing certain lines. And that was partly true. Indeed, every no-excuses educator seemed to have a story for the moment he decided to act differently. For Drew, it was when he found himself hoping a girl's mother wouldn't catch him disciplining her—and realized he never wanted to make that wish again. For Doug, it was the time he yanked a wandering dog out of APR, only to have a student remind him, sagely, "Mr. Lemov! He's just a *dog*!"

Chi Tschang had a story too. It happened midway through his time at KIPP Fresno, when he took some of his students on a field trip to visit the classroom of Rafe Esquith, the California educator and author who influenced many KIPP leaders. After Rafe's students performed a Shakespeare play, all of the students went out together to share a meal. "One of the things that we realized," Chi says, "is that Rafe's kids were so much *nicer* than our kids. So much more refined, more thoughtful and articulate—and more considerate." He and a colleague puzzled over the difference on the bus ride home. "And what we realized is, 'They're 10 times nicer because Rafe is 10 times nicer. Rafe never yells.'" Chi changed—and so did his colleagues.

But reality was more complicated than just deciding to act more humanely. The most thoughtful schools—the ones that Doug ran, the ones like Rise—had wanted to teach their students something more than just compliance from the beginning. And to get there, they did more than simply swing back and forth between two sides of a pendulum: loose and strict. They reflected on the same question Rousseau asked himself, about whether the good outweighed the bad, or whether the bad was even necessary—and they decided that, yes, it *was* possible to push students without crushing them. What was required was not just the right motivation, but the right skill. Discipline was not a black and white choice—tight or loose, structured or joyful. It was, says David Levin, "unstructured structure." And it was much harder. It required skill. Ultimately, that was what the entrepreneurs gained over time—not new ambitions, but the expertise to make their fullest vision come true.

What, then, explained the charter school in Harlem? The one where Rousseau found a building full of teachers, religiously versed in the Lemov taxonomy and yet defying it?

The irony was that Doug's other reason for writing the taxonomy—just as important as his commitment to developing a shared professional language—was to eliminate the possibility of such a school. Like Chi and Drew, Doug had learned some of the most important teaching lessons the hard way, and he'd done so, he knew all too well, on the backs of some children. (Indeed, he not only rejected many of his own early practices; he rejected the "no excuses" label altogether.) Why should other educators have to do the same? "Culture," as he called the discipline of discipline, was one of the teaching problems he'd worked on the most. And he knew it was also one of the easiest to wreck.

Teachers, especially teachers who had taught in dysfunctional schools, had a tendency to glob onto discipline tools "like catnip." "Like rats in the lab, you keep pressing the lever, even when they become bloated and distended," Doug says. By being meticulous about the details, by emphasizing lessons like "purpose not power" and "The J Factor," for joy (Technique No. 46), he hoped to help more schools achieve what a few schools were figuring out how to do—how to get students not just compliant, but invested; not just obedient, but happy.

In some cases, the taxonomy had done just that. Eight or ten years ago, Doug says, "the number of schools that had outstanding culture were very few and far between." Now "it's common. It's common as day to have a charter school that's figured out how to manage behavior and culture." If the taxonomy hadn't worked for all teachers, perhaps it was because—on its own—a book could go only so far.

Rousseau called the difference between the schools where discipline worked and the schools where it just didn't "that intangible piece." What was that extra piece, exactly? Some charter school teachers pointed to relationships. The teachers who really got kids to change, they said, were the ones who built strong personal bonds with them. Mariel Elguero, the dean of instruction at Rise, talked about the importance of expectations. Early on, she said, "We were like, fifth-graders can't do talking during guided practice" (the part of the class when students work on the lesson with teacher oversight)." "They can't get along! That was the perception." Now, "it's like, of *course* they can. I think it's just expecting more. Expecting what you didn't think was possible." Doug, for his part, said the difference boiled down to something even simpler: love. "In your heart, you have to think, 'I love these kids, and I want the best for them,'" he says.

When he became a teacher, Rousseau tried to do all of those things—build strong relationships, expect what didn't seem possible, teach with love. But he found that trying these techniques lacked "that intangible piece." As he saw it, this intangible piece was like the preparation he did to teach history. Getting ready for a lesson, he would force himself to imagine the mental steps the students would need to take to accomplish the goal of the lesson. By walking through an assignment himself first, he could do a "think aloud" when it came time to work with the students, bringing to the surface the invisible leaps that came naturally to him but that the students still needed to learn.

With discipline, Rousseau did something similar, digging into his memory to recall his own lowest moments. "How did I deal with it as a kid?" he'd ask himself. "How do kids deal with it now? How am I dealing with it now? What has helped me to break through now? How can I help a kid break through now with that same thing?" Teaching discipline required the same amount of mental work as teaching history, plus an extra dose of courage.

But soul searching was not the same as teaching. Once Rousseau could see the idea his students were missing, he still had to figure out a way to give it to them. He had to marshal a kind of knowledge that didn't seem to have a name—a knowledge that was neither about teaching in general nor about the subject he was trying to teach, but a combination of the two. Lee Shulman would have called it pedagogical content knowledge, the skills needed to teach a subject. Rousseau needed a special knowledge for teaching discipline.

Deborah Ball's and Magdalene Lampert's research on pedagogical content knowledge in math teaching had parallels in other subjects, from history and science to English and even physical education. But there was no parallel in the discipline of discipline.

Researchers have begun to uncover some of the dynamics of discipline. When working with difficult students, researchers have found, many teachers lean heavily on rules and punishments. And this "operant conditioning" seems to work in the short term, especially when teachers follow the guidelines outlined in the Lemov taxonomy. If the least invasive, most positive, and most private correction is used, students are more likely to comply not just "grudgingly," but willingly. But psychologists have increasingly found that, on its own, this "conditioning" is not enough to help students in the long term. Teachers also have to teach their students what the researchers call "social problem-solving"—mental and emotional approaches to dealing with interpersonal challenges.

But examples of this more complex approach—of a pedagogical content knowledge for discipline—were harder to find. The researcher who came closest, a teacher and education professor at Northwestern named Carol Lee, never intended to study the subject. Inspired in part by Magdalene's and Deborah's work, she decided to videotape her own classroom in an inner-city public high school every day for three years, hoping to gain insight on teaching literature. But Carol found that helping her students become better readers required a focus beyond just academics. "The framework," she wrote in a book reflecting on the project, *Culture, Literacy, and Learning*, "had to address the developmental as well as the cognitive needs of students." By "developmental," she meant "the process through which over time humans learn how to address the challenges of cultivating and sustaining a sense of well-being and of competence, of nurturing interpersonal relationships first within families and later across wider social networks, and of navigating obstacles." Over the course of the three years, Carol thus worked on two kinds of teaching at once. The first had to do with literature; the second focused on discipline and development.

One episode showcasing the latter kind of teaching occurred in 1997, at the start of her students' senior year, when Carol noticed that one student, a girl named Taquisha, was reading that morning's copy of the *Chicago Sun-Times*. A few minutes before, Carol had shown the class a five-minute film, one of the everyday cultural artifacts that she used to prepare students to analyze texts like the Toni Morrison novel *Beloved*. She was in the middle of asking them to comment on what they'd seen when she noticed Taquisha's unconventional choice of reading material.

The moment posed a challenge. As Carol recounts in her book documenting the year, "Taquisha is actually reading the newspaper while I am conducting the lesson." And she had spent enough time in the classroom with Taquisha to know that she was "a very strong-willed young lady . . . the sort of person with whom you do not pick a fight unless you're willing to go to the mat and be ready to strike with definitive force to win."

Carol knew that she had several options for how to respond. "I could have embarrassed her, punished her with additional work, lowered her grade, or sent her to the office." But while she believed that some punishments could teach, she also knew that, in Taquisha's case, a punishment like sending her to the office would give the student exactly what she wanted—"to be removed from any responsibility for active participation." And that was the opposite of Carol's goal.

So instead of jabbing, she struck a playful tone. "Other questions. Other questions," Carol said calmly before making her move. "Taquisha, you have a question inside that paper there?"

"Yup," Taquisha replied emphatically, retaining her fighting pose. *Yes, I am indeed reading the Chicago Sun-Times during your lesson*, Taquisha was effectively saying. The move was a taunt, a second invitation to spar. But instead of taking the bait, Carol deployed a response that she later called "a kind of Tai Chi move." Instead of responding to the "yup," Carol simply tilted the subject in her desired direction. She "deflect[ed] her motion toward me by simply getting out of the way."

"What's your question?" she asked.

Taquisha punched again, saying she wanted to know what the short film *Sax, Cantor, Riff,* by Julie Dash, had to do with the book they were preparing to read, *Beloved*. "Essentially," Carol translates, "Taquisha is publicly assaulting the design of my lesson."

Faced with this third attack, another teacher might have finally given in. But Carol, determined to force Taquisha into the discussion, deployed another Tai Chi deflection. "Well that might be a question for me," she said. Taquisha had, after all, posed a reasonable question—why were they doing what they were doing; what was the purpose?—and Carol wanted to acknowledge it as such.

"Well," Taquisha persisted, her permission to challenge granted, "what does the book have to do with the girl and the man singing?" (*Sax, Cantor, Riff* depicted a sequence that included a woman singing an African American spiritual and a Jewish man singing in Hebrew.) "Say that again," Carol said. "That's a good question." She couldn't quite hear Taquisha's response—other students, apparently curious about the same question, spoke over her. "What does the girl have to do with what?" Carol asked again. "What does the girl [*sic*] have to do with the girl and the man singing?" Taquisha repeated.

Later, watching the exchange on videotape, Carol marveled at the evolution. In just a few minutes, Taquisha had shifted from open defiance to challenging the lesson plan to asking a sophisticated question that was exactly what Carol had hoped for when she first launched the discussion.

The two sequences in the film—the young African American woman singing, on the one hand, and the Jewish man singing, on the other—were disconnected scenes. As far as the viewer knew, the two hadn't even seen each other. But Taquisha made two important assumptions: one, that the author (in this case, the director) had created the work with some kind of intent; and two, that her role as a reader (or in this case, viewer) was to "impose some form of coherence" on the apparently disparate scenes.

"That is a beautiful and sound question," Carol said, after rephrasing it. "Found it in the *Sun-Times* too, didn't you?"

"Yup!" Taquisha said. Except this time, the yup had a different sound. She was no longer resisting.

In part, Carol Lee's pedagogical content knowledge was a perfect analogue of Magdalene's and Deborah's. To teach English, Carol found that she needed to know how people learned it—what distinguished a novice reader from an expert? She also needed to know the mistakes and misconceptions that might cause a young person to stumble—for instance, the fact that incorrectly pluralizing a word like "child" as "childs" is actually a step forward for beginning speakers of English, rather than a step back (the mistake shows that the student grasps the concept that plural words usually end in "s"). And she needed to understand the nuances of the discipline that might escape even an excellent reader or professional writer—like precisely how irony, satire, and unreliable narration differ, and how the three can and cannot intersect.

But Carol added another dimension, one that matched her developmental work. She called it "the ethical and moral" part of teaching. A teacher, she said, "must come to know each student and the life circumstances that student brings with him when he enters a classroom." That didn't mean every single detail—a hopeless task, especially for a high school teacher working with a hundred or more students a year. But, like reading or math mistakes, students' developmental challenges came in relatively predictable patterns, so teachers could get to know the broad strokes. (For her part, Carol drew on a mix of her own experience and the research of the University of Chicago psychologist Margaret Beale Spencer, who describes young people's acts of resistance as "maladaptive coping strategies.") That way, meeting a student like Taquisha, a teacher could quickly predict how she was likely to think and act, without having to take a detailed inventory with each new student.

Whereas charter schools handled discipline separately from academics, Carol blended the two, not only in the same class, but in the same discussion. She responded to Taquisha's resistance not with a conversation, but with a subtle invitation to participate in class more productively—and a careful, gentle modeling of how to do that, all in the context of the close reading of a film.

Similarly, although Magdalene Lampert did not use the same "developmental" frame, she did talk about the work of classroom management. She called it "Teaching Students to Be People Who Study in School," or, more ambitiously, "academic character education." The values she taught were versions of discipline, just fused with the habits that students needed to do well in math class (and, she thought, in life)—an "inductive attitude," "curiosity," and a broad sense of self as "a person who could have ideas." And just like Carol Lee, Magdalene found she could teach these attitudes best by connecting them with math or other academic activities.

The difference in approach had something to do with each woman's identity as a teacher of an academic subject; that was their primary focus, so that was how they looked at everything they taught, even behavior. But it also probably stemmed from their different approaches to teaching academic subjects. A key difference was what their classrooms demanded of students. As James Stigler found in his TIMSS video study, a principal characteristic of American classrooms was the expectation of attention (also known as the ability to lock eyes with an overhead projector, a teacher, or a worksheet). Magdalene Lampert and Carol Lee excelled because they stretched that expectation.

Like teachers in Japan, Carol required more elaborate activities in her classroom. In order to participate well, Taquisha didn't just have to throw away her newspaper and stare at the board. She had to formulate an insightful question. Similarly, in Magdalene's class, Richard, one of the students who struggled with what Magdalene called academic character, needed to do more than just stop fooling around with his friends. He also needed to learn how to get started on the problem of the day without asking Magdalene what to do. He needed to think about math not just as an assignment forced on him by his teacher, but as a challenge that he could be curious about—and a puzzle that made sense. And he needed to figure out how to disagree respectfully, whether about a mathematical idea or something more personal.

In Carol and Magdalene's view, getting Taquisha and Richard to behave was not a step toward getting them to learn—first, pay attention; then, learn. Behavior was, instead, *synonymous* with learning. The two things happened at the same time. That was why Carol responded to Taquisha's resistance not by mounting a discussion about it, but with a series of pointed questions designed to show her how to respond more productively. And it was why Magdalene gave Richard not just a lecture about the need to start on problems by himself, but also a new seat next to two students she knew were "helpful to their peers but not in a way that would be embarrassing." That way, he could work on his problem of the day without the teacher's help by learning to turn to a fellow student first.

Perhaps the entrepreneurs were right to separate discipline into its own subject. By making a separate space for culture conversations, they gave them more credence. And the separate space certainly didn't preclude blending "developmental" and academic work. They could do both.

But it was also true that if they wanted a more integrated pedagogy—one that could simultaneously teach a student multiplication and curiosity—they would have to change the way they taught, and not just the way they taught discipline. Compliance, the end point of a simpler approach to teaching behavior, didn't just make way for more attentive learners. For the entrepreneurs as for so many American teachers, compliance was also often what their math, reading, and science lessons required.

Magdalene Lampert sometimes took the argument even further. Certain kinds of teaching, she argued, were simply more likely to produce resistance than others. Classroom management challenges, she contended, could be dealt with in part by redesigning the activities teachers asked students to do. Carol Lee found something similar in her English class. As the newspaper example made clear, asking demanding questions of Taquisha and her peers did at first make some of them resist. But over time, the approach opened them up. By asking more of students, she also gave them more of a voice. And in this way, Carol could make them feel safer. The classroom belonged to them as much as it belonged to her.

The idea that classroom management challenges could be solved by well-designed lesson plans was exactly the kind of argument that caused some entrepreneurs to reject ed schools in the first place. Yet by 2010, many of the entrepreneurs had begun to wonder whether the academics had a point. In the taxonomy—which Doug published that year in the form of a best-selling book, *Teach like a Champion*—Doug listed five principles for building a positive classroom culture. Predictably, the first four were discipline, management, control, and influence. But the fifth was what Doug called "engagement," the process of getting students to do "productive, positive work."

Rousseau's first teaching assessments illustrated this shift. Observing him, his principal, Stacy Birdsell O'Toole, always said the same thing: he was great at getting the kids to behave, but to what end? "Rousseau is an incredibly charismatic teacher, and his management is incredible. He invests kids wholeheartedly in what he wants kids to do," she says. "But what we really had to work on is, 'What are you asking kids to actually *do*?'"

Later, when Stacy became director of training at the Match Teacher Residency, a program in Boston designed to prepare teachers to work in no-excuses charter schools (including the school associated with the residency, also called Match), she found that Rousseau wasn't the only one working on this problem. All the charter schools she visited were talking about the same thing. Stacy had diagnosed herself with the problem too. "The absence of misbehavior," she had realized, "doesn't mean the presence of high levels of learning." They'd cracked the code of how to get kids to behave. But they were missing a vital academic ingredient. "Rigor," they called it.

THE POWER OF
AN INSIDE JOKE

Seneca Rosenberg entered Teach For America in 2001, eleven years after Wendy Kopp founded the program and half a decade before Doug Lemov began his taxonomy. Placed at Cassell Elementary School in East San Jose two weeks before the start of school, she spent her first weeks as a teacher lurching through a series of trials. First came the dirt, a thick film of which covered every surface of her classroom. Although the school did employ a janitor, his responsibilities apparently did not include scrubbing down desks. Next came the musical chairs. On the second day of the year, after Seneca had dutifully memorized all her fourth-graders' names, the administration assigned her a brand-new class. A month and dozens of new names later, the same thing happened again. "And I didn't get the first class back, of course. I got a new class of fourth-graders," she says.

What struck Seneca most of all, however, was not the chaos of her own assignments, but the radically disparate experiences of her fellow corps members. She noticed this most acutely in her third year, when TFA made her a "learning team leader," charged with coordinating a group of corps members working across the South Bay.

The teachers had almost everything in common. They all came from the same training program (TFA followed by a crash course at San José State University); they had students from essentially the same demographic (fourth- and fifth-graders living in a poor, urban area, many of whom spoke different languages at home); they taught under the same state standards (California's) and in the same district (Alum Rock Union Elementary School District); and they had roughly the same number of years of teaching experience (between one and three). But as Seneca traveled from school to school visiting the teachers' classrooms, or investigated the products of their students' work at monthly meetings, she saw that their teaching differed wildly. From the way they organized their classrooms to the kinds of projects they assigned and the work that hung on the walls, almost nothing about the teachers' approaches was consistent.

The randomness was most visible in students' writing samples. "Length, the strength and clarity of an argument, complexity and variety of sentence structure, the type of vocabulary, the accuracy of conventions"—every aspect varied from teacher to teacher, Seneca remembers. "Despite all that we had in common with respect to training and standards and beliefs, it actually seemed we might be learning quite different things, with pretty deep implications for our students' learning."

Seneca had originally thought that talent alone separated one teacher from another. Some teachers simply figured out how to help their students learn and others didn't. But it didn't take her long to realize that this explanation didn't capture the problem. What mattered most, for her colleagues at least, was not will or natural skill, but luck. What workshop had the teacher happened to stumble into? Whose classroom did she happen to get placed next to? Which mentor happened to take an interest in her work? Thinking back, Seneca realized that her own trajectory had depended on a handful of accidents. If she hadn't taken that specific workshop, or hadn't met her teacher friend, Laura, or hadn't been assigned that particular supervisor, her teaching would have evolved differently. Probably for worse, but who knew? Maybe for better.

The whole arrangement seemed "absolutely insane," she says. How had something so important been left to chance? Searching for explanations, Seneca took to the web. Surely she was not the first to marvel at this randomness; some education researcher must have studied the problem, maybe even suggested a remedy. But instead of answering her question, the policy papers she found skirted the issue.

One typical study, hosted on the website of a leading education school, examined parents—specifically, the kinds of teachers parents requested for their children when enrolling them in a new grade. The study found that preferences differed depending on families' demographic background. Low-income parents of color cared more about teachers' academic records than their popularity with students. Wealthier parents, meanwhile, tended to make the opposite choice. Across the board, many parents—30 percent—requested a particular teacher when given the chance. The implication, the researchers pointed out, was potentially profound. The national trend toward greater school choice might end up exacerbating segregation as parents with different race and class backgrounds looked for different strengths in teachers.

Another study took a novel approach to investigating the challenge of teacher turnover. Instead of looking at data on teachers who left the classroom, the researchers studied teachers who returned to it. By figuring out why those teachers came back, they surmised, they might find a way to prevent the teachers from leaving in the first place. Indeed, the data suggested that the pool of returning teachers was large. More than 40 percent of those in the study who left the classroom later came back. The data also pointed to an intriguing pattern in those who left and then returned. Many of them, especially women, were the parents of young children. When they first taught, they had no children; when they came back, their children were old enough to go to school. The pattern suggested that districts could avoid the costs associated with retraining returning teachers by investing in convenient child care options so that they wouldn't leave in the first place.

The studies asked important questions, but though parent preferences and teacher turnover were *related* to how people learned to teach, they were ultimately different subjects. Then one day, Seneca stumbled onto a professor's web page at the University of Michigan. A photo showed an older man with downcast eyes, smiling in front of a bed of flowers. In contrast to the other studies, this professor's research asked the questions Seneca had been asking herself, only in more formal language. Where she thought about the "randomness" of what her fellow teachers' learned, he described the "inconsistency" of "instructional guidance." Where she diagnosed teachers' varied learning experiences as a "mess," he described "a blizzard of different and often conflicting ideas" that added up to an overall "variability" or, more plainly, "incoherence." Different words, but the same conundrum.

Even more important, he had an explanation for the source of the trouble. Seneca later learned that his students had come to name the quandary after their professor: the "David Cohen coherence problem."

Since leaving Michigan State with his wife, Magdalene Lampert, in 1993, David had been doing more and more thinking about what had gone wrong. And not only in East Lansing, but also in California and all across the country. Why did every American effort to improve teaching seem to fail? From the slow dissolution at Spartan Village to the false revolutions in California, did the disappointments have a common cause?

Over time, David found his answer in his original discipline, history. Specifically, he realized that he could trace the American resistance to reform back to the founding fathers and their disagreement about centralized power. Should the federal government hold the highest power, or should the states? The debate foreshadowed much that was to come in education. Nearly two and a half centuries after the constitutional convention, the question of who should control the schools remained unresolved.

American education was like the story that David's old friend Lee Shulman told about a rabbi mediating a dispute between two men over the ownership of a chicken. After the first man explained why the chicken was his, Lee said in a talk recounting the story, "the rabbi nodded sagely and stated, 'You are right. The chicken is yours.'" When the second man gave his testimony, the rabbi nodded again. "You are correct. The chicken must be yours," he said. Confused, the rabbi's wife spoke up. "My dear, it is impossible for this one to be right, and that one too," she said. "That's correct," the rabbi replied a third time. "You're also absolutely right!"

Similarly, in American schools, the federal government was sovereign and the states were sovereign. Both. And if you thought that situation couldn't possibly hold, you were correct about that too.

Instead of guidance, American schools endured mass confusion. Principals received mandates from the feds and from the state and from the district, sometimes matching and sometimes not (and only sometimes funded). Teachers got advice and orders just as contradictory as the directives their bosses received. Their local curriculum said one thing; their education school another. And the textbook, when there was a textbook, said something else altogether. With fifty states, more than fourteen thousand school districts, and nearly a hundred thousand schools, the law of the educational land was *incoherence*.

Incoherence sabotaged quality. If teaching was a skill or trade to be mastered, then teachers were also apprentices, students of another kind. Like students, they either had to figure out the material on their own, or they had to be taught. The law of incoherence meant that instead of training with one good teacher, they received the equivalent of seventeen bad ones, each one saying something completely different.

The lucky ones made progress against the odds. Like diligent students in chaotic schools, these resourceful apprentices took clear guidance when it emerged and ignored the rest. The majority, meanwhile, took pragmatic steps to inure themselves to chaos. Faced with yet another conflicting order, they responded with what the educator Lovely Billups once described as the American teacher's creed: "This too shall pass." Nod politely, thank the state/district/professional developer/professor for the suggestion, and then, as Billups described in a speech, "close the door and go back to what you believe in." Often, those still open to change ended up like Mrs. Oublier of California, whose teaching "revolution" bore only superficial resemblance to the state's intended reforms. These teachers took the new ideas and incorporated them into the very different kind of teaching they'd learned somewhere else.

Impressed by David Cohen and his work, Seneca decided to go to grad school and learn from the professor himself. Over the next eight years, she found herself especially struck by the flip side of coherence—all the stuff that couldn't exist without it, the institutions and shared knowledge base that *incoherence* had prevented American schools from building. David called this "infrastructure." The dictionary defined *infrastructure* as "the basic facilities, services, and installations needed for the functioning of a community or society"—building blocks like roads, bridges, and power lines. *Educational* infrastructure, as David defined it, was a school system's intangible equivalent, the foundation for all teaching and learning. It comprised three main categories: a common curriculum suggesting what students should study, common examinations to test how much of that curriculum the students had grasped, and teacher education to help the faculty learn to teach exactly what students were supposed to learn.

Acting in an environment of incoherence, the U.S. government had never built educational infrastructure. Without infrastructure, meanwhile, schools also failed to develop other crucial resources. "Chief among these," David explained, in a book he cowrote with the political scientist Susan Moffitt, "is a common language concerning teaching, learning and academic content." Doctors had their *Physicians' Desk Reference*, with its technical terminology and its evolving descriptions of common problems and treatments. Electricians, plumbers, and pilots had continuously updated "standard operating procedures" outlining best practices. Teachers had—well, they had a bunch of question marks. No agreement on what their work should aim to teach, no common vocabulary to describe how to do it, and no standard measures to know whether they had succeeded.

No wonder Seneca and her fellow Teach For America corps members entered a single school district and encountered a dozen different experiences! With no infrastructure, they were like acrobats walking across a moving tightrope blindfolded—no spotter, no safety net, and no map. It was no surprise that so many of them tumbled to the ground.

Seneca arrived in grad school in 2004, two years into the life of the landmark No Child Left Behind education law, which took the standards movement and nationalized it, requiring every state to set learning goals and judge schools according to whether they met them. In many ways, the accountability law would seem to be the perfect solution to the David Cohen coherence problem. Marshaled by a historic coalition that included labor and business leaders, Republicans and Democrats, and representatives of multiple branches of government (not only congresspeople and senators, but also a group representing state school superintendents), NCLB proved that Americans could take common action on schools. And by requiring that states write standards for what students should learn, it took a step toward coherence.

But watching the effects of the law unfold across the country, Seneca saw that No Child Left Behind was not creating the infrastructure that coherence was supposed to bring. In place of common curricula, tests, and teacher education, NCLB created standards, tests, and accountability measures. The only overlap—tests—were hardly the kind imagined in David Cohen's vision. For one thing, the new state tests were rarely tied to a clear curriculum outlining what students should study. That wasn't surprising, given that most states didn't *have* a common curriculum. But standards didn't clarify the matter either. They offered learning goals, whereas curricula provided, in the words of one writer, a "day-to-day, week-to-week, year-to-year road map for reaching those goals." Drawing this road map was still left up to individual school districts or, in many cases, the teachers.

Accountability measures might have acted as a form of teacher education, levying consequences to schools that failed to meet standards and thereby at least suggesting *when* teachers needed to improve. So might tests, which could give teachers a report on what their students had and hadn't learned. But as David knew from his research in California (and as Seneca had learned through her experience in San Jose), standards and matching tests—while a good start—were still no guarantee that teachers would learn to teach in a better, or even uniform, way.

If what education needed was infrastructure, No Child Left Behind was "best understood as a sort of exoskeleton," David wrote. It outlined goals and offered consequences for failing to meet them, but it only skimmed the surface of schools' core work. Teaching—that daily crucible on which change depended—was left untouched. Accountability provided a benchmark, but no guidance for how to get there. As far as David could tell, American schools still operated more or less the same way they had for years, just with more tests.

As David's student, Seneca had no reason to think otherwise. And so, on the day in 2005 that Seneca discovered a case of burgeoning infrastructure in American education, the realization struck her like a "lightning bolt." She was sitting in an auditorium in Washington, DC, with hundreds of other Teach For America alumni, there to celebrate the organization's fifteenth anniversary (at that point, TFA had trained more than ten thousand corps members), when the speaker on stage cracked a joke—some inside line about TFA—and the whole audience laughed. A perfectly banal moment. But to Seneca, it was a revelation: the way a group representing fifteen years of alums laughed with one voice.

"I had just been reading about hallmarks of a profession in other professions," she said, "and thinking about this lack of common language thing, and our inability to communicate in any substance or depth." But here was a room full of strangers—education professionals of varying levels of experience—all laughing at the same joke. That was the lightning bolt. "Ohhhh!" she thought. *"Teach For America!"*

Teach For America was the organization that had introduced her to the coherence problem, but since then, it had built an impressive community for corps members, with shared jokes and an expanding curriculum. And this was nothing compared to what its alumni were building—a new parallel system of public education, composed mostly of charter schools, and increasingly speaking the common language spelled out in Doug Lemov's taxonomy.

Seneca's friends had told her all about this new entrepreneurial world. The school names sounded like Boy Scout badges: the Knowledge Is Power Program, Uncommon Schools, Achievement First, Aspire Public Schools. But until that moment, she had marveled at their work—the strangely deliberate chants, the almost militaristic "no excuses" strictness, the superhuman, TFA-powered workforce of mainly childless young people—without thinking much about what it all meant.

Now she beheld the entrepreneurs in a new light. Seneca had been studying the infrastructure for teaching by examining its absence. Was it possible her old friends were actually building a real-life version of it?

David loved working with Seneca. Like many of his best collaborators, she played Pooh to his Eeyore, balancing out his perpetual cynicism with an unblemished faith in the possibility of change. But when she came to him with her idea about TFA and the no-excuses entrepreneurs, he was incredulous. "I would be shocked—shocked, *shocked*—if any of these organizations were doing something different," Seneca remembers him saying.

There were many reasons to doubt her hypothesis—and not

just the fact that David had spent his entire career documenting the factors that made a spontaneous emergence of American educational infrastructure unlikely. For one, TFA and the
no-excuses schools seemed to be distinguished not by how they
worked, but with whom. TFA famously recruited high-achieving
college students, many of them Ivy Leaguers, the idea being that
they were recruiting not just teachers, but a new generation of
leaders to solve educational inequity. Critics, however, argued
that this merely layered smart people on top of a broken system
rather than creating fundamental change.

Moreover, the program seemed to eschew craft, sending
bright young people into classrooms with just five weeks' summer training. Brand-name diplomas and high hopes, these critics
said, could hardly make up for a lack of training and experience.
Indeed, even the most optimistic researchers found that corps
members had an uneven impact on students' learning. Studies found positive effects on students' math achievement—the
equivalent of about a month of extra instruction, by one estimate; more than two and a half, by another. But when it came to
reading, the best you could say was that corps members did no
harm.

There was also the fact that, after years of searching, the only
contemporary cases of a strong, coherent educational infrastructure that David had ever seen were outside the United States. In
countries like Japan, France, and Singapore, national education
ministries were strong enough to write clear curricula, and the
rest of the educational machinery—education schools, textbooks,
test makers—aligned itself accordingly. As for his own country,
the historic ambivalence about federal power made consensus
impossible. "The dispute has deep roots," David wrote in a paper
with Jim Spillane, "it would be astonishing if it were settled easily
or soon."

David had found only two American programs that came close to infrastructure—a pair of whole-school reform projects called America's Choice and Success for All. Although they did offer real curricula, plus matching tests and teacher training, the projects had to implement their programs on top of the existing school system, which snarled their efforts.

But America's Choice and Success For All *were* promising. And if Seneca's hypothesis was correct, then TFA and the charter networks might represent the next evolution of their model. Operating outside the traditional district system, but not depending on it, charter schools could build infrastructure from scratch. The presumptuousness of the entrepreneurs nauseated some of David's colleagues—the way these arrogant, self-righteous "movement" types marched into public education like they were the first to discover its dysfunction, and especially the way they dismissed their predecessors as part of the problem. Nevertheless, the entrepreneurs had figured out a way to build from scratch, and that was undoubtedly an advantage.

Another problem was that the movement was tiny, especially compared to the vast U.S. school system. In 2005, the number of TFA corps members and alumni working in schools totaled only about seven thousand, less than 1 percent of the 3.6 million teachers then working in all U.S. schools. And that year, a million students were enrolled in charters, compared to almost forty-eight million in traditional public schools. And only a fraction of the charters subscribed to the learning culture that Doug Lemov and his colleagues were shaping. Even so, David *wanted* to believe that infrastructure was possible. His advisee was likely to be disappointed by her research. But why not try and see?

Seneca began with a "really motley crew" of interviews with no-excuses teachers from her personal network. By the end of her research, she'd conducted formal interviews with forty-one of them. She also analyzed the new projects that Teach For America had undertaken since she left it. "I kept this as an empirical question: Were they actually doing something different?" she says. The deeper she looked, the more she felt that they were.

One project was not unlike Doug Lemov's taxonomy. After two decades of observing, interviewing, and surveying the organization's most effective teachers, Teach For America had distilled their common attributes into a framework it called Teaching as Leadership. The framework had become a touchstone—the organization's "intellectual centerpiece," in official TFA-speak. It informed everything from TFA's recruitment of new corps members to its expanding efforts to train teachers, including reliable access to the mentorship opportunities that had arisen so haphazardly for Seneca.

Seneca found herself especially drawn to the work of the charter networks. Selecting one network for closer study, the Achievement First charter schools in New York and Connecticut, Seneca found further evidence of a developing infrastructure. Achievement First employed a standard "Cycle of Highly Effective Teaching" to structure teachers' work, from setting goals to planning units and lessons and then revising to fit students' evolving needs; "scope and sequence" documents for each major subject that outlined periodic learning goals; regular low-stakes tests, called interim assessments, designed to help teachers diagnose how their students were progressing; an "Essentials of Effective Instruction" document naming the twenty-four elements required to teach well, in the organization's view; and a series of trainings directly connected to the rest of the infrastructure, including weekly *jugyokenkyu*-style sessions for teachers.

The program offered Achievement First teachers not only standards, but infrastructure; not only support, but *coherent* support. The cycle of highly effective teaching mapped onto the scope and sequence documents, the scope and sequence documents mapped onto the interim assessments, and the regular professional development sessions were designed to support the entire structure, from "data days" for studying interim assessment results to a formal coaching system pairing every teacher and principal with someone chosen specifically to help them improve.

Infrastructure meant that, where others had four walls and a locked door, Achievement First teachers had a herd. At her old school, an Achievement First teacher told Seneca, the attitude was "do what you will." When she didn't know how to teach a certain topic—she particularly struggled with math—she resorted to the only available recourse. "Guys," she would tell her students, "let's just do multiplication again." Like most American teachers—like Seneca herself back in San Jose—she was on her own. At Achievement First, meanwhile, the teacher had a framework around which to build each day's lesson; prewritten interim assessments to get a regular peek inside her students' minds; special designated data days to dig into the results; and an army of colleagues to help her think through the problems that teaching presented every day. An elementary school teacher, she did not have to plan lessons for all four of the core subjects on her own. Instead, mimicking a common practice in Japanese elementary schools, Achievement First teachers shared the planning work among "grade-level teams," with a more experienced teacher taking responsibility for the toughest lessons, while novices handled the easier plans. When she really struggled with a particular topic, the teacher told Seneca, her coach would literally stand in front of her classroom with her. "Look, this is how you're supposed to do it," the coach would say.

With each new dispatch from Seneca's field notes, David dialed back his skepticism. "Achievement First was building a new education system," he says. "And that was very exciting . . . Here was this organization that was building a version of what America has never—or hardly ever—had."

Seneca had discovered a system through which teaching might be improved. And not just for one or two gifted teachers, but for a whole school district.

When Seneca published her dissertation, in 2012, her final assessment of Achievement First (abbreviated AF in her paper) was overwhelmingly positive. "AF provides a rich and generative new model for thinking about what organizing for quality teaching and learning might look like in the US context," she wrote. But she also described challenges that could impede the organization's success. One had to do with the model's ability to be replicated. The network's infrastructure could easily grow to serve more students. But another key factor—Achievement First's unusually talented and hardworking staff—would be harder to extend. Another challenge was the problem of rigor.

Like Rousseau Mieze's old principal, Stacy Birdsell O'Toole, some leaders at Achievement First worried that their students' learning was too superficial. This was especially true in math. Students did well on state standardized tests—even better on the math tests, in fact, than on the English ones. But did they really understand? Would they continue to learn and eventually be prepared for college?

"I'm watching them count objects to add them together," a third-grade teacher told Seneca in one of her interviews. Given a set of five, the students had to count, "one, two, three, . . ." when they should have just been able to look and know, *five*. Given a set of ten, with five objects on one row and five identical objects lined up right beneath, they couldn't just count the first row and double it. They counted the second one too: one, two, three, . . . nine, ten." "I think all of those should be mastered and solid by the end of second grade," the teacher told Seneca, "and they're not."

The teacher felt just as culpable as the second-grade teachers who sent students to her unprepared. In third grade, students were supposed to master fractions, but she never found enough time to get them to really understand. They moved on to fourth grade able to master the state test, but with very little idea of what kind of number a fraction actually represented.

Seneca thought that the superficiality might have to do with the network's emphasis on posting strong results on state tests. The tests set relatively low bars for learning, emphasizing a wide but shallow set of skills instead of a steady progression of deeper understandings. Many teachers felt that the tests didn't measure the higher-order skills children needed to reach and succeed in college. One academic dean told Seneca that while she and her teachers preferred a curriculum that emphasized deeper understanding—a TKOT-like math textbook called *Investigations*—the curriculum clashed with what students needed to master in order to do well on the state math test, and, therefore, with the "scope and sequence" Achievement First had written to prepare them for it.

And for a network of charter schools, test scores mattered. Scores determined not only whether the schools stayed open, but also whether the infrastructure continued to receive the support of the private donors who looked to the tests as indicators of a school's success. The same forces that enabled Achievement First to build a strong infrastructure for teaching had also conspired to make the teaching within that infrastructure utterly conventional.

Seneca observed a striking contrast between how Achievement First taught its teachers and how it taught its students. Working with their designated coaches, teachers focused their studies on only one or two learning goals at a time. But with students, even when teachers wanted to spend more time on a single, complex goal—like understanding fractions—the state test thwarted them. Taking more time for fractions, after all, meant taking less time for another unit, like money. And when it came time for the test, one educator told Seneca, "you know that you're going to have three questions on money and if you never got to the money unit . . . you're not sure how your kids are going to do."

Having some infrastructure was certainly better than having none. But the big question remained. Could an American infrastructure support *high-level* teaching at scale? Thinking over that puzzle, Seneca found herself turning not to David but to David's wife, Magdalene Lampert.

Both Magdalene and David had been despondent in the years after fleeing Michigan State. For David, the disappointment was an academic problem, another educational failure to analyze. But Magdalene had given her entire self to the work. At Michigan State, she had made herself the template for both the new math teacher and the new ed school professor. The national reform groups had held her up (along with her star protégé, Deborah Ball) as the American exemplar, the one who demonstrated what was possible. When first the Michigan State experiment and then the math reforms failed, one after the other, Magdalene felt that she had failed too.

A moment in 1991 had exemplified the pain. Asked to present to a commission advising President George H. W. Bush on new education standards to take effect by the year 2000, she had gone to DC with what was by then her usual spiel. To highlight the changes that both teachers and students would have to undergo, she described a day in her fifth-grade classroom at Spartan Village. She did not sugarcoat the difficulties. "Unfortunately," she said, "very few Americans—and remember that American teachers are only a subset of Americans—have any idea what a mathematical community is or what a conjecture is or what it would look like to do mathematical reasoning. Most of us have never done that." She went on, "The goal that all students by some year, whether it's 2000 or 2061 or whatever year you want to pick, are going to be able to do this thing that most Americans have no sense of right now, let alone many teachers, seems like a rather ambitious goal."

She was not saying that the country shouldn't try. She was simply drawing the obvious conclusion. Change—real change— would require a lot of learning, a lot of support, and a lot of time.

But instead of embracing these challenges, the commission attacked her. "Let me use an analogy," said the chairman, Roy Romer, the tough-talking, square-jawed governor of Colorado. "In Desert Storm, when the president wanted to move, he called in the generals from Saudi Arabia. You know, flew them in. He said, give me a plan." But the plan they developed called for spending way too much time on the ground—a whole year. So the president demanded another plan, and what did the generals do? "They came up with another plan that did work." The implication was clear. If the work as Magdalene imagined it would take too much time, then she needed to imagine something else.

Later, when she published the research that had informed her testimony to Romer—a detailed, five-hundred-page book documenting a year inside her classroom at Spartan Village called *Teaching with Problems and the Problems of Teaching*—the public's reaction echoed the governor's. "The response initially was, this is way too complicated. If it takes [five] hundred pages, you know, like—this is amazing what you're doing here, but any novice teacher is gonna read this and say, you know, I'll never be able to do this," Magdalene says. "And any experienced teacher is going to say, I don't have time."

She had dedicated her career to making her work accessible to other teachers, but still readers rejected the work as too hard, too complex, impossible to scale. When her sabbatical year arrived, she picked a destination as far away as she could imagine: Rome, where her plan was to spend three months learning Italian. "What I needed was just some time off from being in the center of this controversy," she says.

But after just a few weeks at Italiaidea, her new language school, Magdalene found herself thinking about teaching. She couldn't help it. Her Italian class felt eerily familiar. First, there was the way the class was structured, always starting with some kind of problem (how do you order off a menu? or how do you make a complaint politely?); then moving onto hypotheses made by students, which the teacher wrote up on the board; and finally, ending in a discussion. "In our very, very halting Italian—because you didn't speak a word of English in that school from day one— we were meant to consider each hypothesis and talk about why it made sense or didn't make sense," she says. "And I'm thinking, wait a minute. This is how I teach math! And even though I didn't want to be there as an educational researcher, I started thinking, where did they learn to do this?"

The question struck her again one day early in the course, when, coming back from a break, she noticed that the teacher had rerouted the group. Instead of the task they'd been working on, they now found on their desks photocopies of a newspaper article along with an assignment to underline all the personal pronouns. The change was clearly strategic. Before the break, the teacher had been walking between their desks, observing the students' work. He'd seen that many of them were struggling with the same challenge, the placement of personal pronouns in relation to verbs. The new assignment helped them correct the misunderstanding.

In between Italian classes, Magdalene had been sitting in Roman cafés, editing the page proofs of her book, which devoted considerable space to defining this precise activity—"the work of teaching while students work independently," she called it. "And again I thought, that's really pretty complicated. Where did these tasks come from? Is it only my teacher who's doing this? Did he read my book?"

At first, she asked no questions. After all, she was there to learn Italian, not to do research. And, given Italiaidea's no-English rule, she couldn't have posed the questions even if she'd wanted to. "First of all, I didn't know how to ask," she says. "And secondly, I don't know how I would have understood the answer!"

But as the weeks went by, she noticed patterns. Students at Italiaidea transitioned to a new teacher every month. Magdalene took note of each instructor's style. The routine stayed the same—the same lesson structure, the same teaching while students worked independently, the same habit of regularly revising the plan midclass. Her first teacher was not an exception; at Italiaidea, he was the rule.

The implications for her old work were profound. The students at Italiaidea had all signed up for the class voluntarily, but they had a variety of academic and class backgrounds. So did the teachers, a mix of full- and part-time, experienced and novice teachers who were not particularly well paid, hardworking, or reform-minded. If a modest Italian language school in Rome achieved routinely high-level teaching, why couldn't American schools?

After her sabbatical ended, Magdalene returned to Rome, studying the school deliberately this time, as a researcher. Italiaidea's success, she learned, depended not just on an impressive bank of resources—the newspaper article on personal pronouns was just one of hundreds. It also depended on a teacher education program that carefully trained teachers in the school's special method.

Before Magdalene went to Italy, she knew that what David called "coherence" was technically possible—that countries like Japan had it, and that it enabled them to teach at a high level in large numbers. But until she saw Italiaidea herself, she didn't really understand what coherence could mean for her and for American schools. John Dewey's fantasy about preventing "waste and loss" because "the successes of [great teachers] tend to be born and to die with them" was within reach. Great teaching did not have to perish with the teacher; the right system could teach more than just one person to do it, without sacrificing any complexity in the process.

When Seneca told Magdalene Lampert about the work going on at Achievement First, Magdalene couldn't help but notice the parallels to Italiaidea. Like the language school, Achievement First had created a detailed set of resources that teachers could share, plus an organization designed to help teachers as much as students. Both organizations had created infrastructure. The only difference was the level of teaching. Achievement First had all the supports she'd seen at Italiaidea, but less of the TKOT-like rigor.

Magdalene discovered Seneca's research in 2009. Around the same time, her colleague Anthony Bryk, a sociologist, invited Magdalene to speak at a conference hosted by the NewSchools Venture Fund, a philanthropy whose donations had helped build the entrepreneurial education world. (Out of $248 million that NewSchools invested between 2012 and its founding in 1998, Achievement First received over $6 million; Uncommon Schools, more than $7 million; and KIPP, more than $6 million.) The conference was meant to target one of the charter networks' latest challenges—a "pain point," in NewSchools-speak.

In working groups, conversations, and board meetings, the entrepreneurs all described the same problem. Some called it "human capital." Doug Lemov called it the "build it/buy it" challenge. Either way, the point was the same. In their early days, the charters had hired the best teachers they could find. But as they grew, they could no longer rely on recruiting the cream of the crop ("buy it"). They had to "build it"—to teach their teachers how to teach. The conference was one of a series of events designed to launch a new "portfolio" of funding for projects tackling the training problem.

From Magdalene's perspective, speaking at the NewSchools conference was a risk. She knew the entrepreneurs might lump her together with other ed school professors—as part of the problem. But after talking with Seneca about Achievement First, she was intrigued to meet them. Plus, as Tony Bryk pointed out, not only had she spent most of her career thinking about the best way to train teachers; after her research in Italy she was building a new model at the University of Michigan that had her more optimistic than ever. A summer program for teachers, it built on the ideas she'd learned at Italiaidea's teacher training school. She told Bryk yes.

At the conference, some of the entrepreneurs displayed the bluster that Magdalene feared, making their disinterest in her work clear. But others were friendly. One stunned her by walking up and citing her research. "I read your book," he said, meaning the five-hundred-page tome describing a year inside her classroom at Spartan Village. "It was awesome."

The conference-goer's name was Jesse Solomon. Jesse, Magdalene learned, had taught math in the Boston public schools before teaching at one of the city's original charter schools, City on a Hill. There, after running into his own version of Doug Lemov's build it/buy it problem, he'd started a program called the Teachers Institute to help prepare new teachers. The institute had since grown to serve not just City on a Hill, but the entire Boston public school system. Its new name was BTR, for the Boston Teacher Residency.

Eight years into running BTR, Jesse's challenge, like that facing Achievement First (and, it turned out, most of the other entrepreneurs at the conference), was academic rigor. For Jesse, the problem was especially pressing. A professor at Harvard had just completed a multiyear study of the Boston Teacher Residency, and the results were disturbing. Although BTR graduates were more likely to continue teaching than were their counterparts from other programs, they were no better at raising students' test scores in English than was the average Boston teacher with the same amount of experience. And in math, they were worse. Something had gone wrong, and Jesse needed to make a change.

After watching Magdalene's presentation on Italiaidea, he made the mental leap Tony Bryk had been hoping for. He realized that BTR needed Magdalene Lampert.

9

THE HOLY GRAIL

Jesse Solomon was especially taken with an idea that was at the core of Magdalene Lampert's findings about Italiaidea: the concept of *instructional activities*, or *IA*s.

The hard part about getting teachers to teach at a high level, Magdalene explained, was not to sacrifice complexity for the sake of accessibility. This was not so different from the challenge of helping students who knew very little about math to nevertheless grasp the bigness of it—getting them not just to memorize, but also to reason, conjecture, prove, and understand. It wasn't easy, but with a well-chosen problem a teacher could make the subject's big ideas come alive, even to little children. The same held for teaching: focus on only the simpler parts of instruction, and teachers would learn only superficial techniques. The trick was to get new teachers teaching rigorously right from the start.

At Italiaidea's training school, a place called Dilit, teacher-educators divided Italian teaching into fourteen core instructional activities. Each IA was like a rich math problem. Even a brand-new teacher could try it out, it could be adapted across any grade or competency level, and it was both accessible and rigorous.

Take one IA, called "Conversation Rebuilding." In the classroom, the routine resembled a game of communication Pictionary. The teacher began by pantomiming a conversation, using only gestures and drawings. She spoke no words. Then, letting the students speak only Italian, she invited them to imagine what had been said. What would a person ordering a meal in a restaurant say to get the waiter to bring over a wine list? Once the list arrived, how might the person respond, if she still wasn't sure what she wanted to drink? As students proposed hypotheses, the teacher helped steer them toward an understanding of how the conversation could have actually proceeded. (When a hypothesis made sense, the teacher signaled that by having the whole group repeat it; when it didn't, she said "excuse me," mimed the act again, and got them to start over.) Along the way, the students learned not just new vocabulary words and grammar, but how to feel their way into the language, to communicate.

Steering the conversation demanded a complicated set of maneuvers for a beginning teacher, but Dilit made it easier by spelling out the steps and having the teachers try them out, first with the professor and other students acting in the role of students—the teacher-educator throwing out common student errors—and then with real students. During rehearsals, Dilit teacher-educators gave live suggestions in the middle of an activity. They reminded new teachers not to forget key pieces of the IA, like always making a student repeat a correct hypothesis. Later, as the trainee teachers became more advanced, they learned to analyze students' thinking, ignore likely diversions, and guide students toward increasingly accurate responses. By the end of a session, the whole group began to chime in, giving each other reminders and suggestions about how to proceed.

Before she began working in Boston, Magdalene had been trying to do the same thing at the Summer Learning Institute she had built in Ann Arbor. IAs, she said, were like "containers." They let new teachers learn what they needed to know. One piece of that learning consisted of practices, the actions required to help children learn. In the "Choral Counting" IA, for example, teachers learned how to lead a group of students in counting aloud by a particular number (tens, say, or twos); how to write the sequence on the board (for instance, using columns, so that, counting by twos, 2, 12, 22, and 32 would sit side by side, helping the children see a pattern); how to stop the count at a deliberately chosen number to ask a question, like "What's the next number?"; how to help the students look for patterns; and, finally, how to facilitate a discussion leading to the key mathematical idea.

The IAs also let new teachers work on the core math knowledge they needed to teach—the stuff Deborah Ball and Hyman Bass had named "Mathematical Knowledge for Teaching," or MKT. (In Choral Counting, this included an understanding of mathematical patterns, the common ways students come to understand numbers, and representations that teachers could use to advance the students' understanding.) Following the Dilit model, the Summer Learning Institute had groups work together between rehearsals to give each other feedback and contribute ideas and techniques to improve students' number sense. Finally, they tried the IAs with local children enrolled in the summer program.

Jesse Solomon wanted to incorporate IAs into the Boston Teacher Residency. Within a year, the rest of the BTR leaders had traveled twice to Michigan to watch the Summer Learning Institute in action. By 2011, they had asked Magdalene to come work with them full time to redesign the entire BTR program.

The Boston program posed greater challenges than the summer program in Ann Arbor. Residents were placed in some of the city's most difficult schools, including several "turnaround" schools, representing Boston's portion of the country's five thousand worst-performing middle and high schools. While the students Magdalene had worked with in Michigan were racially and culturally diverse, the students in Boston were more likely to be impoverished, more likely to be new speakers of English, still learning the language, and more likely to struggle with learning and emotional difficulties (20 percent of students in the Boston public schools are classified as needing special education).

And yet, when touring the Boston schools, sitting in classrooms that were often chaotic and unruly, Magdalene always had the same thought. The problems she saw, all the challenges—they were difficult, but they were also solvable. The BTR teachers, she knew, could get their students to learn. They only needed to be trained. So, when Jesse asked her to leave Michigan and work at BTR full-time, Magdalene said yes.

Two years later, Magdalene Lampert found herself standing in the first-grade classroom of a BTR resident named Sabine Ferdinand, holding up an iPad to record a lesson that would help determine whether BTR would award Sabine the certification she needed to teach in Massachusetts. Technically, the classroom belonged to Ilene Carver, a fifteen-year veteran teacher. But over the course of the year, Sabine had taken more and more responsibility, becoming just as much the teacher as Ilene, at least in the eyes of the students. That day, she was leading an activity called "Quick Images," an IA adapted from the math curriculum used throughout Boston elementary schools.

The lesson began with Sabine counting down—"eight, seven, six, . . ."—as the students arranged themselves on the classroom's rectangular rug, sitting on masking tape X's with their names written in marker. "Three, two, one," Sabine said, pausing patiently between each number. "The expectation is that you're in your rug spot with your pencil."

Sabine sat in the usual teacher spot: the corner closest to the door, near the place where the class's cloth calendar hung on the wall. "MARCH," it said, counting out the days in bright red and white.

"You're sitting on your bottoms, crisscross applesauce," she said, warmly. "I don't want to remind you again. Thank you."

Then she shifted into the work of the moment. "Who here remembers early on, when we used to do Quick Images, with the dots?" Hands shot up. One squealing student gulped and jumped from her bottom to her knees in glee.

They reviewed the rules: The teacher flashes each image only twice, and only very briefly each time. After each flash of the image, the students write down what they've seen. But while the image is up, they can only think—no pencils.

On this day they were working on geometry, so the images Sabine showed wouldn't be dots to count, but shapes to draw. "Ready?" she asked. "One, two, three." The students took in deep breaths as Sabine flashed the drawing, rotating it for everyone to see, Vanna White–style. A perfect square on a white sheet of paper.

After the second viewing, she pinned the drawing to an easel on her left. "All right," she said. "So my question is, how can we describe this shape?" There was another show of hands, but Sabine waited patiently, giving more students an opportunity to think. "How can we describe this shape?" she repeated. "Rafael?"

"Uhh," Rafael said thoughtfully. He was a heavyset child with a big, nervous smile. "It's a square." Sabine could have left it there—yes, a square—and moved on to the next shape. But she continued to probe as Magdalene watched.

"Who agrees with Rafael?" she asked, holding up a model thumb to her chest to suggest how students could signal their answer, up or down. "Stephanie," she asked. "Do you have anything you want to add on? What else—how can you describe your shape?"

Stephanie, an energetic girl who sat in a special chair on the side of the rug, presumably to keep her focused, mulled that over. "Um," she said, and then announced: "It is *not* long!"

"Can you say more about that?" Sabine asked. "What's not long?"

"The sides are not long," Stephanie offered.

Malcolm had his hand up too. "Malcolm, what do you want to say?" Sabine asked. "It has"—he paused to count—"four sides!"

They were getting more specific, but Sabine decided they could say even more. "Now," she said, "what do we notice about these sides?"

"They're medium-sized," offered Oscar, from the back.

"True," she said. "Danica," she continued, turning to someone else, "what do you notice about the sides?"

"I want to add on to what Oscar said," Danica said thoughtfully. Magdalene took note of her phrasing—here was a first-grader engaging in a mathematical discussion, in the classroom of a first-year teacher. It was remarkable.

Danica went on. "They are large," she said, "but on the top of it—they are large—on the sides, they're even longer." Danica's description wasn't accurate, of course; the shape was a square, and so the sides were actually equal. But she was the first in the class to compare the lengths at all, and that pulled the discussion in an important direction. Sabine repeated the observation, pointing to the drawing on the board: the sides, Danica was arguing, were even longer on the left and right than they were on the top and bottom. "Interesting," Sabine said.

The students were treading into significant mathematical territory, and at just the right developmental moment. By the spring of first grade, these students clearly grasped the difference between broad geometric categories, like triangles versus squares. But grappling with finer distinctions—the difference, for instance, between a right triangle and an isosceles triangle, or in this case, between a rectangle and a square—proved more of a challenge. The children's ideas suggested they had some understanding of the difference (the relationship between the sides), but they were struggling to describe it. Were the left and right sides longer than the top and bottom ones, or were they the same?

The discussion now moved into more important terrain: the shift from what the psychologist Jean Piaget called "animism"— the idea that objects have their own consciousnesses, like people, and so can move and change, rather than staying stable and constant—to a more abstract understanding of a square as a category describing shapes with four equal sides of unchanging lengths. For children still thinking animistically, a square was not a solid and permanent fact, but an object that could decide to expand in any direction if it chose to do so.

Not long after Danica's misguided comment about the square's longer vertical sides, a girl named Luisa made the observation that tugged the class in the correct direction. The shape, she said, actually had four *equal* sides.

"Luisa," Sabine had asked, seizing the opportunity to underscore an important point, "why were you sure to say *equal* sides? What does that mean?" Clarifying for the rest of the class's benefit, Luisa had replied that *equal* meant "the same as."

Yet some students still seemed confused. Building on Danica's comment, Oscar, the eager boy in the back, had propped himself up on his knees to share an idea. "If you put it a little up, and a little up," he said, motioning to show how he could move the top and bottom sides farther apart, then, he explained, "it would be longer, because you're putting it a little *upper*." But while the right and left sides then would have to get longer, the top and bottom would become shorter, he said.

"So are you saying if we were to squish this shape?" Sabine asked, to confirm. "Yeah," he said, nodding.

One purpose of studying math in school, Magdalene knew, was to help children wrestle with just the ideas Oscar was working on. Could squares really squish themselves? Or were they more stable than that?

"But," Sabine asked Oscar, "what did Luisa tell us about this shape? Malcolm?"

"She said it's four equal parts," Malcolm said.

"Equal parts," Sabine repeated. "Equal sides."

As a more experienced teacher, Magdalene knew that there were other ways Sabine could have helped the students work on these ideas. To get them closer to grasping the distinction between a rectangle and a square, for instance, she could have used Danica's incorrect observation about the sides as an opportunity. "I could have pulled out a picture of a rectangle and said, 'Are these the same or are they different? In what ways are they the same and in what ways are they different?'" Magdalene says.

But that kind of response takes longer to cultivate (starting with learning to recognize what all this strange squishing was about—no simple thing), and she didn't expect a first-year resident to figure it out on the fly. What Sabine was doing was exactly what Magdalene hoped for. Using a routine she'd rehearsed many times before, she was able to keep the students focused—and, at the same time, to listen to their math. Her preparation had helped her learn not only what to do (the steps of choral counting) but how to make sense of the math the students were working on. As a result, she had gotten the kids thinking about fundamental concepts in geometry, and when wrong ideas arose, she didn't just swat them away; she put them on the table for the class to probe. Ultimately, she had managed to elicit the pivotal idea about four equal sides from Luisa. So when Oscar brought up his animistic idea that the shape could "squish," Sabine could hold it out against Luisa's more sophisticated conjecture, helping Oscar to reconsider what it meant to be a square.

Even if the students didn't end that particular discussion fully grasping the difference between a rectangle and a square, or the difference between an abstract shape and a living, elastic object, they had made important progress. "They're struggling with a fundamental concept, and they should be," Magdalene said. It was more than could be said of many first-grade classrooms. It was exciting.

Later, after they finished the Quick Images IA, Sabine introduced a problem about addition. She showed the students a puzzle and then gave them a chart that tracked the blocks she'd used to complete it—"two hexagons, zero trapezoids, one blue rhombus, zero squares, three tan rhombuses, and seven green triangles," she read out loud. Now their challenge was to find the total number of blocks.

Magdalene knew Sabine had selected the numbers deliberately to add up to a sum greater than 10 (13). They'd been working on more complicated methods of adding numbers, like "counting up" from the largest number or breaking an unfamiliar problem into familiar parts or using a number line to skip from one number to the next. A problem with a solution larger than 10 would nudge the students to try out the new methods for themselves, rather than using the one that many of them still preferred: counting on their fingers.

Indeed, just as Sabine had hoped, the students walked through all kinds of novel combinations of the methods they'd been working on. Magdalene watched as one girl, lying on her stomach, wrote out two number sentences—3 + 3 = 6 and 6 + 7 = □ —and then filled in the empty box by starting with 7 and then drawing 6 lines:

$$7 \quad | \quad | \quad | \quad | \quad | \quad |$$
$$ \quad 8 \quad 9 \quad 10 \quad 11 \quad 12 \quad 13$$

She caught another student writing out different sets of number sentences:

$$2 + 1 = 3$$
$$3 + 7 = 10$$

Another student, Faith, took a similar approach. "That is very cool," Magdalene told her, as Faith showed off what she'd done:

$$2 + 1 = 3$$
$$3 + 7 = 10$$
$$2 + 1 + 3 + 7 = \boxed{13}$$

Later, as the lesson moved from individual work time to group discussion, Sabine invited a quiet boy named Kevin to share his strategy.

"I did three plus seven equals ten and then—" he began, before Sabine interrupted.

"How did you know that three plus seven equals ten?" she asked.

"Because I knew my combinations of ten," Kevin replied.

"So three and seven's just another combination of ten," Sabine repeated, turning to the rest of the students to make sure they'd understood Kevin's strategy. "So you can use what you already know to help you figure out this problem. So he knew three plus seven equals ten." She turned back to Kevin. "Go on."

Kevin described his next step. He was left with 2 and 1, and he knew that $2 + 1 = 3$, so he added up the two final sums, 10 and 3. "And you got?" Sabine asked. "Thirteen," he said. Sabine added that to the board, where she was chronicling each student's steps:

$$3 + 7 = 10$$
$$2 + 1 = 3$$
$$10 + 3 = 13$$

But before she could summarize the important point—once again, Kevin had used a combination he already knew to find the final sum—another boy blurted out an idea from the carpet. Earlier, he'd been squirming and talking out of turn. But now he was interrupting with an observation about Kevin's strategy. "If you take away the zero," he said, pointing to 10, "and put the three, it's thirteen!"

Sabine looked at Magdalene. A common course for young children was to see "3 + 10" and mistakenly add the three and one together, since the one is closest to the three, getting 4. Then, not knowing what to do with the zero, and not fully grasping the difference between the tens and the ones places, they would write a zero next to the four: $3 + 10 = 40$. This boy, still just a first-grader, had leapt headfirst into the correct idea: three ones and one ten meant that the three could effectively replace the zero: 13. He had intuited place value.

Sabine and Magdalene smiled at each other. "I see what you're saying," Sabine told the boy. And the class moved on.

Jesse Solomon wasn't the only entrepreneur to seek help from the academics. Heather Kirkpatrick, a leader at the Aspire charter network in California, came to the Learning to Teach summit focused on the same problem as the others. "We looked so good on paper; we were kind of killing it," Heather says. "But we all felt like, jeez, when we walk into the classroom, we're not where we want to be."

What they wanted was rigor—more specifically, something they called "academic discourse." To them, *discourse* meant four things. First, adults couldn't do all the talking (and therefore all the thinking). Second, the students had to talk about the academic idea at hand and, third, they had to talk using academic vocabulary. Finally, they had to do what Aspire called "bringing evidence to bear"—quoting the text in English class, citing a primary source in history, reasoning through a proof in math, pointing to experimental evidence in science.

"It was those four things. And we said we should be able to see that in math, science, English language arts, history. That is the holy grail," Heather says. "Then we said, okay, how do we get there?"

Heather was struggling with this question when someone suggested she talk to Pam Grossman, a professor at Stanford's ed school and one of Lee Shulman's first students after Lee left Michigan State for Stanford. Pam had come to grad school after nearly a decade of teaching high school English. During her time at Stanford, Lee dispatched a group of his students to study the teaching of individual academic subjects; Pam selected English. Over time, she came to think of Lee's students in family parlance. With Lee as their shared mentor, Deborah Ball and the others were like Pam Grossman's academic "cousins," working on the same questions, just at different universities and in different subjects. There was one other difference for Pam: instead of experimenting with her own teaching, she studied other teachers' work.

One episode, caught on videotape, showed seven students at a struggling urban high school in San Lorenzo, California, discussing "The Yellow Wallpaper," the short story by Charlotte Perkins Gilman. Their teacher was not visible in the video, but the students carried on as if he was right there, paging through the Xeroxed story in front of them and even calling on each other to speak.

"What do you have to say, Jim?" a blonde girl named Amy was asking the boy across from her when the clip opened. "My interpretation of this," Jim said, "goes back to what Ms. McWilliams"—his student teacher—"said before we even read the story, about how it gave her chills." Jim wore glasses and had a knack for the theatrical pause. "And actually, my interpretation of this is that she was dead from the very end of page thirty."

The other students looked up from their papers. The story, written as a series of diary entries by a woman suffering from anxiety, used the word *dead* only once, and that was to describe the paper on which the woman wrote her diary. But while the diary did chronicle the woman's worsening condition after her husband, a physician, ordered that she isolate herself from work and society, it never mentioned that the woman was not alive. Now Jim was saying she'd been dead since page thirty. "What?" one student asked.

"That whole conversation" on page thirty, Jim continued, "the very last line says, 'I am securely fastened now by my well-hidden rope—you don't get ME out in the road there!'" The line described how the narrator, after feeling trapped behind the wallpaper of her isolated room, had used a rope to escape it. Jim continued, "I think at that point, she's dead. This is her talking to John"—the narrator's husband—"as a ghost."

"Ah!" exclaimed Jade, a girl in denim who had been listening quietly, with one eye on the page and another on Jim. She bolted up, putting a hand over her mouth. The girl next to her, Sariah, had her mouth wide open too.

"She's free in the house," Jim went on, "but she is never, like, free—"

"—OUTSIDE OF THE HOUSE!" Jade and Sariah shouted in unison, as the rest of the group talked over each other in an excited rush.

But Amy, the one who had called on Jim in the first place, wasn't buying Jim's idea. "So then, wait, wait," she said. She pointed to another passage that didn't seem to fit Jim's story. The line about the "securely fastened" rope was preceded by another, speculating that other women might have made the same escape as the narrator, fleeing from behind the room's oppressive wallpaper.

"Right there," Amy said, "it says, 'I wonder if they all come out of that wallpaper as I did?'" How did that description jibe with Jim's interpretation? "Does that represent the people who died just before her, or something? Other people who've died?" A few students attempted an explanation before Jim spoke. "I wonder if it sort of represents society," he said. "Because she's freeing herself, and she's wondering, are all the other women doing this too?"

"So her way of freeing herself was killing herself," Amy replied, repeating his point. You could connect the two passages, Jim was saying, by interpreting all the women's escapes from behind the wallpaper as suicides.

Soon Jade had a question. "But what about this house?" she asked. "This house! This house! This house has to represent something too." Amy took the opportunity to offer her own interpretation of the story. "Maybe," she said, "maybe the house and the area can represent life, right? There are parts of life, places in life you want to go, things you want to do, right? She was talking about that one room she wanted, but her husband said no."

Jade nodded. She was persuaded by this interpretation too. "The different rooms could be different lifestyles!" she said, jumping in. "Or different things she can or cannot do," Amy said. "Or," Jim said, quietly, "different parts of her life." "Yeah," Amy said, pointing at him with her pencil and nodding. They had different interpretations, but they were on the same page.

The video showed just the kind of conversation Heather and her team wanted to cultivate at Aspire—a pristine example of "academic discourse." The teacher, Peter Williamson, might not have been on the screen, but, as Pam explained, his work was all over the lesson. More specifically, he had set the students up to have a productive discussion, first having them write out two types of questions, literal and interpretive; then having them go over the questions with each other, getting feedback on how to improve on them; and finally, after they'd finished talking, leading a debriefing of the conversation centered on how they could have gotten even more out of talking to each other. (That was one reason Peter, who later became a professor of teacher education at the University of San Francisco, had videotaped the session—so that the students could watch it and think about what to do better next time.)

And these steps were only what Peter had to do to prepare for the single "Yellow Wallpaper" lesson. It had taken him more work to get the students to that point. Eventually, Pam and her graduate students broke the practice of English teaching down into key parts—"core practices," Pam called them, an English counterpart to Magdalene's instructional activities.

Among the practices Pam outlined was "modeling." This was a

core part of the best English teachers' repertoire, a way of walking students through the processes they needed to perform in English class—not just reading and writing, but their component parts, like annotating a text to help understand its meaning or using evidence to construct an explanation. To teach students each part, a teacher not only had to walk them through what, for instance, an annotation looked like (*here are my highlights!*) or show them an explanation (*this sentence right here!*); she also had to break the activity down into its invisible mental steps. Pam called this "making your thinking visible."

Modeling worked best on texts that resonated with the students. Even better, the teacher could use the students' own work. For instance, a teacher might take the draft of a student's persuasive essay and use it to model, say, the writing of explanations, walking step by step through the evidence and narrating how a writer might think about using that evidence to support a point. "'So what?' is the question I need to ask," the teacher could tell the students. "And my answer should tell you . . . *oh*, that's why this evidence is so important!"

Another category in Pam Grossman's taxonomy of English teaching, "classroom discourse," helped teachers work with students on their ideas. A classroom discussion shouldn't operate as a floating alternate reality, the entertainment before the real work begins. At their best, discussions were the first step in the writing process, verbal editing sessions in which students worked together to sharpen their ideas. What did the text literally mean? What did it mean symbolically? If the discussion went well, then, by the end of the lesson, a classroom full of bland observations would transform into thirty well-articulated interpretations.

When Pam started grad school, scholars of English teaching had written about the importance of discussion in a literary class.

Studying American classrooms, they had also discovered how rare it was. But few had thought about how to help teachers do more of it and do it better. Pam and her students "decomposed" discussion, breaking the practice down into teachable parts.

What they found was that great discussions did not happen by accident. They required serious, deliberate preparation. One teacher whose practice Pam studied—Yvonne Divans Hutchinson, who taught in the Los Angeles Unified School District at a high school lodged between the neighborhoods of Watts and Compton—handed her students detailed lists of what she called "stock responses," possible ways of participating in a discussion, including half a dozen alternatives to a shrug:

- *You don't know the answer?* Try saying, "I don't know, but I will try to find out the answer and get back to you."
- *You didn't come prepared to talk?* "I regret to say that I am not prepared."
- *You didn't understand the question?* Just ask, "Would you please repeat (or restate) the question?"
- *You did the homework and understood the question, but still couldn't come up with an answer?* How about, "Please come back to me; I'm still thinking."

The stock responses might seem forced, but without them there was no guarantee students would talk at all. "You're not born with a gene that tells you how to talk about *Beloved*," Pam says. "Actually, that's something you learn to do over time, and there are things that teachers can do to make kids successful."

Yvonne also wrote out suggestions for ways of making a contribution. To disagree, first say so: "I respectfully disagree." Then give your opposing idea—"and justify it." To agree and then extend, say, "I want to add to what (person's name) said."

Other rules added to the class's discursive repertoire. To make sure a wide variety of students spoke, and to increase the likelihood of getting an answer, Yvonne took advantage of peer pressure and had students call on each other. Asked for a response by a peer rather than the teacher, she found, teenagers were more likely to comply. She also prepared for the case of a student with nothing to say. She often reminded her classes to pause, giving the students Yvonne called "reticent" more time to put their thoughts together. And through her modeling, the students learned how to coach each other too, coaxing contributions from even the quietest peers.

That was just the beginning. In Yvonne's class, every discussion began with an "anticipation guide," a list of questions designed to get the students thinking about subjects covered in a reading before they began it. Next came a "reading response prompt" that each student answered individually, complete with reminders about the best way to read—"mark up the text in the way you choose," the instructions said, "including the use of highlighters and metacognitive marking"—and instructions asking the students to write questions of their own. (In Yvonne's class, even questions had a careful taxonomy, from basic factual "right there" questions [level one] to "global" questions [level three] that took a text's substance and expanded beyond it; for one prompt, the students were to write two level-one questions, three level twos, and one or two level threes.) Finally, in the minutes before the whole-group discussion, they held miniconversations in small groups. "If they come to the work with their own frame of reference, then they're much more apt to be engaged," Yvonne explained.

The planning got the students to the starting line, but to pull off a lively and productive discussion, Yvonne had to teach in the moment too. Pam and another one of her grad students, Lisa

Barker, used videos from Yvonne's class and others to further break down the art of leading a discussion. Drawing on a term coined by early scholars of classroom discussions, Pam and Lisa called one of the practices Yvonne often deployed "uptake." A teacher practiced uptake when she listened to a student's contribution and then repeated it in some way, by summarizing the idea (*So her way of freeing herself was killing herself*), elaborating on it, or pushing the student to do the same.

Working with Pam, Lisa broke down "uptake" into nine subparts, which teachers used at different times. "Restatement," the simplest, involved summarizing a student's claim, but this time adding academic language, such as better grammar or more precise terminology. "Revoicing," a subset of restatement, summarized a student's contribution for the even more specific purpose of aligning it with the particular side of the discussion it belonged to—*Amy is clarifying Jim's statement about "freeing herself" in order to support his interpretation that the woman is a ghost.*

Other moves had the teacher directly pushing students for better contributions. A "challenge" move responded to a claim by taking the opposite stance, just for the sake of argument. "Press" asked the speaker for more information—evidence of a claim, maybe, or clarification of meaning. "Post" held up a student's claim and solicited comments on it—*Who thinks they can articulate what Jim is trying to say?*

Not only had Peter Williamson, the teacher who assigned "The Yellow Wallpaper," mastered classroom discourse himself; his mastery served as a model for his students, who used uptake to discuss the story on their own. Amy knew to ask for clarification; Jade knew to repeat Jim's claim to make sure she understood it and to press him to elaborate on the idea when she wanted to challenge it; and at the end, when Amy put forward her own interpretation, Jim knew how to use "uptake" to build on the idea, listening as she described the house's symbolic meaning and then helping her burnish her explanation. The rooms represented not just "different things she can or cannot do," but "different parts of her life."

Heather Kirkpatrick loved Peter's video. She talked with Pam, and in no time, Pam and Lisa were coming to Aspire to teach a session at its summer retreat.

One way to think about what the academics offered the entrepreneurs was "content." Whereas the entrepreneurs like Doug Lemov looked at teaching generically, across all kinds of subjects, Magdalene Lampert looked only at math and Pam Grossman, only at English.

But just as important as their content knowledge, and maybe more so, was the academics' theory of learning. Ironically, this was a legacy of the same academic structure that had once hindered research on teaching: the close relationship between education research and psychology. It was true, as Lee Shulman's predecessor Nate Gage had discovered, that the science of teaching was not simply the inverse of the science of learning. But the corollary was also true. It wasn't possible to understand teaching without understanding learning.

Perhaps unintentionally, the charter school educators had adopted a linear model of learning. Learners, they assumed, started with the basic fluency skills needed to do what they called "higher-order" work. In math, that meant memorizing the multiplication tables before working on problem solving; in English, it meant mastering simple vocabulary words before learning to construct an argument. They thought of learning as if it were architecture: a fantastic design was nothing without the materials to build it. Something complex and beautiful could not be accomplished without first mastering the mundane.

The idea that facts laid the foundation for concepts yielded a basically behaviorist theory of learning. If learning began with facts, and facts began with memorizing—because memorizing (or "fluency") was separate from concepts ("critical thinking")— then the best method to teach children to learn was not so different from what Edward Thorndike had hoped to accomplish with his cats. Practice, practice, practice, with regular punishment and rewards. The "rigor" could come later.

The resulting teaching style was especially clear in the handling of mistakes. In a behaviorist model, every mistake should be greeted with a quick and firm correction. Otherwise, students won't learn that an idea is wrong. The best charter school teachers took this maxim seriously. One math teacher, heralded as one of the best in the KIPP network, decided never to give his students chances to practice problems at homes that they hadn't already been taught how to solve. The danger, he explained, lay in the likelihood that, alone at home without the teacher to stop them, they would practice doing the steps wrong. Absent a response that corrected or approved the step, the mistake might be ingrained in the category of uncorrected, and therefore accurate, truths.

Several of the techniques in Doug Lemov's taxonomy (for example, "Do It Again") rested on this belief. Teaching behavior, in the world of the taxonomy, often boiled down to the imperative of responding to every visible *mis*behavior. A teacher was bound to give a swift and clear correction to every mistake. Doug applied the idea to teaching academic content too. Writing about how to teach children to "decode," the work of deciphering a string of letters into a pronounceable word, he emphasized the importance of letting no error go unnoticed. "Given the bedrock importance of decoding at every level," he wrote, "teachers should strive to correct decoding errors whenever possible, no matter what subject or grade level they teach." "Punch the

Error" was the name he gave the technique of notifying a student swiftly of her mistake.

But by the time Pam, Deborah, and Magdalene started their study of teaching in the 1980s, research had begun to show the limits of this behaviorist view. Learning among humans, psychologists were discovering, was more than just a sum of experienced stimulus-and-response yes-no pairs, and concepts didn't wait for facts to accumulate; the two were enmeshed together.

The best memorizers, for instance, succeeded by embedding their object of study within a more abstract map of big ideas. One psychologist, studying a college student he called "S.F.," found that the student could memorize long strings of numbers only by attaching the digits to others that held more meaning. A competitive runner, S.F. translated numbers into race times; 3492, for instance, became "3 minutes and 49 point 2 seconds, near world-record mile time." Just 3.492 wouldn't have been enough; he also had to place the number in a context that *made sense to him*. After a year and a half of using the racing mnemonic, the number of digits S.F. could memorize had grown from 7 to 79. The only cases where he stumbled were numbers that simply couldn't be mapped back to a memorable race.

Children, similarly, learned to add and subtract through strategies that built on their intuitive sense of numbers, not what their teacher told them was correct. Like the Brazilian street children selling fruit, who managed to make multidigit calculations in their heads, they counted, grouped, and regrouped until they arrived at a solution that corresponded to what they knew about how numbers worked.

Humans appeared to practice this reasoning—"critical thinking" or "rigor," the entrepreneurial educators might call it— practically from birth. In experiment after experiment, psychologists studying infants showed that they looked at the world not via a system of rewards and punishments, but through a web of generalizations, rules, and principles derived from observations.

In one experiment, psychologists pushed a blue cylinder down a ramp until it hit a toy bug. Their six-and-a-half-month-old subjects watched as the blue cylinder propelled the bug forward, so that it traveled all the way to the middle of a horizontal track. Then the researchers rolled down two more cylinders, a larger yellow one and a smaller orange one. Predictably, the larger yellow cylinder knocked the bug farther along the track, all the way to the end. But the orange cylinder, although smaller than both of the other cylinders, nevertheless moved the bug to the end of the track as well. Presenting the same strange events to adults, researchers found that they reacted with surprise. But would infants, who had never been taught the laws of physics, do the same?

They did. Shown the surprising case of the smaller orange cylinder that knocked the toy bug farther than made sense, infants stared longer than a control group of infants shown a sequence of events that did not violate physics. They'd been on Earth for under a year, and certainly had never been given a gold star for knowing that larger cylinders have greater mass than smaller ones. But after taking in the world's data—all the times that large objects pushed things farther than smaller ones—they had come up with the abstract mental model that made sense.

The takeaway message was not that conceptual understanding is more important than memorization; it was that the two are inextricably enmeshed. Any supposed dichotomy between them was false. Magdalene summarized the lesson in a single phrase. Children, she said, were "sense makers." Like the babies staring at the cylinders, they took in data and reasoned about it, working from their own evolving grasp of how the world worked. Educators who imagined otherwise—assuming, for instance, that memorization took place outside the context of concepts and principles, or that repeated rewards and punishments were enough to help a person learn—did so at their own peril. Children would try to make sense of rules, even rules that made no sense. Then, when violations inevitably arose, they would apply the rules anyway, as the California teacher who overemphasized subtraction with regrouping found when her student, told of the importance of borrowing, began doing so on every problem, no matter what size the bottom number was.

Magdalene and Pam and Deborah's kind of teaching, TKOT, was more academically rigorous not because their problems were harder, or their expectations higher, or their grading curve steeper, but because their vision of learning was more refined. Not only had they read the general research on learning. They had also studied the specific rules of "knowing"—the *epistemology*—for the individual subjects they taught. Each field had its own specialized definition of what it meant to know something—of the way, in math, conjectures built to proofs, or, in literature, evidence became explanation and finally interpretation.

Because the definitions were not all the same, neither was the teaching they argued for. In math, for instance, the "You, Y'all, We" lesson pattern popularized in Japan (as well as in Magdalene and Deborah's math classrooms) made sense for structuring investigations of big ideas, like the meaning of fractions or negative numbers. In English, meanwhile, where students needed to learn specific reading and writing strategies—how to figure out the meaning of an unfamiliar word, for example, or how to build ideas for an essay—the "I, We, You" pattern of modeling followed by guided practice was more appropriate. And within each subject, different topics could call for different structures.

Drawing on these very specific traditions, Magdalene, Pam, Deborah, and their colleagues had an easier time achieving the academic rigor that the no-excuses teachers also longed for. They taught by helping students see the world differently, pushing their intuitive knowledge closer to the bank of understandings and rules of operation that mathematicians (and scientists, historians, literary theorists, and so on) have arrived at over centuries. Teaching, in this view, began with listening. "Part of interacting with kids," Magdalene said, "is assessing where they are and thinking about what experiences you can give them that will challenge their way of seeing the world."

The different approach to learning also led Magdalene, Pam, and Deborah to take a different view of children's mistakes. In TKOT, mistakes were not worrisome ills to stamp out on sight, but precious opportunities to begin the longer process of correcting misunderstandings over time. One purpose of teaching, in their view, was to draw out mistakes. The best English teachers, Pam saw, helped children write better by showcasing real examples of student writing that needed work—and then, holding weak models up against the strong, by describing exactly what students could do to improve. Magdalene and Deborah, similarly, built their problems of the day around the goal of eliciting misunderstandings that could move the class toward more accurate ideas.

Some Japanese teachers took this notion even further. In Japan, the portion of the lesson that Magdalene called "teaching while students work independently" actually had two competing names: *kikan-shido* and *kikan-junshi*. The first, *kikan-shido*, described the act of observing students' efforts to solve the problem of the day and, when necessary, intervening to resolve their confusion by offering a hint or an extra instruction. But the second, *kikan-junshi*, adopted by a contingent of purists, described observing without comment. When a student made a mistake or became confused, the teacher simply noted the error (maybe on a pad of paper or maybe just in her head), nodded, and walked on by. An English translation clarified the difference: *kikan-shido* meant "between desks instruction," whereas *kikan-junshi* meant "between desks patrolling."

Students learned better when they saw the error of their ideas on their own, the *kikan-junshi* purists felt. And the teacher made sure they did see it, in the course of the "We" part of the lesson, the group discussion.

In this regard, Doug Lemov seemed conflicted. On one hand, as the "Punch the Error" technique exemplified, much of his taxonomy was built around the eradication of mistakes. Yet Doug also wrote about the importance of making class a safe space for errors. Indeed, "Normalizing Error" was Technique No. 49, the last one in the taxonomy. It described how teachers could get students feeling comfortable with mistakes. And so, in *Teach like a Champion*, on the same page that Doug emphasized the importance of fixing errors "as quickly as possible," he also called them "a normal and healthy part of the learning process."

The tension was much less apparent in Doug's work teaching adults, his teacher training. In this regard, the entrepreneurs and the academics took a strikingly similar approach. At taxonomy workshops, attendees practiced techniques in simulations that looked practically identical to those used at Dilit in Italy. Doug always emphasized that teachers should use these evolving techniques only *if they made sense.* The job of administrators, meanwhile, was not to punish bad performers for poor teaching. It was to give them opportunities to learn. To teach them.

And over time, even without direct intervention from the academics, the entrepreneurs' approach to teaching children was beginning to bear more resemblance to their approach to teaching adults. In 2013, Doug began crafting "Taxonomy 2.0," a second edition of *Teach like a Champion*, in which he revised large portions of his approach to error. Instead of focusing on ways that teachers could eliminate mistakes as soon as they arose, the new document tried to give them tools to use errors as learning opportunities, naming new techniques they could use to help students feel comfortable making mistakes.

As Doug's changing ideas made clear, the biggest question was not whether the entrepreneurs' teaching would evolve over time. Their teaching already *was* evolving, even without the academics' help. The biggest question was whether the rest of the country's teaching would change too. Academics like Pam, Magdalene, and Deborah still made up only a minority of ed school professors. The entrepreneurs, meanwhile, were growing in number, but by 2011, charter schools still reached only 4 percent of American public school students. And although the outside world was paying more attention to the charters, the lessons that observers drew didn't necessarily reflect the reality inside. Instead, as usual, the observers focused on the idea that had spawned charter schools in the first place: accountability.

10

A PROFESSION OF HOPE

In 2004, as Doug Lemov began thinking about his taxonomy, Deborah Ball found herself talking about her future with two of her mentors—David Cohen and the University of Michigan's provost, Paul Courant.

After spending eight years at Michigan State, Deborah had followed David and Magdalene Lampert to the University of Michigan in Ann Arbor in 1996. There, her career had blossomed. Her videotapes of Sean, Mei, and the rest in her classroom at Spartan Village had gained a growing following among academics and math teachers, and so had her research. She had cowritten several papers with David describing the infrastructure problem. And, working with the mathematician Hyman Bass, she had built on the corpus of Mathematical Knowledge for Teaching, MKT, expanding the focus from content knowledge to accompanying practices that could be taught.

And that year, another prestigious university had begun recruiting her for its ed school. She was discussing her options with David when he asked her a question. "Something like, 'What do you actually want to do?' Like, not where do you want to live, but what do you actually want to *do*?'" Deborah recalls.

The answer spilled out. "I want to completely change the way teacher education works in this country." Very little had changed over the two decades she'd been studying teaching. The new entrepreneurial sector was an intriguing exception, but it served only a tiny fraction of American students. The vast majority of kids still learned with teachers who were as unprepared as Deborah had been when she first came to Spartan Village. At university ed schools, aspiring educators still sat in five-hundred-person lectures like the ones Lee Shulman had taught at MSU in the 1970s. Even Teach For America, despite its improvements, struggled to ensure that all its corps members entered the class-room ready to help students learn at a high level.

The classroom was no different. Curricula still varied from state to state, district to district, even school to school. Tests still confused rather than complemented each curriculum—or simply overrode it. Professional development was haphazard at best. The David Cohen coherence problem, in other words, was still alive, well, and widely ignored: Americans still lacked any discernible agreement on what students were supposed to learn, and teach-ers were still left alone to help them learn it. The whole education world lived with the consequences of incoherence every day, yet the number of people who really understood what educational infrastructure meant could be counted on a first-grade pattern block set, and all of them seemed to work in the same building in Ann Arbor.

What did Deborah really want to do? She wanted to build the infrastructure to support "responsible teaching" (the phrase she preferred over "TKOT")—and not just for her students at Michigan, but for teachers and students all across the country. By David's definition, *infrastructure* had three key elements: a common curriculum suggesting what students should study; common examinations to test how much of that curriculum they learned; and finally, teacher education to help teachers learn to teach exactly what students are supposed to learn. Since her expertise was in the third category, Deborah thought she could start there.

Deborah started looking ahead. It was currently 2004. For the 2007–08 school year, nearly two hundred thousand new teachers would enter classrooms for the first time, up from sixty-five thousand just twenty years earlier. By 2011, 3.7 million people would work in the profession. And the modal number of years of experience of the American teacher—fifteen years in 1987—was now just one. If these new teachers were going to come to the classroom ready to teach, somebody needed to help them prepare.

At Michigan, Deborah could test a model that would arm teachers with the knowledge and practices they needed to teach students well. If the model worked, she could expand it to the rest of the country.

David and the provost gave Deborah their full support. If what she wanted to do was transform teacher education, they said, "then that's what you should be doing." She decided to stay in Ann Arbor, where she became director of the university's teacher education program, and received a significant grant from the provost to reshape the program from scratch. The next year, she became dean of the school of education.

As Deborah's project took off—the Teacher Education Initiative, she decided to call it—her timing began to look remarkably apt.

Of the three elements of a David Cohen–esque infrastructure, she'd picked teacher education partly because it seemed especially important and partly because it was what she knew best. But soon, signs of the other two elements—a common curriculum and assessments to match—also began to emerge. The driving force were the Common Core standards, a new attempt to write national education goals for all American students. The Common Core standards weren't themselves a curriculum, and they weren't assessments either, but they paved the way for both. At first, the effort seemed just as quixotic as Deborah's Teacher Education Initiative. Every previous effort to write national standards had imploded. Close reading of the master document always set off debate; critics found too many instances of Harriet Tubman and too few of Robert E. Lee, or a reading goal matched to third grade instead of first, and poof!, the coalition backing the standards would disintegrate.

But the agitators for the Common Core had learned several lessons from their predecessors. They assembled the standards in relative solitude, avoiding a big public campaign. They deliberately sought input from states, organizing not through a federal government agency, but through the National Governors Association, and thereby preempting cries of federal intrusion. They also had the advantage of time; after several rounds of math and reading wars in the 1980s and 1990s, certain ceasefires had been wrought. Reading experts now largely agreed that both phonics instruction and an emphasis on comprehension were important for teaching children to read, and a core group of mathematicians had come to accept that educators might be onto something with their "fuzzy math." Inevitable disagreements remained, especially in the less organized middle and high school English community. Nevertheless, less than two months after the standards were released, in June 2010, twenty-seven states had vowed to adopt the standards. By the end of 2013, the number was forty-five (plus the District of Columbia). With so many states signing up, common curricula and common assessments weren't far off.

The remaining leg of the infrastructure triangle, teacher education, was perhaps the hardest to build. After all, reformers had been trying to reinvigorate teacher education for decades with little success. But here again, Deborah's timing gave her a unique opportunity. By 2004, when the Teacher Education Initiative began, researchers knew more than ever about how to teach teachers to teach. In large part, this was Judith Lanier's legacy. Her own reform effort might have failed at Michigan State, but the faculty she and Lee Shulman had recruited twenty-five years earlier had, over two and a half decades, uncovered a great many practices that successful teachers employed. They had begun to codify "the wisdom of teachers." That meant they could lay out in detail the things a new teacher needed to learn how to do. And as Magdalene Lampert and Pam Grossman showed with their instructional activities and core practices, they had also begun to develop ways of passing that wisdom on to new teachers.

Judy Lanier's faculty members at Michigan State had been confined to general goals like "connect teacher education more closely to the classroom" or "make the academic preparation of teachers more intellectually sound." By 2004, Deborah and her faculty at the University of Michigan could be much more specific. Drawing on the research from Judy Lanier's Institute for Research on Teaching, they could draft a curriculum for new teachers that described a full course of techniques: "high-leverage practices," the Michigan faculty called them.

The first high-leverage practice, for instance—"making content explicit through explanation, modeling, representations, and examples"—drew on the focus by Pam Grossman and other researchers on modeling. Both Pam's and Magdalene's work, meanwhile, inspired the second high-leverage practice ("leading a whole-class discussion") as well as "eliciting and interpreting individual students' thinking," which was high-leverage practice number three. And the practices related to mathematical knowledge for teaching, Deborah's MKT, helped ground high-leverage practice numbers five and six: "recognizing particular common patterns of student thinking in a subject-matter domain" (like the tendency of elementary school children to mistake the "R" in their remainder findings for a decimal point—turning, say, "1 R 5" into "1.5") and "identifying and implementing an instructional response to common patterns of student thinking" (like deciding on a way to help fifth-graders notice the importance of defining the whole of any fraction).

Collaborating with her colleague Francesca Forzani—a Michigan graduate student who had begun working with Deborah on the project—Deborah also drew on the work of the entrepreneurial education movement (of which Francesca, a Teach For America alum and former staffer, was a member). Like the academics, the entrepreneurs were busy codifying teaching. In particular, Deborah drew from the curriculum at a teacher residency program spun off from the Boston charter school Match—the one where Rousseau Mieze's former principal, Stacy Birdsell O'Toole, worked.

Inspired by the school's founding principal, a beloved educator named Charles Sposato, who died of cancer in 2007, the Match training program distilled Sposato's magic into a teachable science. A key element was the way he had established exceptionally strong relationships with students and their families through methodical habit. Every August, before school started, he would telephone each family to build what he called "relationship capital." He continued calling throughout the year, making sure to vary the kinds of conversations so that he didn't always bear bad news. The Match training program, in turn, required that each of its teacher candidates practice six different types of phone calls, from the "praise quickie" to the "powwow." The curriculum also required several hours of calls to different parents each week: one hour a night each weekday and two hours each weekend.

"When he called, you didn't know what he was calling for," says Venecia Mumford, the mother of two Match graduates, who saved a voicemail from Sposato, left just before he passed away, for years after he died. "Hey Venecia," he said in the message, "I'm so proud of Ed." (Venecia's son Ed had just made the honor roll during his first year at Virginia State.) "Would you tell him congratulations and please keep the hard work up? And thank you for always thinking of us. I love you."

The idea of methodical relationship building resonated with Deborah, who had made regular contact with her students' families at Spartan Village and found it immensely helpful. So, in addition to modeling, leading discussions, and eliciting thinking, the nineteen high-leverage practices included "engaging in strategic relationship-building conversations with students" and "communicating about a student with a parent or guardian."

None of the high-leverage practices were easy. All required diligence, care, thought, and a certain amount of courage. But they had an outsized impact; if a teacher was going to spend her time on something, it would best be spent on one of the high-leverage practices. And if teachers were encouraged to make habits of the practices from their first day in ed school, they might continue them for the rest of their careers.

Deborah's final stroke of luck came from an unexpected source—not the school of research on teaching launched by her own mentor, Lee Shulman, but the other one, created by the economist Eric Hanushek.

When Eric Hanushek first proposed the accountability idea back in 1972, arguing that education spending didn't matter unless it was paired with expectations, he was received as a gadfly—"the neighborhood kook," Hanushek says. But by the first decade of the twenty-first century, as first Republicans and then many Democrats came to agree with him, the idea became policy in states across the country. With the passage of the No Child Left Behind law, the kook became the establishment.

But the second piece of Hanushek's argument took longer to catch on. That was his case for what he called "Teacher Accountability." Since his early work studying teachers in California, Hanushek had continued to find that large differences in effectiveness existed between the best and worst teachers. The gaps persisted even as he refined his "value-added" calculation, the statistical technique that he borrowed from the literature on the productivity of industrial factories. Each finding reinforced the idea that by using the value-added estimates to reward top teachers and fire the lowest performers, American education could be fundamentally transformed.

One Hanushek calculation compared American students' educational performance and that of their Canadian peers, who performed, on average, half a standard deviation higher on international tests. (Canadian students were above average, among the top ten of young people in countries belonging to the Organisation for Economic Co-operation and Development, whereas American students just barely escaped the bottom ten.) The entire gap could be wiped away, Hanushek realized, by eliminating the bottom 6–10 percent of American teachers as judged by value-added scores, or, at a school with thirty teachers, by firing two.

Among the early skeptics of Hanushek's value-added calculations for teachers was Tom Kane, another economist studying education. Kane didn't believe the value-added numbers. At least, he didn't believe anyone should take them too seriously. In 2002, when the Federal Reserve Bank of Boston invited Kane to respond to a new paper of Hanushek's, he aired his concern. "Value-added might be a useful concept," his thinking went, "but there's so much noise in the measure that it's hard to imagine it ever being a useful thing."

Kane had good reason to be skeptical. A year before, as Congress began considering President George W. Bush's proposed education bill—the one that would become No Child Left Behind—he and another economist, Douglas Staiger, ran an analysis of the year-by-year test results that would determine whether schools received rewards or penalties. They found widespread variability. A school on a mostly good trajectory could have one bad year and thus, in the eyes of the bill, be deemed a failure. Kane and Staiger summarized their findings in an op-ed in the *New York Times*. "Because the average elementary school has only 68 children in each grade," they wrote, "a few bright kids one year or a group of rowdy friends the next can cause fluctuations in test performance even if a school is on the right track."

The variability was so pervasive that if No Child Left Behind had been enacted in North Carolina and Texas as the bill was written, only 2 percent of the states' schools would have met its standard of continual progress—and that was in a period when both states showed significant academic growth. "At the typical school, two steps forward were often followed by one step back." If the legislation remained as written, they concluded, the law "is likely to end as a fiasco."

At the Federal Reserve Bank of Boston, Kane's remarks about teachers reflected his experience studying schools. If schools' year-to-year test score results fluctuated that much, each teacher's had to be even more volatile. After all, the core cause of variability for schools seemed to be the small sample size of students they worked with each year. Teachers had even fewer students per year than schools had, meaning that more variability was practically guaranteed. Surely, value-added data for them would prove even less trustworthy than the accountability data on schools.

After Kane and Staiger's study attracted publicity, Congress rewrote the bill's definition of what was called "adequate yearly progress," significantly reducing the impact of the year-to-year variability. Struck by the influence of his research compared with the relatively small amount of work he and Staiger had put into it, Kane decided to take on the next natural question—teachers. "We thought, 'Oh it's gotta be worse at the teacher level, because the sample sizes are smaller,'" Kane says. They set to work on a data set of their own, from the Los Angeles Unified School District.

The data took them by surprise. Just as they had predicted, teachers' value-added scores fluctuated from one year to the next, the same way schools' results did. But the fluctuations were not nearly as arbitrary as Kane had expected. Indeed, the teacher scores had the same predictive power as the school scores, despite the smaller sample size. "There was," Kane says, "more signal to detect." The effect of the individual teacher was, in other words, actually stronger than the effect of the school—so much so that it resonated even through the statistical haze of assorted bright kids and rowdy friends. Indeed, the effect of a teacher was stronger than the effect of any other educational variable that Kane and Staiger could identify. Put a student with a top-rated teacher, they found, and she scored an average of 5 percentile points higher than a similar student assigned to a middle-rated teacher. Put her with a bottom-rated teacher, and her scores fell an equal amount in the opposite direction.

Kane and Staiger ran a few calculations, and the results astonished them. The size of the achievement gap between black and white students, they knew, was about 34 percentile points. "Therefore," they estimated, "if the effects were to accumulate, having a top-quartile teacher rather than a bottom-quartile teacher four years in a row would be enough to close the black-white test score gap."

The findings matched almost perfectly what Hanushek had discovered thirty years earlier. Kane had to concede that the other economist was onto something. Noisy signals might be distracting, he said, but "if the underlying effects are big enough," that would outweigh the problem of variability. Take smoke detectors. They might give some false alarms, but "we don't completely ignore them," Kane said, "because they could save our lives."

And unlike in 1972, when Hanushek first made his value-added calculations, in 2006, when Kane, Gordon, and Staiger published their findings, the rest of the world seemed ready to listen. By that time, the accountability idea was not only conventional wisdom but, judging by the well-publicized successes of charter schools like KIPP, it seemed to be working. And the key to the success of schools like KIPP, observers increasingly concluded, was not just school expectations, but teacher accountability. Unfettered by unions, charter schools were able to do just what Hanushek had suggested—hire and fire on the basis of performance alone. They improved education by holding their teachers accountable in ways no school had ever done before.

In the wake of Kane and Staiger's findings, gathered together and published for popular consumption by the Brookings Institution's Hamilton Project, Hanushek's second kooky idea finally began to go mainstream. Indeed, Kane and Staiger's Hamilton Project paper—cowritten with Robert Gordon—produced even more impressive results than their work on No Child Left Behind. In 2007, presidential candidate Barack Obama referenced the Hamilton Project findings in his major education speech. "From the moment our children step into a classroom," he said, "the single most important factor in determining their achievement is not the color of their skin or where they come from; it's not who their parents are or how much money they have. It's who their teacher is."

"Perhaps," wrote *New York Times* columnist Nicholas Kristof two years later, citing the calculations, "we should have fought the 'war on poverty' with schools—or," he added, "with teachers."

For Deborah Ball, the sudden swell of interest in teachers seemed to offer the final boost her project needed. The Common Core offered coherence, the research on teaching and teacher education offered a starting point for a curriculum, and the entrepreneurs added passion and a laboratory for experimentation. Now economists like Eric Hanushek and Tom Kane provided a warrant to proceed. If teaching really was the most important of all the educational interventions, then the only logical conclusion was that American educators ought to build a coherent infrastructure—clear goals, accurate tests, trained instructors—to teach teaching.

Tom Kane didn't know Deborah Ball, and he didn't know about the David Cohen coherence problem. He only knew what his data told him. So, when he wrote up his Hamilton Project report with Doug Staiger and the policy maker Robert Gordon, he made a different suggestion.

Looking at value-added scores, Kane and his colleagues had been surprised to find that the identity of a student's teacher not only dwarfed the power of key "school-level variables," predicting success more reliably than the size of their classes or the funding allotted to each student. They also outpaced every factor currently used to hire, fire, and reward teachers.

Whether a teacher was certified, for instance, bore almost no relationship at all to whether the teacher's students performed well on achievement tests.

Nor did the scores correlate with a teacher's level of graduate education, even though most school districts rewarded advanced degrees with salary increases. Trying to find something to contradict this finding, Kane and some colleagues ran a study they jokingly called the "kitchen sink" test, looking at everything from SAT scores to "extraversion" in New York City teachers. No meaningful exceptions emerged.

Writing about the findings in the *New Yorker*, Malcolm Gladwell named the dilemma the "quarterback problem." Just as the NFL Combine's predraft tests (bench press, forty-yard dash, and so on) appeared to bear no relationship to a quarterback's abilities in the game itself, there seemed to be no way to predict whether a teacher would succeed until he or she actually taught.

Professions like football addressed this problem with ruthless pragmatism. When quarterbacks failed, coaches pulled them out of the game and, eventually, cut them from the team. School systems, meanwhile, did almost the exact opposite, investing heavily in the factors that predicted teachers' success the least. Likewise, they ignored the one area where the research suggested teachers could be graded accurately. Almost no states performed on-the-job evaluations using value-added scores, the measure the economists had found to be most predictive of success. Many states even prohibited the collection of the data that would allow districts to calculate these scores. When districts did perform evaluations, they rarely used value-added metrics—and rarely found poor teachers. Surveying fifteen thousand teachers in twelve school districts across the country, a research group at The New Teacher Project found that, of all the teachers in all the districts they polled, less than 1 percent had ever been deemed unsatisfactory.

In the Hamilton Project paper, Kane, Staiger, and Gordon laid out the obvious conclusion, the same one that Hanushek had reached thirty years earlier: if all the variables currently used to hire, fire, and reward teachers were useless at predicting student achievement, then they should not be used at all. Instead of erecting barriers to entry, districts should hire at will (or randomly), steering the best teachers to the neediest students and then weeding out the worst with evaluations—evaluations with real teeth. Using value-added measures to determine whether a teacher kept her job, for instance, could give students a substantial academic boost. Kane, Staiger, and Gordon estimated that, in Los Angeles, letting go of teachers who scored in the bottom 25 percent would raise student test scores by about 14 percentile points—a boost equivalent to as much as $169,000 extra in each student's career earnings. (In 2013, working with a more precise data set, Raj Chetty, John Friedman, and Jonah Rockoff reached a similar conclusion. Replacing a teacher in the bottom fifth percentile with an average teacher, they found, would increase students' lifetime earnings by roughly $250,000 per classroom.) All schools needed to do was think more carefully about how they sorted teachers *after* they hired them—which ones they kept, which ones they rewarded, and which ones they let go—and they could generate dramatic change.

Gladwell summarized the suggestion in his *New Yorker* article, with only slight exaggeration. "Teaching," he wrote, "should be open to anyone with a pulse and a college degree—and teachers should be judged after they have started their jobs, not before."

The argument was seductive, especially because it seemed to explain the success of the rising entrepreneurial education movement. Hadn't charter schools like Doug Lemov's succeeded by acting like the most cutthroat NFL franchises, recruiting and keeping only the very best teachers? Unfettered by the usual union and tenure protections, they had made gains by discarding those who couldn't keep up.

But what sounded to the economists like simple logic—try a lot of teachers, keep the best, fire the rest—sounded to Deborah like a recipe for educational malpractice. Drop an unprepared quarterback in a game, and the only risk was lost points. Put an unprepared teacher into a classroom, and the students would suffer. The economists' own value-added research showed how grave a risk that was. By Kane, Gordon, and Staiger's estimates, a year with one weak teacher added up to a drop of 5 percentile points in academic performance rank. The study by Chetty, Friedman, and Rockoff had gone even further, connecting strong teachers not only to their students' future earning levels, but also lower teenage pregnancy rates and higher college attendance.

The idea not only discounted and ignored the needs of the children that "anyone with a pulse" would be responsible for helping. It also flouted the previous twenty-five years of research on teaching, all of which suggested that good teaching was not an innate quality, a mysterious idiosyncrasy some people were randomly assigned at birth. Just as most brilliant future mathematicians couldn't reinvent calculus on their own, even the most talented future teachers had to be taught. But given rigorous and regular opportunities to work on the core practices of teaching, a new teacher could learn to help her students.

Deborah also knew that most of the so-called hurdles the economists pilloried—the credentials and licenses and master's degrees that determined who could teach—were, in practice, not much of a hindrance. Pretty much anyone with a college degree could become a teacher. In New York, for instance, the pass rate for the teacher certification exam in 2009 was 92 percent. By comparison, the pass rate for the cosmetology certification exam was 59 percent.

As for successful charter schools, they might not have labor contracts or district guidelines on who to hire and fire. But that didn't mean they used their freedom to dump the bottom quarter of their teachers each year. As Seneca had discovered, in the charter school world, performance evaluation was just one of many spokes in the complex infrastructure that helped teachers achieve their mission. Places like Uncommon Schools (where Doug Lemov worked), KIPP (the network where Drew Martin and Shannon Grande taught at Rise Academy), and Achievement First (the infrastructure-building network that Seneca Rosenberg studied) evaluated their teachers' performance, and they did let some unsuccessful teachers go. But they also worked on recruitment, selection, incentives, material resources like textbooks and tests, and professional development. One study of Achievement First by the group Education Resource Strategies found that the charter school network spent less than 1 percent of its operating budget on teacher evaluation, compared to nearly 10 percent on time for teachers to learn.

Indeed, what the entrepreneurs were clamoring for was not more evaluation, but more guidance. How can we get more rigorous? they asked. And when they saw something promising, they leapt to try it.

Their efforts to adjust to the new Common Core standards made that clear. "Thank goodness someone—not someone, a group of really thoughtful people, did this," said Joe Negron, a middle-school math teacher and the founding principal at KIPP Infinity in Harlem. As a teacher, Joe's reputation crossed state lines. Ryan Hill, the founder and executive director of the Newark KIPP schools, called Joe one of the best math teachers in the entire network. When Drew Martin at Rise found himself competing to hire a teacher, KIPP Infinity was one of the only rivals that made him nervous. But Negron had spent the years before the Common Core feeling deeply frustrated. The students practiced strategies and memorized techniques until their "eyes popped out," but ask them to explain what the strategy meant, or to reason about why their answer made sense, and they couldn't even begin. "I would go home and be like, 'I'm making robots,'" he says. "But I didn't know how not to."

The Common Core changed Joe Negron's whole approach. For instance, he'd always taught the division of fractions through mnemonics. "Keep it, switch it, flip it" reminded students to keep the first fraction the same, switch the division sign to multiplication, and then flip the second fraction ("THAT'S IT!" he sang in a song to remind them called "Fractions and We Know Them," modeled off of the song "Sexy and I Know It" by LMFAO). Now, reading over the standards and other resources he found (he especially appreciated books by the California math educator Marilyn Burns, who helped teachers learn a TKOT-style approach), Negron created tasks that helped students understand what dividing fractions really meant. He wanted his students to understand fractions as their own kind of number, participants on the number line. He made them not only write out the equations, but also draw pictures describing what the fractions represented.

But for all the exciting changes, Negron was struggling to keep up. That year, he'd passed the principalship of KIPP Infinity to a colleague in order to return to teaching full-time. The switch should have given him more free time. Instead, he found he was working just as hard, if not harder. Every night, he stayed up late, reworking his lesson plans from scratch. What he needed was guidance. Help. A coach.

The Hamilton Project report looked at high-performing teachers like Joe Negron (who presumably achieved a high value-added score) and saw stars. By the report's logic, Joe and other teachers who outperformed their peers would get rewards but receive no further training. But as Deborah saw it, leaving the Negrons of the world to their own devices would be like telling talented high school musicians they'd made the symphony—and then asking them to learn the repertoire on their own. If she and Francesca had their way, the Common Core would be just the beginning, engendering materials to help all teachers achieve the standards and to propel talents like Joe to new levels of expertise. If the Hamilton Project argument was sustained, the Common Core would become one more piecemeal mandate handed to teachers without any guidance on what to do. Another incoherent layer in an incoherent system.

"We have a moment when we could do something different," Deborah said one day, sitting in a coffee shop in Ann Arbor. "But if everybody does it their own way, forget it. It's going to be the same thing again."

For better or worse, the Hamilton Project paper gained traction. In 2007, Bill Gates read a copy. A few weeks later, Tom Kane met him in Manhattan to discuss it. The next year, Gates announced a major shift in his philanthropy. Instead of investing hundreds of millions of dollars in small high schools, his first big idea about how to improve schools, the Gates Foundation would now devote its education resources to the teacher quality problem. The old project, Gates explained in a TED talk, "had a good effect. But the more we looked at it, the more we realized that having great teachers was the very key thing."

Gates described the differences between top and bottom teachers as measured by Hanushek's value-added statistics. "If the entire U.S., for two years, had top quartile teachers, the entire difference between us and Asia would go away. Within four years we would be blowing everyone in the world away." The conclusion, he said, was "simple. All you need are those top quartile teachers." His answers echoed the Hamilton Project paper: use on-the-job performance data to keep top performers (and not others), steer them to the neediest students, and give them raises.

To help districts do that, Gates promised to invest $45 million toward designing better teacher evaluations. He hired Kane to lead the project, called the Measures of Effective Teaching project, or MET. Four school districts were already on standby, ready to implement the MET conclusions.

Evaluation was not the only investment Gates made in his efforts to improve teaching. From the beginning of his efforts to grow what he called "teacher effectiveness," he also wanted to help them get better, according to his lead education adviser, Vicki Phillips, a former superintendent and teacher. Indeed, Phillips says that from the beginning, the foundation sought to build "development and evaluation systems." But, especially for the first several years of their work, it was the evaluation work that came out first, and the evaluation work that got the most attention.

Then came a new force that pushed the country even more in the direction of evaluation. The impetus came from Barack Obama. Now president, he had hired Robert Gordon, Kane and Staiger's coauthor, to help lead his Office of Management and Budget. And in 2009, announcing his own education plan, Obama echoed the Hamilton Project paper once again. Recommendation five of the paper read:

> Provide federal grants to help states that link student performance with the effectiveness of individual teachers over time.

The Obama administration called the grant program it created "Race to the Top." A competitive fund, Race to the Top offered grants only to those states that were willing to overhaul their teacher evaluation systems—identifying, promoting, and rewarding effective teachers and removing those "who aren't up to the job."

Race to the Top didn't only recommend evaluation. The legislation also included other policy suggestions, like urging states
to give teachers "effective support" and improving their local
teacher preparation programs. But of the total five hundred
points available in the competitive scoring system, the largest
portion came from a category called "great teachers and leaders."
And within that category, the largest factor by far, at fifty-eight
points, was "improving teacher and principal effectiveness based
on performance," meaning evaluation. A special condition further encouraged evaluations by disqualifying states that banned
assessing teachers by students' test scores—a restriction that led
several states to revise their laws.

With Race to the Top nudging them along, school districts
increasingly saw teacher evaluations as their most important
tool for improving teacher quality. By 2012, all twelve states that
were awarded Race to the Top grants, and many that weren't,
had overhauled their teacher evaluation systems, including, in
many states, raising the stakes so that well-rated teachers stood
to receive bonuses, higher salaries, and tenure protection, while
poorly rated teachers could be denied tenure or fired.

Exactly how school districts expected tougher evaluations to
lead to better teaching depended on the district. One common
theory, stemming from the Hamilton Project paper, claimed
that achievements would be gained through better sorting. By
steering the best teachers to the students who needed them
the most and removing the worst, districts could arrange their
teaching force so that they had "the right people standing in
front of the classroom," as Kane, Staiger, and Gordon put it.
Interviews with thirteen state policy makers showed that some
education leaders had picked up on the idea. They intended to
improve the teacher pool by weeding out the bad ones. "We're
talking employment decisions," one interviewee told research-

ers. "Two years of ineffective teaching means that a teacher shall not be reemployed."

Increasingly, however, education leaders were voicing a third idea, one that didn't come from the Hamilton Project paper: the idea that evaluations could serve not as sorting tools, but as diagnostic tools. By knowing how they performed, teachers could figure out what they needed to do to improve in the next year. "The purpose behind it is really to help teachers that are struggling to be better teachers," another state official told the group of researchers. "We're hoping," said another, "that the evaluation is designed to give very specific and actionable feedback to teachers." Measure something, the thinking went, and it will get better. "Simple," as Bill Gates said.

Could evaluations really help teachers get better? There was some evidence to support the idea. One teacher evaluation program in Cincinnati gave teachers focused feedback on specific teaching practices, from the level of classroom discourse to the quality of the questions they asked. A study of the Cincinnati program found that students performed better in the years after their teachers received focused evaluations. But evaluations, as they had been conceived by most states, were essentially a two-step process. The teacher was observed, and then the teacher received a grade. Asking teachers to learn granular teaching practices from this system would be like asking students to figure out trigonometry from their SAT scores.

Another effort, led by Pam Grossman, took an observation rubric that had been studied as a possible evaluation device and adapted it into an actual professional development tool for use with a group of urban teachers, with impressive results. The rubric, called PLATO, for the Protocol for Language Teaching Observations, was one of several that Tom Kane and the Gates

Foundation used as part of their MET study. Comparing twenty-five thousand videotapes of three thousand teachers at work against the rubrics, the study had sought to discern whether certain teaching practices led to gains in students' learning. Many of the practices did, including several of the elements in PLATO, suggesting that the rubrics could be used to evaluate teachers.

Pam's professional development project began, like MET, by scoring teachers' lessons against the PLATO rubric. At first, the teachers' PLATO scores roughly matched those from the MET study: on average, teachers' scores were a disappointing 2 out of 4; on the crucial "strategy instruction" component, the score was 1.33.* In interviews, only one teacher demonstrated an understanding of what strategy instruction was. Among the eleven who didn't, one teacher who mentioned using a strategy talked about teaching "organization and self-direction"—not anything to do with the skills students needed for English class. But by the end of Pam's project, just as in Cincinnati, things had changed.

The teachers noticed the difference as much as the researchers. After the first PLATO training session, Lorraine McLeod, a twenty-five-year veteran who taught sixth-grade English in the San Francisco Unified School District, said she immediately "started doing things differently in my classroom." She'd always prided herself on her charisma with the students. Her "Pharaoh Game" lesson, in which she dressed up as an Egyptian monarch and theatrically mimicked knocking down the students' paper "pyramids" when they weren't sturdy enough, got students hys-

---

*The poor performance matched the disappointing teaching quality that the MET researchers found nationally. Nearly two-thirds of teachers scored less than proficient on PLATO's measures of "intellectual challenge" and "classroom discourse," and more than half of all lessons were rated unsatisfactory for "explicit strategy use and instruction" and "modeling."

terical every year. Her writing lessons helped even her many students for whom English was a second language craft decent persuasive essays. But PLATO stretched her ideas in new and helpful ways.

PLATO's "strategy instruction" unit, for example, helped Lorraine break down the drafting and revising processes into smaller parts. In the case of a persuasive essay, for example, students should learn not just to identify evidence, but to discover ways to collect it (by highlighting and making deliberate annotations) and explain it (build it into an argument by describing its importance). Lorraine designed specific lessons about each strategy. By modeling what it looked like to identify and then explain evidence, she helped her students to take their writing (and their thinking) to a higher level. As a result, when she assigned an essay on whether Emperor Qin was an effective leader, her students didn't just declare that the emperor was an effective leader because he standardized currency; they explained that, by standardizing currency, he had helped strengthen the economy, thereby improving the lives of his subjects. PLATO's "classroom discourse" unit, meanwhile, helped her structure paths for her discussions to assist children in learning how to talk about ideas.

The PLATO approach turned even Lorraine's favorite lessons into gems. One, a unit on poetry in which students listened to Billy Joel songs, had always been fun in the past. (She loved getting her young charges to fall for her old music.) But the class usually got stuck when she tried to transition them from singing along with the songs to thinking about the metaphors in the lyrics. "They didn't get it, and I had to explain it over and over and over again," she says. Even then, "only some kids got it."

Inspired by the PLATO trainings, Lorraine revamped the unit, injecting it with strategy instruction and discussion. Instead of just listening to the song, she had the children listen while filling out blank words in a handout. Then, when all the words turned out to be landforms, she transitioned into a strategy lesson on how to spot a metaphor—and then another on how to write one. From there, the students filled out a graphic organizer, brainstorming four different landforms and their possible associated emotions and personifications. Only then did they write poems modeled after the Billy Joel songs.

For the first time in her career, not just a few, but all, of the poems showed metaphorical skill, at least for sixth-graders. "A mountain of anxiety/full of fear . . ./A mysterious swamp/you better veer"; "A plateau as flat as bird wings/passionate but blind"; "The feeble cliff of old age"; "A volcano throwing furious fists." Before PLATO training, she knew in theory that all kids were capable of symbolic expression. After PLATO, she saw the evidence. "It wasn't just you have to have poetry in your soul," she said. Any student, properly taught, could make words sing.

Lorraine wasn't the only one. By the spring of the PLATO study's first year, teachers across the project were describing big changes in their classrooms. PLATO training, one experienced teacher told Pam and her students, "has taught me how to teach." When the researchers rescored the teachers, the improvements were confirmed. After just three cycles of professional development, the average PLATO score had significantly improved.

Pam was quick to point out the differences between PLATO as used in the MET study and PLATO as used in their professional development program. They had the same name and the same foundational ideas about good English teaching, but that was about it.

For teachers, the PLATO rubrics used for evaluation meant that either someone came into your classroom to watch you teach, or you installed a video camera for a day or two and someone you never met watched the footage. The only opportunity to improve would arrive when the scores came back, especially if the person who'd seen you teach or reviewed your tape helped you think about how you might do better next time. But at most, the review would consist of a series of conversations. The evaluation's main function, at least as it was used in the Gates MET study, was identification (who taught well and who taught weakly?), not improvement.

PLATO as a teaching tool drew on studies of learning. Like children, adults needed chances to make connections between new content and what they already understood. They also needed resources to help them make the connections, and they needed to feel ownership of their own learning. As a result, the PLATO training began not by giving teachers their individual scores, but by sharing their aggregate scores—the group average, broken down by each of the program's thirteen elements. Then Pam and her team of grad student collaborators let the teachers decide which two of the elements they wanted to improve. Lorraine's group picked strategy instruction and classroom discourse, the two elements on which their scores had started out the weakest.

In the workshops that followed, Pam and her grad students dissected the two elements. Teaching teachers to use the elements forced the team to develop materials beyond what was in the rubric. The starting point was description. A core practice like "uptake," for instance, includes three submoves—pressing, revoicing, and connecting to the speaker's ideas—all of which required definitions of their own. Next, Pam and her team devised real examples of these moves in practice, drawing on preexisting classroom videotapes or creating their own. Finally, they came up with what Pam called "approximations of practice," exercises designed to give the teachers a chance to try it for themselves. Pam assigned different teachers to different activities according to their starting points. Those like Lorraine, with more experience leading a discussion, practiced "uptake" in a simulated whole group. Those with less experience practiced in a small group.

As a result, when Lorraine worked on strategy instruction or classroom discourse with her students, she had more to turn to than vague buzzwords or the scores on her evaluation. She now drew on tangible examples (she especially liked videos of Pam's old collaborator from Los Angeles, Yvonne Divans Hutchinson) and her experience practicing with fellow teachers. She even adopted special materials designed by Pam and her team, like sentence stems to help students participate in a discussion and anticipation guides to get them thinking about the reading before discussing it with their peers. In fact, Lorraine didn't realize that PLATO had any evaluation aspect at all. As far as she knew, it was professional development—the rare kind that actually helped her grow rather than wasting her time. PLATO the development tool was much more than an evaluation system; it was an education in how to teach.

Might the states' evaluation systems offer this kind of learning experience? The early signs were not promising. One challenge was that, at the district level, most of the observation instruments were generic, meaning they could apply to any academic subject, from math to English to history to science. Generic instruments saved money, but using them meant that any feedback would be generic as well.

And though the MET study did not produce clear findings about classroom practice, it did reveal that teachers needed the most work not on the generic elements of teaching—classroom management challenges like keeping the students focused and engaged—but on academic ones, like facilitating discussions, speaking precisely about concepts, and carefully modeling the strategies that students needed to master.

It would be difficult for evaluators to explore these specific shortcomings with each individual teacher, especially given that the designated observer in most states was not someone with the same subject-matter specialty, but the school principal. Principals often had teaching experience themselves, but rarely did they have experience across every grade and subject.

Early studies indicated that principals lacked the kind of pedagogical content knowledge—like MKT in math, or the equivalents in English, history, and science—that would be required to help a teacher, say, come up with a better representation of dividing fractions. One pair of researchers asked 430 principals to comment on a teaching case study—the exact activity they would do when evaluating their teachers for the district. In the example, a teacher encouraged students to discuss whether 5 can be divided by 39. In their responses, almost half of the principals made no reference to the math at hand, and another 25 percent made only cursory references.

The ability of evaluations to improve teaching was also hindered by the individual value-added scores that made up a substantial portion of teachers' ratings. Kane had demonstrated that teacher effects were less meaningfully volatile than school-wide results. And in the long term, the scores seemed to be impressively predictive of a teacher's performance. But that didn't mean the scores were perfect measures. While a teacher judged effective one year by value-added techniques was likely to continue to be judged effective the next year and the year after that, in practice many teachers still wound up mislabeled. Measurement error and statistical realities of large numbers meant that some teachers who were good would inevitably be labeled neutral or even bad by their value-added score, even if the percentage of the misidentified was relatively low. Other teachers would receive value-added scores calling them ineffective one year, then very effective the next—and vice versa.

It was one thing to use the estimates to study the teacher population in the aggregate and quite another to use them to make decisions about individual teachers' careers. When the economist Sean Corcoran looked at value-added scores of New York City teachers, roughly 12,000 of whom received ratings in the 2007–08 school year, he found that 31 percent of English teachers who ranked in the bottom quintile of teachers in 2007 (that is, those who were less effective than 80 percent of teachers) had jumped to one of the top two quintiles by 2008 (more effective than 60 percent). In other words, assuming half of the rated teachers taught English, of the 1,200 "worst" English teachers in New York, 372 of them became above average just one year later, at least according to the value-added rankings. If the bottom quintile had been fired, the district would have lost nearly four hundred teachers who were destined for effectiveness.

Of course, nobody was suggesting that value-added rankings stand alone. Even the strongest supporters of the measures advocated using them as just a portion of a teacher's rating. But that portion—50 percent in some cases—still had power.

In a paper summarizing the challenges of using evaluation as an improvement tool, Pam Grossman and Heather Hill wrote, "Changing practice is slow, steady work." If policy makers wanted to help teachers improve, they said, they had to "engage in the kind of high-demand, high-support policies that . . . help teachers learn."

Deborah Ball approached the challenge of responding to what she called the "evaluation tidal wave" in the way that felt most familiar: as a teaching problem. Thanks in large part to the value-added research publicized by Tom Kane's Hamilton Project paper, people all across the country were beginning to see the importance of high-quality teaching. What they still didn't understand—what Deborah and others needed to teach them—was the best way to get more teachers to do it.

Just as she had always done with her students, Deborah targeted her response at what seemed like the root of the misunderstanding: the widespread idea that teaching was a natural gift, something you either could or couldn't do. Following that logic, it made sense to try to improve teaching through sorting. If some teachers were simply born to the job and some destined to fail, the logical course of action was to throw "anyone with a pulse" into the classroom, and then, after seeing how they did, dispense with the duds and save the stars. But in fact, as Deborah explained to anyone who would listen—a group that began to include state lawmakers, philanthropists, and congresspeople—teaching was anything but natural work. She could prove that with those same math problems she'd developed back in grad school, the ones that only a trained teacher could solve. She could also prove it with simple logic.

Think, she told people, about all the ways good teachers need to depart from normal human protocol. In everyday life, when conflict emerged, the polite approach was to smooth it over, smiling away differences of opinion or pretending not to notice when a friend made a mistake. Teachers, by contrast, had to deliberately "provoke disequilibrium," Deborah and Francesca Forzani wrote in an essay. Similarly, while everyday life called for immediately helping people in need, teachers, in order to help their students really learn, sometimes first had to let them struggle. And while everyday norms required people "to assume commonality with others' understanding of ideas and arguments and with others' experience of events," teachers could not rest on the comfortable presumption of common ground. They had to probe.

The unnaturalness of the profession, combined with the specialized knowledge and skill it required, meant that improving teaching simply by sorting the better and worse among the untrained would be not only ineffective, but irresponsible. "We would do that in no other sector," Deborah said in a speech in 2012. "In no other sector in this society would we think the way to supply . . . skillful work, would be to go find people, hope they do it well, leave them on their own to figure it out. We don't do that with nursing, and we don't do that with surgery. We don't do that with hairdressing," she joked, "and I'm pretty happy about that, to tell you the truth." Her punch line comparison was pilots. "Every single time I get on a plane," she said, "I'm really glad that the plane is not being flown by someone who just always loved planes . . . But that's what we do in this country. We take people who are committed to children, and we say here. You know, it's individual, work on it, figure it out."

By 2013, Deborah thought she was, if not winning, at least getting much better at explaining. A combination of private donors and support from the University of Michigan had helped Deborah and Francesca take their Teacher Education Initiative national, forming a new organization called TeachingWorks. At the University of Michigan, the School of Education faculty had incorporated high-leverage practices and restructured the teacher education program. Prospective teachers now had chances to learn the core skills and then practice them in increasingly authentic settings. And students couldn't graduate until they passed a series of assessments deliberately designed to measure whether they'd mastered the key practices.

At TeachingWorks, Deborah and Francesca designed a common curriculum for teacher education, complete with everything from models ("exemplar" videos of teachers working on the high-leverage practices) to instructional activities (the best way to help a future teacher learn discussion leading, for instance), to assessments that could be used by any training program, whether at the school, district, or state level. The new TeachingWorks curriculum also included a revision of the high-leverage practices and added a new list of "high-leverage content," the topics in the K–12 curriculum that all teachers needed to know, no matter their subject (things like how to write a thesis statement, but not a more granular and less essential idea like the intricacies of rhyme and meter in poetry).

Some researchers remained skeptical about the possibilities of helping teachers learn to teach. Pointing to the reams of studies showing no positive effects of professional development, Eric Hanushek, for his part, deemed efforts to revamp it a fool's errand. But others demurred. That group included Bill Gates and Tom Kane, who now emphasized the power of "feedback" and coaching in addition to evaluation. After leaving the foundation, Kane returned to Harvard to take on a major new study examining the effect of targeted feedback on teaching quality. And the Gates Foundation, in turn, issued a major grant to help TeachingWorks expand its infrastructure-building efforts.

But while the infrastructure idea was understandable enough in theory, enacting it was much more difficult. It would be one thing simply to inject the TeachingWorks curriculum for teacher education into the entrepreneurial world that was already building an American version of educational infrastructure. But Deborah and Francesca wanted to reach a larger group of teachers than that, so they had to work with the patchwork that *did* exist—incoherence and all.

Deborah also saw the growing signs of a backlash developing against evaluations that swung in the opposite (but equally flawed) direction. Like the charter school educators, Magdalene Lampert, David Cohen, Pam Grossman, Heather Hill, and the teachers in Japan, Deborah didn't oppose teacher evaluation. She just didn't think that, on its own, evaluation could improve teaching. But as the evaluation movement gained momentum, many teachers understandably turned their frustration with accountability into an argument for its opposite. The only way to get better teaching, they argued, was to leave teachers alone—"liberate" them, one columnist put it, and "let them be themselves." Yet leaving teachers alone was exactly what American schools had done for years, with no great success.

The Common Core standards, vital to establishing coherence, came under a similar pressure. In June of 2013, Deborah watched with dismay as lawmakers in her state, Michigan, voted to block funding that would have supported implementation of the new standards. Later, legislators voted the funding through, but at the end of 2013 they were still debating whether to fund new Common Core–aligned tests. Other states were backing away from the standards by opting out of the tests that were being built to measure them. The standards were, their critics said, an unwelcome federal intrusion or even, according to some, a march toward fascism. ("If this isn't Nazism, Communism, Marxism and all the 'ism's,' I don't know what is," one critic said.) The tide was turning toward autonomy. But autonomy offered the same prescription as unsupported accountability: an absence of infrastructure.

Even if Deborah and Francesca could write a curriculum for teacher education that would receive wide support—and they believed they were doing just that—the two educators still faced a slew of tactical questions. How quickly should they expand the TeachingWorks curriculum, and to how many teacher-training institutions? And how could they ensure that the new teacher trainers would teach the TeachingWorks curriculum effectively?

A growing number of ed school professors and entrepreneurs who taught teachers were embracing an approach that Pam Grossman called the "practice-based teacher education" movement. They appreciated teaching that aspired to get students really thinking and learning, striving toward TKOT. And they had experience doing it themselves. But they were still a minority.

Even the entrepreneurs' infrastructure of practice was full of uncertainty. Doug Lemov might have been working on a more rigorous taxonomy 2.0, and schools like Rise Academy might be evolving their approach to discipline. But whether the rest of the movement would follow them was not clear.

Rousseau Mieze's experience at the Harlem school presented an alternative path, and not necessarily a better one. Many charters maintained high standards for teacher training, but under pressure to replicate their schools quickly, they sometimes failed to extend the learning culture to every new franchise. Some became merely superficial replicas, enforcing certain techniques without inculcating an understanding of why they made sense— or, even more important, revising them when they didn't. There was a real tension between the desire to scale programs and the imperative to preserve those programs' quality.

For her part, Deborah's most optimistic estimate was that TeachingWorks would take at least ten years to have an effect. Yet even this cautious outlook fell short of expectations; everyone else she dealt with operated on much tighter timelines. The state and federal education officials and the national philanthropists they depended on for support wanted schools better not a decade from now, but tomorrow. "Everyone gets impatient, but ten years from now, if we had a different system, that would be a revolution, not a modest change," Deborah says. The question was whether the pieces could actually fall into place without their backers moving on to the next big thing.

Deborah is not the kind of person to let these challenges deter her. In her office hangs an excerpt from Lewis Carroll's *Alice's Adventures in Wonderland*:

> "There is no use in trying," said Alice; "one can't believe impossible things."
>
> "I dare say you haven't had much practice," said the Queen. "When I was your age, I always did it for half an hour a day. Why, sometimes I've believed as many as six impossible things before breakfast."

Teaching, David Cohen once said, is a profession of hope. It requires, on top of everything else, a leap of faith. A willingness to believe that something that does not currently exist might one day come to life. Deborah was a great teacher because she had spent a long time learning how to teach. But she was also a great teacher because she knew how to hope.

Whoever made the *Alice in Wonderland* poster for her had highlighted the last line: *sometimes I've believed as many as six impossible things before breakfast.* Deborah hung it on her door, like a conjecture made by one of her Spartan Village students. Every time she left her office, there it was, reminding her.

Epilogue

HOW TO BE A TEACHER
(Part Two)

O ne day in 2013, midway through the writing of this book, I finally let one of the teachers I had been observing beat me in an argument.

I met Andy Snyder at an event hosted by the news organization where I work, Chalkbeat (then GothamSchools). Later, a mutual friend (himself an excellent teacher) told me that Andy was the best teacher he'd ever seen. Students, the friend said, actually post photographs of the whiteboard in Andy's classroom on their Facebook profiles. That's how much they admire him.

Our mutual friend was right. Andy, who teaches high school social studies in the New York City public schools, is an extremely skilled teacher. Sitting in his classroom, I often felt the same buzzing sensation that I got watching old tapes of Magdalene Lampert and Deborah Ball, sitting in the classrooms of Mariel Elguero and Shannon Grande, or observing lessons in Tokyo. The material was for students half my age, but I could still feel myself learning.

The argument between me and Andy went like this: He thought that I would be a fraud to write a book on teaching without ever doing it myself. Did I really want to join the ranks of those who pontificate about teaching but have never attempted it themselves? I responded that if the only warrant for writing about something was doing it, then why not also suggest that political journalists stop covering government until they themselves hold office? Teaching shouldn't be exempted from outsider inquiry just because so many people underestimate it as personal, natural work.

I lost the debate. At least, I lost the argument about whether or not I should try to teach. And so, on a gray morning in March of 2013, I woke up exceedingly early, and, with my heart pounding, rode the subway from my apartment in Brooklyn to a Manhattan high school called the School of the Future, where I was to teach Andy's class.

Two days earlier, planning the lesson, I'd felt an ethereal mania. The thrill and pleasure of putting together a plan had taken me by surprise. I was having *fun*. But my exuberance was shattered when I sat down with Andy to make final preparations. A fellow teacher happened to walk into the room where we were meeting, and he and Andy each talked about the first class they had taught. Andy asked the other teacher whether he'd cried, explaining that Andy had, his first time—more than once. Then he looked at me. "You might cry," he said. "I just want to warn you."

The following evening, the night before class, I had a nightmare. The details evaporated as soon as I woke up, but the gist was clear: utter, spectacular failure. The students already knew everything I wanted to teach them. Presented with my lesson, they handed me back indifference. Waking up that night in an exam-level panic, I tossed and turned and never fell back to sleep.

The lesson went by fast. I had just remembered to look at the clock to see how much time we had left—and like that, it was done. Andy and I had one period to debrief, and then it was on to the next batch of students. Although he had several more classes that day, I taught only two.

In one way Andy misjudged me. I did not cry, though I came close, feeling, in the period between lessons, an exhausted, washed-out emptiness after all the wild excitement receded and my sleep loss set in. But Andy was right in another, more important way. Trying to teach showed me things I could never have known from watching and interviewing teachers. Doing it myself, I relearned everything that Deborah Ball, Magdalene Lampert, Pam Grossman, and Doug Lemov had taught me, but in more profound, permanent ways.

I had understood that teaching was difficult intellectual work from the first time Deborah Ball gave me a Mathematical Knowledge for Teaching test. But I hadn't understood *how* difficult until I worked with Andy. To plan the lesson, the first in a unit he was building on biographical writing, I spent hours thinking about what it meant to do biography, what made it hard, and where a student of the craft needed to start. I wondered if it was more important to focus on the claims biographers make about people, how they come to make them—or, alternatively, whether the claims are fair. Was it even possible to separate those problems and work on only one at a time? Paging through books and journalistic profiles for passages that raised the issues I thought we should focus on, I thought about what questions and texts I could use to get students thinking about these issues. Then I spent hours selecting excerpts we could read and discuss in a sixty-minute lesson—short enough to be understandable, yet complex enough to address key topics I wanted the students to consider.

Yet even after all that, on the day of the class Andy and I still struggled to articulate the "goal for today," which he always wrote out on the same spot on his class whiteboard. Trying to distill the purpose of the lesson into a single sentence, I wrote and rewrote. By the time the lesson started, crumbles of dry-erase marker already covered my palm.

I learned (again) what Lee Shulman said about pedagogical content knowledge: knowing the content was simply not enough. I also needed to know the students. Sitting down to plan earlier in the week, I had proudly shown Andy the stack of books I'd selected, with bookmarks flagging the pages containing passages I thought we could use. He leafed through them quickly and, one by one, pronounced them not good enough. One, a brilliant section of Taylor Branch's book *Parting the Waters* that introduced the civil rights activist Bayard Rustin, was too "boring" to hold eleventh- and twelfth-graders' interest. So was another Branch passage I'd chosen, introducing Roy Wilkins. Another passage, by Michael Lewis, which I took from his book *The Big Short*, might be okay—the character being described, the hedge fund manager Vincent Daniel, grew up nearby in Queens, and there were some saucy details, like the fact that his father was murdered, "though no one ever talked about that." But I needed to make the selection much shorter. And it was still pretty boring, according to Andy. He gave me a stack of biographies the students were currently reading—a possibility I had not anticipated. Try these, he suggested.

The assessment stunned me. I'd spent hours selecting these texts, and I thought the Bayard Rustin one was particularly good. But though I'd considered ways that I could use the passages with the students—questions I could ask and problems we could think about together—"boring" was never a factor that occurred to me. I'd spent hours interviewing Pam Grossman about English teaching and the importance of picking not only canonical texts, but ones that students would actually find interesting. But somehow it was only when Andy described how students would react to even the most brilliant biography that I really understood. What you assigned them meant nothing if they didn't read it.

When the lesson began, I learned that modeling is just as powerful as Pam Grossman says. Andy and I had planned for this part to happen right before the whole-group discussion—five minutes when we would sit in the middle of the students' circle, reading one of the passages together and posing the questions we wanted the students to learn to ask. "What is the author claiming about his subject?" "Imagine the moment when the author first decided to write about the subject. What actions do you think he took to learn about him? What thinking did he do? What choices did he make?" We used one of the passages Andy had thrust at me the day before, from Mitch Albom's book *Tuesdays with Morrie*. Later, after the first lesson, when Andy gathered a few students to give me feedback, they pinpointed this moment as one of the most helpful. One student, Marcus, told me he'd never thought about the fact that authors had to learn about their subjects before writing about them until we broke down how Albom might have learned about Morrie. As a journalist, the challenge of overcoming that unknowing was part of my daily life. But how were high school students supposed to know that? Of course they didn't know. They had to learn. And so, of course, they had to be taught.

I learned, again, that what Heather Kirkpatrick had told me about "academic discourse" was brutally accurate. Discussions are wonderful in theory and eyeball-yankingly difficult to facilitate in a live classroom. I had tried to arrange the lesson in three parts: modeling, to start; then individual practice working through the questions with a different text (in the end, I took a risk and used the Michael Lewis passage; nobody fell asleep), and finally a group discussion of what the students had learned that would, I hoped, make the specific ideas become more abstract, taking them from what one author did to what *they* might do, if they were to write a biography of their own.

But when I began the discussion, in the first period, I realized quickly that I was in way over my head. Trying to keep track of the students' ideas in my notebook as they came, I wrote gibberish instead. And the note-taking disrupted my working memory. Someone said something, and I was so distracted by everything I had to do—keep everyone focused, watch the clock, think about where I wanted them to go next, remember their names, call on this and that student who'd written down an interesting idea while not ignoring the students whose ideas were more conventional—that I forgot to listen. I just nodded blankly, and called on someone else.

In the second period, Andy and I decided to give up the discussion entirely. It was simply better not to try. Not surprisingly, the class went much more smoothly, and I spent much less time freaking out. Maybe the lesson simply didn't call for discussion. Or maybe, like so many teachers, I took the path that felt best: easier, but not necessarily better.

I learned, again, what the early studies had found while searching for the optimal teacher personality. Character traits and teaching skill are not the same thing. They interact, but personality does not lead to skill, or vice versa. In some ways, I was a natural. During our debriefing, Andy pointed out that when I walked into the room, the students immediately treated me as the teacher—no questions asked. Without earning it, I had their full attention, if not yet their respect. Many teachers aren't that lucky, Andy said. Something in their gait or their posture just makes it harder for them to hold the spotlight.

But while I had some "it" in me—"Strong Voice," in Lemov taxonomy parlance—in other ways my personality betrayed me. My friends and colleagues know my habit of blurting comments that come out rude or, as my friends never ceased telling me in high school, "awkward." As an adult, I've worked to temper this filterless part of myself, at least with people I've just met. But in the crucible of the classroom, I reverted. When a girl with her hair in a skull-tight ponytail said something I didn't understand, instead of asking her politely for clarification, I said something like, "How could you think *that*?" as if she must be an idiot to have such a strange idea. My words slaughtered her. As soon as I said them, the spell I'd managed to cast was broken. Suddenly, all twenty-some students were looking at me and laughing, and not in a good way. The most awful part was that I couldn't have picked a worse student to offend. The girl in the ponytail was the most defiant student in the class, the one most determined not to buy in. I offended her just by existing, and now she was lost.

I learned, again, what I'd learned reading Magdalene Lampert's book about a year in her classroom. A single lesson is not the important unit in teaching. My initial metric of success was, "Did they learn anything?" But as the weeks went by, and I stayed in touch with Andy as he continued, day after day, with the unit I'd launched, I realized how silly that was. Learning in school happens over weeks and months, not periods of sixty minutes. By the time Andy and the students finished the biography unit, they'd made progress, then hit a dead end, restarted, and recovered the very territory Andy and I thought we were sowing the day of my lesson. By the time he finally got them to produce biographical essays that they could all get excited about, no assessment on Earth could discern the effectiveness of my single lesson.

The first and last thing I relearned—the one that stuck with me the most—had to do with that four-letter word, *love.* Many times, Doug Lemov had earnestly explained to me the importance of love in teaching. Good discipline, he told me, required that teachers work with the students "from love." When Doug said this, I always nodded. But it wasn't until I taught Andy's class that I understood what he meant.

Just before the lesson started, Andy and I stood in the Xerox room in the school's basement, frantically making copies of the passages I'd brought and the graphical organizers I'd made. I had a million questions, and Andy answered them patiently, one by one. He gave his own advice too, but I can't remember what he said. Something about how to work the Xerox machine, maybe, or exactly what time class began and ended and what to say when I walked into the room. Then he turned around, his shirt disheveled from near oversleep and his eyes red.

"Here's another thing," he said, "and this might be the most important point. You have to look at them with love in your heart. Once they know that you care about them, then they can relax a lot." It was the only thing I managed to remember when I made that comment to the girl in the ponytail and nearly turned the entire class against me. Staring at the girl I'd offended, the one who'd unwittingly caused me to cede my command—the only thing I had, really—I forced myself to follow Andy's instruction. The girl looked like she wanted to throw me out the window. Staring back at her, I thought about how she was a human, a person I cared about. I decided that I loved her.

I managed to keep going. And later, when I grabbed her as she walked out the door at the end of class to tell her, privately, how sorry I was for putting her on the spot like that, she gave me the most precious gift. She turned up her lips in the tiniest approximation of a smile, finally looked me in the eye, and shrugged. *Whatever*, her face said. But it was the first thing she'd communicated to me all period since our incident. I could have hugged her.

Teaching that lesson, I relearned one more thing: a person absolutely *can* learn to teach. Working with Andy, I didn't do a great job; I did okay. But I know with mortal certainty that if I had tried the same thing before I began the reporting for this book, I would have done dramatically worse.

I could tell how far I'd come when I talked to friends who aren't teachers about what I was doing. "What will you teach?" they asked me, a question that repeatedly took me aback. "What will you teach them to *do*?" the question suggested. In their questions, I heard my own voice, circa 2009, imagining classroom work as a presentation of expertise. Possible answers to their question passed through my mind: I will teach them to make a sandwich, to write a headline, to dance, to blog, to juggle—to do anything they had never encountered. "What is the theme of the speech?" another friend asked, conflating a lesson with a lecture (a form of teaching, certainly, but just one part of it).

My own question was not so much what would I teach, but how would I manage to do it? I thought not just about topics, but also about activities and ideas. What could I help the students learn, and how could I help them learn it?

I shudder to imagine how I would have prepared for the lesson if it had happened three years earlier—had I, like so many new teachers, gone into the classroom without understanding how teaching really works. Probably I would have been like the filmmaker who had come to teach Andy's class the week before me. Obsessing over my lesson—its goals, content, and sequence— I had forced Andy to exchange multiple e-mails with me and then sit down for more than two hours, going over what I'd do, step by step. The filmmaker, Andy said, had resisted planning altogether, and then came in and bombed, failing to keep the students engaged, much less working with them on anything interesting.

I still needed a ton of help, and no amount of reading and watching and interviewing could substitute for real practice working with students. But at least I had an understanding of what made teaching work—and that carried me farther than either Andy or I could have imagined.

Acknowledgments

"The teaching I write about in this book is not mine alone," Magdalene Lampert declares in the opening of her book, *Teaching Problems and the Problems of Teaching*. To crib her one last time, this book is not mine alone.

Thank you to those who opened your hearts, minds, and classrooms and became my teachers as well as my sources. The list is led by but in no way limited to Deborah Loewenberg Ball, David Cohen, Pam Grossman, Magdalene Lampert, Doug Lemov, Drew Martin, Rousseau Mieze, and Akihiko Takahashi. You gave me the most incredible gift, and I have tried my best to give it back to everyone who reads this book.

Thank you to Aaron Pallas for introducing me to Deborah Ball, and to Norman Atkins and David Levin for introducing me to Doug Lemov.

Thank you to the many people who provided the time, space, and resources that this project required. Paul Tough gave me the magazine assignment that became the book and then committed his trademark grit to seeing me through to the very bitter end, despite many moments when giving up would have been substantially easier. Paul also introduced me to Vera Titunik, another terrific editor whose mark lasts here. My superstar agent, Alia Hanna Habib, along with David McCormick, helped me see that what began as a magazine story could become a book and then shepherded me into just the right hands. Those belonged to Tom Mayer, whose expert knowledge and skill—poured into innumerable editing sessions—will be examined in our next collaboration, *Building a Better Editor.* Thank you also to Louise Brockett, Erin Lovett, Ryan Harrington, Stephanie Hiebert, and the rest of the incredible team at W. W. Norton.

Thank you to LynNell Hancock, Nicholas Lemann, and the other brilliant minds behind the Columbia Graduate School of Journalism's Spencer Fellowship in education journalism. Thank you to Mike McPherson and the Spencer Foundation for supporting this project not once but twice, not to mention for supporting a healthy portion of the actual research articles that make this book possible. Support from the Abe Fellowship for Journalists at the Social Science Resource Council was invaluable in sending me to Japan and making sure I thrived once I got there; I am especially grateful to Nicole Restrick, Fernando Rojas, and Takuya Toda-Ozaki. Akihiko Takahashi and Toshiakira Fujii generously facilitated many life-changing classroom visits in Tokyo. Also in Tokyo, Yvonne Chang offered translation, interpretation, directions, and good company.

Thank you to team Chalkbeat, especially Philissa Cramer, Alan Gottlieb, Sue Lehmann, and Gideon Stein, for ensuring that I didn't have to give up one dream for another. I am also indebted to Jill Barkin, Daarel Burnette II, Geoff Decker, Scott Elliott, Todd Engdahl, Anna Phillips, Maura Walz, and the ever-growing ranks of our fellow nuance crusaders, all of whom also helped pick up slack when I was away. You have all taught me so much, and you inspire me every single day.

Thank you to the generous friends and colleagues who read this book in early and last-minute stages and made it so much better with your comments—namely, Drew Bailey, Jessica Campbell, David Cohen, Philissa Cramer, Rachel Dry, Nick Ehrmann, Alia Hanna Habib, Ryan Hill, Timothy Pittman, Andy Snyder, Emma Sokoloff-Rubin, Ira Stoll, Paul Tough, and Maura Walz. I am also in debt to Elana Eisen-Markowitz, Nitzan Pelman, and Dale Russakoff for conversations that left a big impression.

Thank you to Jessica Campbell. Your research assistance and fact-checking improved this book from start to finish.

Thank you to my teachers, especially (in order of appearance) Lesley Wagner, Ralph Bunday, Nanette Dyas, John Mathwin, and Darra Mulderry, who added immeasurable value.

Thank you to my friends, who kept me grounded and understood every time I could not leave my apartment.

Thank you to the Epstein family for unwavering support and many quiet writing rooms.

Thank you to my grandparents—including, among them, three first-generation college graduates, a normal school alum, a nonprofit media entrepreneur, and a former math teacher.

Thank you to Andrea Weiss, John Green, Daniel Green, and Benjamin Green, my first and best teachers, readers, fact-checkers and friends.

Finally, thank you to David Epstein, who teaches by example and looks at me with love in his heart.

Notes

The reporting for this book included many dozens of interviews with teachers, administrators, policy analysts, and researchers over the course of more than five years. In addition to interviews, I relied on a large number of research articles, books, and records of teaching, including classrooms that I observed directly and others made accessible to me after the fact through videotapes, transcripts, lesson plan books, and other records.

For space considerations, I have not included a comprehensive list of all these interviews, texts, and classrooms. These notes list sources that directly informed the words on the page but are not otherwise obvious from the text.

Except where noted otherwise, pseudonyms to replace children's names were provided by the author.

Prologue

page

1 *whose names are printed on the attendance ledger*: The student names in this classroom scene are pseudonyms invented by Magdalene Lampert.

6 *"Does anyone* agree *with this answer?"*: The classroom scenes in this chapter were described in Magdalene Lampert, *Teaching Problems and the Problems of Teaching* (New Haven, CT: Yale University Press, 2001); in many interviews by the author with Lampert between 2010 and 2013; and in videotapes obtained from Lampert.

6 *to reveal the "sense of humor" that "he had always had"*: James Hilton, *Goodbye Mr. Chips*, Project Gutenberg Australia, http://gutenberg.net.au/ebooks05/0500111h.html, accessed September 2013.

6 *thousands of studies conducted over dozens of years*: Thousands is not an exaggeration. Even in 1929, the researcher Seneca Rosenberg reports, scholars of teaching described "an unwieldy mass of information . . . too large for assimilation in a lifetime"; and by 1974, another pair of researchers estimated that more than 10,000 teacher-effectiveness studies had been published. Rosenberg, "Organizing for Quality in Education: Individualistic and Systemic Approaches to Teacher Quality" (PhD dissertation, University of Michigan, 2012).

7 *extroverts or introverts, humorous or serious, flexible or rigid*: See, for instance, A. S. Barr et al., "Wisconsin Studies of the Measurement and Prediction of Teacher Effectiveness: A Summary of Investigations," *Journal of Experimental Education* 30, no. 1 (September 1961); and Jonah E. Rockoff et al., *Can You Recognize an Effective Teacher When You Recruit One?* NBER Working Paper, no. 14485 (Cambridge, MA: National Bureau of Economic Research, 2008), http://www.nber.org/papers/w14485.

7 *described to me as "voodoo"*: Jane Hannaway, interview by the author, January 13, 2010.

9 *"He who can, does. He who cannot, teaches."*: George Bernard Shaw, *Maxims for Revolutionists*, Project Gutenberg, Kindle edition, http://www.gutenberg.org/ebooks/26107, accessed October 2013.

12 *"It's who their teacher is"*: Barack Obama, "Our Kids, Our Future" (speech, Manchester, NH, November 20, 2007), American Presidency Project, http://www.presidency.ucsb.edu/ws/?pid=77022.

12 *thereby improving the overall quality of the teaching force*: Barack Obama, "Remarks by the President on Education" (speech, US Department of Education, Washington, DC, July 24, 2009), White House, http://www.whitehouse.gov/the_press_office/Remarks-by-the-President-at-the-Department-of-Education.

13 *teachers "are not rated; they are trusted"*: Chicago Teachers Union, *The Schools Chicago's Students Deserve: Researched-Based Proposals to Strengthen Elementary and Secondary Education in the Chicago Public Schools* (Chicago: CTU, 2012), http://www.ctunet.com/blog/text/SCSD_Report-02-16-2012-1.pdf.

14 *roughly the same size as Apple's global employee base*: "U.S. Jobs Supported by Apple," Apple.com, http://www.apple.com/about/job-creation, accessed July 27, 2013.

14 *and, finally, teachers (3.7 million)*: Deborah Loewenberg Ball, "The Work of Teaching and the Challenge for Teacher Education" (lecture, Vanderbilt University, September 11, 2008). Data are based on an analysis by Francesca Forzani of the Household Data Annual Averages from the Bureau of Labor Statistics.

14 *[number of Americans in different professions]*: This presentation was made in 2008. The latest Census Bureau data continue to establish teachers as the largest occupational group in the United States. See Richard Ingersoll and Lisa Merrill, *Seven Trends: The Transformation of the Teaching Force*, CPRE

Working Paper, no. #WP-01 (Philadelphia: Consortium for Policy Research in Education, 2012).

14 *more than three million new teachers between 2014 and 2020*: William J. Husser and Tabitha M. Bailey, *Projections of Education Statistics to 2020*, 39th ed. (Washington, DC: National Center for Education Statistics, 2011), http://nces.ed.gov/pubs2011/2011026.pdf. See Table 16, p. 53.

15 *But the district still needed six hundred new teachers*: Nancy Slavin (then director of recruitment, Chicago Public Schools), interviews by the author, December 4 and 18, 2009.

15 *start work at public and private schools every year*: Husser and Bailey, *Projections*, Table 16, p. 53.

15 *She'd rather not be caught watching someone else do it*: Steven Farr, interview by the author, January 18, 2010.

18 *better working conditions and more flexibility*: Susanna Loeb, Linda Darling-Hammond, and John Luczak, "How Teaching Conditions Predict Teacher Turnover in California Schools," *Peabody Journal of Education* 80, no. 3 (2005): 47.

19 *an average household income in the country's top ten*: "2011 American Community Survey," US Census Bureau, http://www.census.gov/acs, accessed November 2011.

19 *"the greatest art in all the world"*: Francis W. Parker, *Notes of Talks on Teaching*, reported by Lelia E. Patridge (New York: E. L. Kellogg, 1891), 21, http://books.google.com/books?id=9aLsAAAAMAAJ&printsec=frontcover&source=gbs_ge_summary_r&cad=0%2522%20%255Cl#v=onepage&q&f=false, accessed December 29, 2013.

19 *and he did not intend to give them up*: Ibid., xii.

19 *Even another teacher called him a fool*: William Milford Giffin, *School Days in the Fifties: A True Story with Some Untrue Names of Persons and Places* (Chicago: A. Flanagan, 1906), 125, http://books.google.com/books?id=P449AAAAIAAJ&pg=PA63&dq=school+days+in+the+fifties+francis+parker&hl=en&sa=X&ei=z-HAUvikIdWvsQTK6ICYDg&ved=0CC0Q6AEwAA#v=onepage&q&f=false, accessed December 29, 2013.

20 *"The general public was against it"*: Orville T. Bright, Homer Bevans, and John Lancaster Spalding, "Addresses Delivered at the Memorial Exercises Given by the Public-School Teachers of Chicago and Cook County, Auditorium, April 19, 1902," *Elementary School Teacher and Course of Study* 2, no. 10 (June 1902): 728.

20 *destined to behold his promised land only from afar*: William R. Harper et al., "In Memoriam. Colonel Francis Wayland Parker, Late Director of the School of Education, University of Chicago," *Elementary School Teacher and Course of Study* 2, no. 10 (June 1902): 715.

20 *letting great teachers' secrets live and die with them*: John Dewey, *The Sources of a Science of Education* (New York: Horace Liveright, 1929), Kindle edition, http://www.archive.org/stream/sourcesofascienc009452mbp#page/n13/mode/2up, p. 10.

20 *"can be communicated to others"*: Ibid., 11.

20 *both died before seeing "educational Palestine"*: Harper et al., "In Memoriam," 715.

Chapter One

23 *he joined the prestigious new Bureau of Educational Research*: David Berliner, "Toiling in Pasteur's Quadrant: The Contributions of N. L. Gage to Educational Psychology," *Teaching and Teacher Education* 20, no. 4 (May 2004): 329–40.

23 *with barroom storytelling late into the night*: The following portrait of Nate Gage as a teacher and scholar is based on David Berliner, "Toiling in Pasteur's Quadrant," and on interviews by the author with David Berliner (February 7, 2012), Barak Rosenshine (February 19, 2012), Frank Sobol (February 27, 2012), Lovely Billups (February 4, 2012), and Garry McDaniels (February 17, 2012).

23 *to fall asleep in the middle of his lectures*: Berliner, interview.

24 *eye color, clothing style, and strength of grip*: The studies referenced in this paragraph are summarized in Thomas L. Good, Bruce J. Biddle, and Jere E. Brophy, *Teachers Make a Difference* (New York: Holt, Rinehart, and Winston, 1975), 14; and in A. S. Barr et al., "Wisconsin Studies of the Measurement and Prediction of Teacher Effectiveness: A Summary of Investigations," *Journal of Experimental Education* 30, no. 1 (September 1961), 103.

24 *"cruel, depressed, unsympathetic, and morally depraved"*: Quoted in Egon G. Guba, "Review of *Handbook of Research on Teaching*, by N. L. Gage," *Theory into Practice* 2, no. 2 (April 1963): 114.

24 *called, unhelpfully, "teaching skill"*: Donald M. Medley, "Early History of Research on Teacher Behavior," *International Review of Education* 18, no. 4 (1972): 431.

25 *or improving teacher-education programs*: Quoted in Good, Biddle, and Brophy, *Teachers Make a Difference*, 13.

25 *"I think there are about six weeks of it"*: Geraldine Joncich, *The Sane Positivist: A Biography of Edward L. Thorndike* (Middletown, CT: Wesleyan University Press, 1968), 156.

25 *Edward Thorndike, another foundational figure*: David Berliner, "The 100-Year Journey of Educational Psychology," in *Exploring Applied Psychology: Origins and Critical Analyses*, eds. Thomas K. Fagan and Gary R. VandenBos. (Washington, DC: American Psychological Association, 1993), 193.

25 *calling the trips a "bore"*: Joncich, *Sane Positivist*, 163, 230.

25 *"Do? Why, I'd resign!"*: Ibid., 217.

26 *"Never will you get a better psychological subject than a hungry cat"*: Edward Lee Thorndike, *Animal Intelligence* (New York: Macmillan, 1911), 54.

26 *But he did not study teachers*: Ellen Condliffe Lagemann, *An Elusive Science: The Troubling History of Education Research* (Chicago: University of Chicago Press, 2000), 56–66.

26 *Dewey set his work in education aside*: Ibid., 55–56.

26 *and universities did not hire Jews*: The portrait of Nate Gage in this paragraph draws on an interview by the author with David Berliner on February 7, 2012; as well as on David C. Berliner, "Toiling in Pasteur's Quadrant: The Contributions of N. L. Gage to Educational Psychology," *Teaching and Teacher Education* 20 (2004): 329–40.

26. *by scouring psych departments' reject lists*: Barak Rosenshine, interview by the author, February 19, 2012.

26. *"and uncommon commonsense"*: Quoted in Arthur G. Powell, *The Uncertain Profession: Harvard and the Search for Educational Authority* (Cambridge, MA: Harvard University Press, 1980), 48.

27 *"the lord deliver us therefrom"*: Quoted in Willis Rudy, "Josiah Royce and the Art of Teaching," *Educational Theory* 2, no. 3 (July 1952): 158–69.

27 *the number of teachers alone was nearing one million*: The enrollment and staffing figures in this paragraph are taken from Thomas D. Snyder, ed., *120 Years of American Education: A Statistical Portrait* (Washington, DC: National Center for Education Statistics, 1993), 34.

28 *"or Mendel in raising his peas"*: A. S. Barr et al., "Report of the Committee on the Criteria of Teacher Effectiveness," *Review of Educational Research* 22, no. 3 (June 1952): 261.

28 *in the messy cauldron of a real school*: See, for example, John Dewey, *The Sources of a Science of Education* (New York: Horace Liveright, 1929), Kindle edition; and Lagemann, *Elusive Science*, 48–51.

28 *to find out which teachers had explained it best*: This paragraph draws on N. L. Gage et al., *Explorations of the Teacher's Effectiveness in Explaining*, Technical Report, no. 4 (Stanford, CA: Stanford Center for Research and Development in Teaching, 1968).

29 *"I do not know if you have ever heard of the book . . ."*: The description of Barak Rosenshine's research draws on Gage et al., "Explorations," 48.

29 *so did a high level of right-to-left movement*: Gage et al., "Explorations," 39–40.

30 *the only two giving papers on the topic*: Berliner, "Toiling in Pasteur's Quadrant," 339.

30 *the volume sold 30,000 copies*: Ibid., 334.

30 *the pamphlet had sold 130,000 copies*: Nancy J. Hultquist, "A Brief History of AERA's Publishing," *Educational Researcher* 5, no. 11 (December 1976): 12.

30 *to convert his findings into usable lessons for teachers*: Lovely Billups, interview by the author, February 4, 2012.

31 *but with transforming it*: Richard Nixon, "Special Message to the Congress on Education Reform" (speech, Washington, DC, March 3, 1970), American Presidency Project, http://www.presidency.ucsb.edu/ws/?pid=2895#ixzz1njSzPyoX.

31 *"was to change the field"*: Garry McDaniels, interview by the author, February 17, 2012.

31 *a young professor visiting from Michigan State named Lee Shulman*: The

account of the NIE's support for teaching research draws on Garry McDaniels, interview by the author, February 17, 2012.

31 *"Doesn't Nate realize that behaviorism is on life support?"*: Lee Shulman, interview by the author, November 2010.

32 *psychology had to reckon with cognition*: For more background on the origins of cognitive science, see Howard Gardner, *The Mind's New Science: A History of the Cognitive Revolution* (New York: Basic Books, 1985).

33 *what Lee had always found fascinating was thinking*: This chapter's portrait of Lee Shulman is drawn from interviews by the author in November 2010, January 2011, and February 2012, as well as records captured by the Inside the Academy project at Arizona State University. See http://insidetheacademy.asu.edu/photo-gallery-lee-shulman and http://insidetheacademy.asu.edu/lee-shulman.

33 *"he thinks of clouds and a coming shower"*: John Dewey, *How We Think* (Boston: Heath, 1910), Kindle edition.

33 *"there is blind groping in the dark"*: John Dewey, *Logic: The Theory of Inquiry* (Henry Holt, 1938), Kindle edition.

35 *far more complex than the textbooks portrayed*: The description of Lee Shulman's research on medical problem solving is drawn from Arthur S. Elstein, Lee S. Shulman, and Sarah A. Sprafka, *Medical Problem Solving: An Analysis of Clinical Reasoning* (Cambridge, MA: Harvard University Press, 1978); Lee S. Shulman and Arthur S. Elstein, "Studies of Problem Solving, Judgment, and Decision Making," *Review of Research in Education* 3 (1975): 3–42; and interviews by the author with Shulman (November 2010, January 2011, and February 2012) and Elstein (February 6, 2012).

35 *quite what form the transformation would take*: In addition to the work on teacher thinking that Lee Shulman's work on medical problem-solving eventually inspired (described later in this chapter), Shulman also coauthored, with Arthur Elstein, an article more straightforwardly examining the early work's implications for education research during that year at Stanford: Lee S. Shulman and Arthur S. Elstein, "Studies of Problem Solving, Judgment, and Decision Making: Implications for Educational Research," *Review of Research in Education* 3 (1975): 3–42.

36 *and called them "information processors"*: Lee S. Shulman et al., "Teaching as Clinical Information Processing," ed. N. L. Gage, Panel 6 Report (Washington, DC: National Conference on Studies in Teaching, 1975).

36 *"And from there, all was commentary and interpretation"*: Gary Sykes, interview by the author, February 20, 2012.

37 *especially Mary Budd Rowe's study of "wait time"*: See, for example, Mary Budd Rowe, "Wait Time: Slowing Down May Be a Way of Speeding Up!" *Journal of Teacher Education* 37, no. 1 (1986): 43–50, http://jte.sagepub.com/content/37/1/43.abstract.

37 *"blessings dipped in acid"*: Lee S. Shulman, *The Wisdom of Practice: Essays*

on Teaching, Learning, and Learning to Teach, ed. Suzanne M. Wilson (San Francisco: Jossey-Bass, 2004), 263.

38 *"it is far more germane"*: Ibid., 258.

39 *and he decides to do another thing instead*: Jerome Bruner, *Actual Minds, Possible Words* (Cambridge, MA: Harvard University Press, 1986), 17.

39 *they mean "teacher"*: Shulman, *Wisdom of Practice*, 197.

39 *"much less generating or predicting"*: Shulman et al., "Teaching as Clinical," 19.

40 *"said [Connecticut congressman Abraham] Ribicoff"*: United Press International (UPI), "Was School Racial Report Buried?" August 18, 1966. Versions of the report ran in many papers, including the *Boston Globe*.

41 *overcome the challenges of their environments*: James S. Coleman et al., *Equality of Educational Opportunity* (Washington, DC: U.S. Department of Health, Education and Welfare, 1966).

41 *"and more money into schools to try and improve them?"*: Eric Hanushek, interview by the author, March 31, 2009.

41 *across ninety-three different variables*: Richard John Murnane, "The Impact of School Resources on the Learning of Inner-City Children" (PhD dissertation, Yale University, 1974), 22–23.

41 *a data set from a school district in California*: Eric A. Hanushek, *Education and Race* (Lexington, MA: Heath, 1972), 36.

41 *whether individual teachers had an effect as well*: Richard John Murnane, "Impact of School Resources," 26, explains the limitations of the Coleman Report data.

42 *as measured by test scores*: A clear summary of the findings is in Eric A. Hanushek, "Throwing Money at Schools," *Journal of Policy Analysis and Management* 1, no. 1 (1981): 29.

43 *"conceptually the problem appears soluble"*: The description of "Teacher Accountability" is in Hanushek, *Education and Race*, 115.

43 *Hanushek gave his method a name: "value-added"*: To my knowledge, the first appearance of the term *value-added* came in a footnote in Eric A. Hanushek, "Education Policy Research—An Industry Perspective," *Economics of Education Review* 1, no. 2 (1981): 8.

44 *That is, classroom teaching and learning*: Hanushek, *Education and Race*, 15.

Chapter Two

45 *"and I knew I was home," she says*: The following account draws on interviews by the author with Mindy Emerson on March 30, 2012, and July 17, 2012.

47 *"FROM THE DESK OF JESSIE J. FRY"*: The portrait of Deborah Loewenberg Ball's teaching career in this chapter draws on many interviews by the author with Ball from April 2009 to November 2013, as well as on records of the period obtained from Ball and from Jessie Fry (now known as Jessie

Storey-Fry), including photographs, curriculum materials, and lesson plan books.

49 *to grow cotyledons and brine shrimp?*: Deborah worked with an experimental science curriculum developed through the Science Curriculum Improvement Study, which was supported by a grant from the National Science Foundation beginning in the 1960s.

50 *reflecting on the experience in an essay*: Magdalene Lampert and Deborah Loewenberg Ball, *Teaching, Multimedia, and Mathematics: Investigations of Real Practice* (New York: Teachers College Press, 1998), 14.

50 *when she assumed they were learning?*: Ibid.

50 *a new experimental curriculum for elementary school math*: The Michigan State professor whom Ball consulted was Perry Lanier. The curriculum he introduced her to was called the Comprehensive School Mathematics Program, or CSMP. CSMP's creation was heavily influenced by two Belgian math educators, Georges Papy and Frédérique Papy-Lenger.

51 *as a way to begin a lesson on negative numbers*: CSMP Mathematics for the First Grade: Teacher's Guide (Aurora, CO: McREL Institute, 1992), http://ceure.buffalostate.edu/~csmp/CSMPProgram/Primary%20Disk/FGRADE/TOTAL.PDF, p. 4-473.

52 *What about to subtract (for example, 3 minus –5)?*: Ball recounts her teaching of negative numbers through an elevator problem in Deborah Loewenberg Ball, "With an Eye on the Mathematical Horizon: Dilemmas of Teaching Elementary School Mathematics," *Elementary School Journal* 93, no. 4 (1993), 378–81.

53 *"mentally and emotionally crushing at worst"*: Deborah Loewenberg Ball, "Knowledge and Reasoning in Mathematical Pedagogy: Examining What Prospective Teachers Bring to Teacher Education" (PhD dissertation, Michigan State University, 1988), 1, http://www-personal.umich.edu/~dball/books/DBall_dissertation.pdf.

54 *and suddenly it would make sense*: The description of Ball's experience in Joseph Adney's class draws on interviews by the author with Ball in September 2010, as well as on Ball's description in Lampert and Ball, *Teaching, Multimedia, and Mathematics*, 16.

55 *What should Deborah do tomorrow?*: The description of Ball's summer school section draws on interviews by the author with Ball (September 2010 and May 26, 2012), as well as on Lampert and Ball, *Teaching, Multimedia, and Mathematics*, 16–18.

55 *didn't become casualties of the experiment*: Lampert and Ball, *Teaching, Multimedia, and Mathematics*, 17.

55 *asked a class of rising sixth-graders to consider a rectangle*: The description of a day at the Elementary Math Lab that follows draws on the author's personal observations on July 23, 2012.

56 *a girl named Anya*: The pseudonyms in this scene were provided by the Elementary Math Lab.

60 *Deborah added the problem to the warm-up*: The author's observations at the Elementary Math Lab were supported by many participants. This description draws especially on the insights of Hyman Bass, Catherine Ditto, and Brian Cohen.

60 *"How can we have this?" Betsy asked Jeannie*: The pseudonyms in this scene were provided by Deborah Ball.

60 *"Twoths. I mean halves."*: Deborah Loewenberg Ball, "Halves, Pieces, and Twoths: Constructing and Using Representational Contexts in Teaching Fractions," in *Rational Numbers: An Integration of Research*, eds. T. P. Carpenter et al. (Hillsdale, NJ: Erlbaum, 1993), 192.

61 *and gave it to education majors about to graduate*: The following description draws on Ball, "Knowledge and Reasoning."

63 *explained a teacher named Rachel*: Ball, "Knowledge and Reasoning," 52.

63 *but the perfect mix of the two*: Lee S. Shulman, *The Wisdom of Practice: Essays on Teaching, Learning, and Learning to Teach*, ed. Suzanne M. Wilson (San Francisco: Jossey-Bass, 2004), 203.

65 *The remaining eight came up with nothing*: Ball, "Knowledge and Reasoning," 65.

66 *"This Kind of Teaching" would do fine*: I first heard the term "This Kind of Teaching" and its abbreviation, TKOT, from Sharon Feiman-Nemser, now the Mandel Professor of Jewish Education at Brandeis University. According to Feiman-Nemser, the term was developed by her and her then colleagues at Michigan State's National Center for Research on Teacher Education as part of the university's Teacher Education and Learning to Teach project. "This Kind of Teaching" also appears in Lampert and Ball, *Teaching, Multimedia, and Mathematics*, 31–35. Although neither Magdalene Lampert nor Deborah Ball uses the term TKOT today, I use it throughout this book for the sake of clarity. For a description of Michigan State educators' thinking at the time about "teaching for understanding," see David K. Cohen, Milbrey W. McLaughlin, and Joan E. Talbert, eds., *Teaching for Understanding: Challenges for Policy and Practice* (San Francisco: Jossey-Bass, 1992).

66 *her teaching was a kind of "existence proof"*: Magdalene Lampert, "When the Problem Is Not the Question and the Solution Is Not the Answer: Mathematical Knowing and Teaching," *American Educational Research Journal* 27, no. 1 (Spring 1990), 36.

68 *and writing about his teaching, all at once*: The colleague on whose unique mix of pursuits Magdalene Lampert modeled her own career is Marvin Hoffman, a longtime teacher, teacher educator, and currently the associate director of the University of Chicago Urban Teacher Education Program and founding director of the UChicago Charter School North Kenwood/Oakland Charter Campus.

68 *all an observer would have to do was click a button*: Magdalene Lampert, *Teaching Problems and the Problems of Teaching* (New Haven, CT: Yale University Press, 2001), 39.

69 *which days they would take notes*: A description of the project's methodology is in Lampert and Ball, *Teaching, Multimedia, and Mathematics*, 38–60.

69 *"It was just a very compelling story"*: Kara Suzuka, interview by the author, July 2012.

70 *"to developing direct performance incentives"*: Eric Hanushek, "Throwing Money at Schools," *Journal of Policy Analysis and Management* 1, no. 1 (1981): 19.

71 *that looked, at first glance, ordinary*: The following account of a scene in Deborah Ball's classroom and Hyman Bass's experience watching it is based on interviews by the author with Bass (July 2012) and Ball (also July 2012), and on videotape and transcripts obtained from the University of Michigan's Mathematics Teaching and Learning to Teach Project.

72 *hijacked by a tall boy named Sean*: The pseudonyms in this scene were invented by Deborah Ball.

78 *"that are entailed by the actual work of teaching"*: Hyman Bass, "Mathematics, Mathematicians, and Mathematics Education," *Bulletin of the American Mathematical Society* 42, no. 4 (2005): 429.

79 *neither (to the subjects' horror) did other mathematicians*: Deborah Loewenberg Ball, Heather C. Hill, and Hyman Bass, "Knowing Mathematics for Teaching," *American Educator*, Fall 2005, 14.

79 *by interviewing witnesses about their characteristics*: An archive of materials documenting *Square One TV* is available at http://www.squareonetv.org, accessed October 27, 2013.

Chapter Three

80 *a college alternative that thrived in the early twentieth century*: An excellent history of normal schools is available in Francesca M. Forzani, "The Work of Reform in Teacher Education" (PhD dissertation, University of Michigan, 2011), 16–71.

82 *a "sideshow to the performance in the center ring"*: Judith Taack Lanier et al., *Tomorrow's Schools of Education: A Report of the Holmes Group* (East Lansing, MI: Holmes Group, 1995), 17.

82 *"anything but schools of pedagogy"*: Harry Judge, *American Graduate Schools of Education: A View from Abroad: A Report to the Ford Foundation* (New York: Ford Foundation, 1982), 42.

82 *"with at least a courtesy appointment in another department as well"*: Ibid., 10.

83 *not to have to work with "dumb-assed teachers"*: Ibid., 31.

83 *The ed department became "our dumping ground"*: Ibid., 21.

83 *they rarely strolled in before 10:00 a.m.*: Forzani, "Work of Reform," 191.

84 *much less to discern what made them succeed*: Ibid., 179.

84 *"a prolonged fit of absentmindedness"*: Judge, *American Graduate Schools*, 21.

85 *"how to help children dress for recess"*: Forzani, "Work of Reform," 198.

85 *a 25 percent increase for future initiatives focused on her mission*: The percentages are based on an interview by the author with Lee Shulman in November 2010. In a separate interview (September 2013), Judy Lanier—now Judith Gallagher—could not confirm whether these precise numbers were correct, but she did confirm the general strategy of cutting more in the short term in order to win a larger budget tailored to her vision in the future.

85 *working at both Oxford and MSU*: David Carroll et al., eds., *Transforming Teacher Education: Reflections from the Field* (Cambridge, MA: Harvard Education Press, 2007), 12.

87 *"rather than by the inductions of reason"*: Quoted in Suzanne M. Wilson, *California Dreaming: Reforming Mathematics Education* (New Haven, CT: Yale University Press, 2003), 9.

87 *"'Tis here, 'tis there, 'tis gone'"*: Alfred North Whitehead, *An Introduction to Mathematics* (New York: Holt, 1911), 7–8.

87 *"some of the beauty and power of mathematics"*: Wilson, *California Dreaming*, 13.

88 *"the statements of the assigned text"*: Larry Cuban, *How Teachers Taught: Constancy and Change in American Classrooms, 1880–1990*, 2nd ed. (New York: Teachers College Press, 1993), 28–29.

88 *diagnosing "mindlessness" across the board*: Charles Silberman, *Crisis in the Classroom: The Remaking of American Education* (New York: Random House, 1970), 10–11.

89 *without wondering about the difference from his first calculation*: Terezinha Nunes Carraher, David William Carraher, and Analucia Dias Schliemann, "Mathematics in the Streets and in the Schools," *British Journal of Developmental Psychology* 3 (1985): 6.

89 *(software, video games, cell phone calls)*: Linda Darling-Hammond, *The Flat World and Education: How America's Commitment to Equity Will Determine Our Future* (New York: Teachers College Press, 2010), 4.

90 *was less than a fourth, having to do with 4*: A. Alfred Taubman, *Threshold Resistance: The Extraordinary Career of a Luxury Retailing Pioneer* (New York: HarperBusiness, 2007).

90 *they paid again for their own*: Ibid.

90 *"it was no exaggeration to speak of a 'movement' for school reform"*: David K. Cohen and Heather C. Hill, *Learning Policy: When State Education Reform Works* (New Haven, CT: Yale University Press, 2001), 14.

91 *and how were they going to learn it?*: Paraphrase of Magdalene writing about Ruth Heaton in Ruth M. Heaton and Magdalene Lampert, "Learning to Hear Voices: Inventing a New Pedagogy of Teacher Education," in *Teaching for Understanding: Challenges for Policy and Practice*, eds. David K. Cohen, Milbrey W. McLaughlin, and Joan E. Talbert (San Francisco: Jossey-Bass, 1992), 53.

92 *the sound of no one thinking*: Ruth Mary Heaton, "Creating and Studying a Practice of Teaching Elementary Mathematics for Understanding" (PhD

dissertation, Michigan State University, 1994), 130. See also Ruth M. Heaton, *Teaching Mathematics to the New Standards: Relearning the Dance* (New York: Teachers College Press, 2000).

93 *the student, a boy named Richard*: Pseudonyms for all of Ruth Heaton's students were invented by Ruth and published in her dissertation ("Creating and Studying a Practice of Teaching Elementary Mathematics for Understanding").

93 *and he said it again*: "000, 111, 000": Heaton, "Creating and Studying," 131–34.

93 *"I felt like I was floundering today"*: Ibid., 136.

93 *(a more fertile way of responding to students' ideas)*: Heaton and Lampert, "Learning to Hear Voices," 55–58.

95 *and construct a response to pull them there*: The description of this teaching episode draws on interviews by the author with Ruth Heaton in August 2012, and on Heaton and Lampert, "Learning to Hear Voices," 62–70.

96 *counting out the calculation with checkers*: Ruth used a counting tool called a *minicomputer* to help students learn mental computation skills. A set of multicolored cardboard sheets on which children laid checkers, the minicomputer allowed students to use a small number of checkers to convey large numbers. Placing the checkers on squares of different colors conveyed different values. For example, on one sheet, a checker on a purple square represented 4, while a checker on a red square represented 2—a total of 6. On a second sheet, each square represented 10 times the value, so one checker on a purple square became 40, and one checker on a red square became 20—a total of 60. Remarkably, working with a skilled teacher, young children quickly become fluent in using the minicomputer to add, subtract, and multiply. The minicomputer was created by the Belgian mathematician and math educator Georges Papy, who, with his wife Frédérique Papy-Lenger, was a major influence on the experimental curriculum that Ruth, Deborah, and Magdalene all used at the Spartan Village school.

97 *"How do I keep it up?"*: The description of this teaching episode draws on interviews by the author with Ruth Heaton in August 2012, and on Heaton, "Creating and Studying," 173–224.

100 *"Facilitating," she called it*: The preceding description of Sylvia Rundquist's teaching draws on Deborah L. Ball and Sylvia S. Rundquist, "Collaboration as a Context for Joining Teacher Learning with Learning about Teaching," in Cohen et al., *Teaching for Understanding*, 13–37.

101 *"This course has enlightened me to a whole world"*: Magdalene Lampert and Deborah Loewenberg Ball, *Teaching, Multimedia, and Mathematics: Investigations of Real Practice* (New York: Teachers College Press, 1998), 35–155.

101 *or "surrender their franchise"*: Judith Lanier, *Tomorrow's Teachers: A Report of the Holmes Group* (East Lansing, MI: Holmes Group, 1986).

102 *from colleges and universities all across the country*: Frank Murray, interview by the author, February 18, 2010.

102 *"could think and reason in such advanced ways"*: David K. Cohen and Deborah Loewenberg Ball, "Relations between Policy and Practice: A Commentary," *Educational Evaluation and Policy Analysis* 12, no. 3 (Autumn 1990): 333.

104 *even some that were obviously far off*: The description of Mrs. Oublier's teaching draws from David K. Cohen, "A Revolution in One Classroom: The Case of Mrs. Oublier," *Educational Evaluation and Policy Analysis* 12, no. 3 (Autumn 1990): 311–29.

104 *"To a one, we never saw radical change"*: Wilson, *California Dreaming*, 207.

104 *she moved on*: Deborah Loewenberg Ball, "Reflections and Deflections of Policy: The Case of Carol Turner," *Educational Evaluation and Policy Analysis* 12, no. 3 (Autumn 1990): 250–51.

105 *had adopted for old worksheets*: Wilson, *California Dreaming*, 207.

105 *"teaching for misunderstanding?"*: Cohen and Ball, "Relations between Policy and Practice," 331.

106 *"had remained essentially the same"*: Wilson, *California Dreaming*, 55.

106 *to make sure the students' answers are correct*: Ibid., 85–93.

107 *here's the framework; good luck*: Cohen, "Revolution in One Classroom."

107 *"in terms of the productivity expected for tenure"*: Quoted in Forzani, "Work of Reform," 246.

108 *"That's just not enough people to make it work"*: Ibid., 253.

108 *at the insistence of the same colleagues who later questioned it*: Judith Gallagher, interview by Jessica Campbell (fact checker for the author), November 2013.

109 *"and other instruments over the heads of her colleagues"*: Ibid., 257.

110 *to deal with both school business and teaching practices*: The following account of the Spartan Village school's struggle in sustaining its reforms is based on multiple interviews by the author with Jessie Storey-Fry between April and August 2012, a review of records from the time provided by Storey-Fry, and interviews by the author with several former Spartan Village teachers.

111 *Others joked about being "bugged"*: A photograph provided by Jessie Storey-Fry records an arch note from her staff. "We're so glad you'll be leading us through the hard times ahead. We're happy we can continue to work in a bug-free environment," the teachers wrote to her.

Chapter Four

113 *She'd opened her remarks with a warning*: For this chapter the author relied on two trips to Tokyo, Japan, in November–December 2011 and April 2012, where interviews and observations were translated by the reporter Yvonne Chang.

114 *better than those with the highest scores in Minneapolis*: Reported in Richard Lynn, "Mathematics Teaching in Japan," in *New Directions in Mathematics Education*, ed. Brian Greer and Gerry Mulhern (London: Routledge, 1989).

114 *especially in matters of science and math*: For background on studies of international math achievement, see Ina V. S. Mullis and Michael O. Martin, "TIMSS in Perspective: Lessons Learned from IEA's Four Decades of International Mathematics Assessments," in *Lessons Learned: What International Assessments Tell Us about Math Achievement*, ed. Tom Loveless (Washington, DC: Brookings Institution Press, 2007).

114 *the top 1 percent of students around the world*: T. Husen, *International Study of Achievement in Mathematics: A Comparison of Twelve Countries* (New York: Wiley, 1967).

114 *better than roughly 98 percent of Americans*: The Illinois-Japan Study of Mathematics, reported in Richard Lynn, "Mathematics Teaching in Japan," in *New Directions in Mathematics Education*, ed. Brian Greer and Gerry Mulhern (London: Routledge, 1989).

114 *while the United States ranked number eight*: Associated Press, "Test Results 'Embarrass' U.S.," December 12, 1983.

115 *"in a manner comparable to the heralded 'economic miracle'"*: Edward B. Fiske, "Japan's Schools: Intent about the Basics," *New York Times*, July 10, 1983.

115 *when they gave children a test of cognitive ability*: Harold W. Stevenson, Shin-ying Lee, and James W. Stigler, "Mathematics Achievement of Chinese, Japanese, and American Children," *Science* 231, no. 4739 (February 14, 1986): 695, 696.

115 *"and your teachers are teaching you these things"*: James Stigler, interview by the author, August 30, 2012.

117 *including a variable to account for classroom teaching*: James W. Stigler and James Hiebert, *The Teaching Gap: Best Ideas from the World's Teachers for Improving Education in the Classroom* (New York: Free Press, 1999), Kindle edition.

118 *"was more significant than we had thought"*: Ibid., Kindle locations 720–30.

118 *Zero of the Japanese lessons did*: Ibid., Kindle locations 814–17.

119 or what new questions do you have, if any? *(We)*: The description of a lesson is drawn from a fourth-grade class observed at Koganei Elementary School on April 17, 2012.

120 *and neither of the Americans asked a "check status" question*: The ministudy of four lessons is reported in James W. Stigler, Clea Fernandez, and Makoto Yoshida, "Traditions of School Mathematics in Japanese and American Elementary Classrooms," in *Theories of Mathematical Learning*, ed. Leslie P. Steffe and Pearla Nesher (Mahwah, NJ: Erlbaum, 1996), 149–75.

120 *in Japanese lessons that number was 40 percent*: Stigler and Hiebert, *Teaching Gap*, Kindle locations 901–3.

121 *why converting to like denominators makes more sense*: Ibid., Kindle location 1183.

122 *forty-five minutes' worth of insights served teachers better*: Ibid., Kindle locations 957–73.

122 *"Now push the equals sign. What do you get?"*: Ibid., Kindle locations 1377–1379.

123 *advice about how to compete with their Asian counterparts*: John Holusha, "W. Edwards Deming, Expert on Business Management, Dies at 93," *New York Times*, December 21, 1993.

124 *"I came to the wrong class"*: The quotes by Akihiko Takahashi in this section come from an interview by the author on December 21, 2011.

124 *math is indeed the same all around the world*: Toshiya Chichibu, interview by the author, November 27, 2011.

130 *"and I cannot go back anymore"*: Akihiko Takahashi, interview by the author, November 29, 2011.

131 *as weak teachers are called in Japan*: Harold Stevenson et al., *The Educational System in Japan: Case Study Findings* (Washington, DC: National Institute on Student Achievement, Curriculum, and Assessment, 1998), 201. A principal interviewed in the report also cited the term *nimotsu*, meaning "baggage."

132 *or breaking up the numbers mentally*: The description of a typical postlesson discussion includes excerpts reported in Clea Fernandez and Makoto Yoshida, *Lesson Study: A Japanese Approach to Improving Mathematics Teaching and Learning* (Mahwah, NJ: Erlbaum, 2004), 110–112.

134 *without having to be told*: The description of a postlesson discussion is based on the author's personal observation of a research lesson at Tokyo's Wakabayashi Elementary School on December 7, 2011.

134 *than making the same mental step for area*: The postlesson discussion about the lesson on angles, which the author observed, occurred at Tokyo's Hashido Elementary School on April 25, 2012.

135 *hadn't gotten to dig into much math*: The research lesson on angles, which the author observed, occurred at Tokyo's Hashido Elementary School on April 25, 2012.

140 *"Potatoes!"*: The author observed Mr. Hirayama's lesson on April 18, 2012, at Takehaya Elementary School, one of four *fuzoku* schools affiliated with Tokyo Gakugei University.

142 *the most productive path to understanding*: Toshiakira Fujii, interview by the author, April 25, 2012.

144 *just like in the United States*: Heidi Knipprath, "What PISA Tells Us about the Quality and Inequality of Japanese Education in Mathematics and Science," *International Journal of Science and Mathematics* 8, no. 3 (June 2010): 389–408.

144 *("field schools," lab schools are called in Finland)*: Evidence of Singapore's conscious efforts to learn from Japanese lesson study is drawn from interviews with officials at the Singapore Ministry of Education, April 2012, and from lectures at the World Association of Lesson Study conference, 2011. China's version of lesson study is described in Liping Ma, "Profound Understanding

of Fundamental Mathematics: When And How Is It Attained," chap. 6 in *Knowing and Teaching Elementary Mathematics: Teachers' Understanding of Fundamental Mathematics in China and the United States* (Mahwah, NJ: Erlbaum, 1999). Finland's "field schools" and their role in the country's recent education reforms are described in Pasi Sahlberg, *Finnish Lessons: What Can the World Learn from Educational Change in Finland?* (New York: Teachers College Press, 2011), 17.

145 *to make a perfect rice pillow*: See *Jiro Dreams of Sushi*, directed by David Gelb (2012).

145 *where students spent decades mastering the special poses*: Tokunaga Kyoko, "The Kabuki Actor Training Center," *Nipponia* no. 22 (September 15, 2002), http://web-japan.org/nipponia/nipponia22/en/feature/feature02.html.

146 *"as a reason why they would do this study"*: James Stigler, interview by the author, August 30, 2012.

146 *"with unlike denominators," in sixth-grade math*: The examples of standards are from New York State's English Language Arts and Mathematics standards, published in May and March 2005, respectively. See http://www.p12.nysed.gov/ciai/mst/math/standards.

146 *would grow to forty-eight*: Margaret A. Jorgensen and Jenny Hoffmann, *History of the No Child Left Behind Act of 2001*, Pearson Education, August 2003 (revision 1, December 2003), http://images.pearsonassessments.com/images/tmrs/tmrs_rg/HistoryofNCLB.pdf?WT.mc_id=TMRS_History_of_the_No_Child_Left_Behind, p. 5.

147 *"to push us along the path to success"*: Stigler and Hiebert, *Teaching Gap*, Kindle locations 130–37.

147 *"to achieve our goals for students"*: James Stigler, interview by the author, September 29, 2011.

148 *teachers had invented new words to describe them*: The vocabulary here draws on interviews by the author with teachers in Tokyo, and on Fernandez and Yoshida, *Lesson Study*.

149 *"and then suddenly, you're in this good restaurant"*: Deborah Ball, interview by the author, May 16, 2012.

Chapter Five

151 *"He writes on the fourth-grade level"*: The quotes by Doug Lemov throughout this passage are from an interview by the author on November 10, 2009.

152 *"and means the revolution has begun"*: Jane O. Reilly, "The Housewife's Moment of Truth," *New York Magazine*, December 20, 1971.

153 *struggle to keep up with her peers*: Wendy Kopp, *One Day, All Children . . . : The Unlikely Triumph of Teach For America and What I Learned along the Way* (New York: PublicAffairs, 2003), Kindle edition, locations 114–15.

154 *"was the problem they were creating"*: Irving Kristol, "The Best of Intentions, the Worst of Results," *Atlantic Monthly*, August 1971.

154 *vowed to "end welfare as we know it"*: Jason DeParle, "President Would Not Limit Welfare Plan's Public Jobs," *New York Times*, June 13, 1994.

155 *"but the taproot is ignorance"*: Quoted in David K. Cohen and Susan L. Moffitt, *The Ordeal of Equality: Did Federal Regulation Fix the Schools?* (Cambridge, MA: Harvard University Press, 2009), 45.

155 *rising from $2,835 to $7,933 in constant dollars*: National Center for Education Statistics, *Digest of Education Statistics*, Table 191 ("Total and Current Expenditures per Pupil in Public Elementary and Secondary Schools: Selected Years, 1919–20 through 2008–09"), http://nces.ed.gov/programs/digest/d11/tables/dt11_191.asp.

156 *essentially a money-back guarantee*: Charles A. Radin, "Charter School Offers a Guarantee: If Student Fails, Parents Get Tuition Free," *Boston Globe*, April 7, 1998.

157 *were held standing up*: This account of the Academy of the Pacific Rim draws on interviews by the author with half a dozen staff from the time, as well as on interviews with former students.

160 *"(It has always been fun)"*: George L. Kelling and James Q Wilson, "Broken Windows: The Police and Neighborhood Safety," *Atlantic Monthly*, March 1, 1982.

163 *the "single cell of instruction" model*: Dan C. Lortie, *Schoolteacher: A Sociological Study* (Chicago: University of Chicago Press, 1975), 15.

167 *"Stand still. They'll respond."*: Doug Lemov, *Teach like a Champion: 49 Techniques That Put Students on the Path to College* (San Francisco: Jossey-Bass, 2010), 3.

168 *"like language class"*: Jay Altman, interview by the author, October 1, 2011.

168 *"the Massachusetts charter schools that had opened"*: Linda Brown, interview by the author, September 13, 2012.

168 *only twenty-two schools had opened so far*: *The Massachusetts Charter School Initiative* (Malden, MA: Massachusetts Department of Education, 2001), http://web.archive.org/web/20061019161538/http://www.doe.mass.edu/charter/reports/2001/01init_rpt.pdf, p. 62.

168 *An "educational 'start-up,'" Bronson called it*: Po Bronson, *What Should I Do with My Life?: The True Story of People Who Answered the Ultimate Question* (New York: Random House, 2002), 338–39.

168 *and all went on to four-year colleges*: Katherine Boo, "The Factory," *New Yorker*, October 18, 2004.

169 *in math and science proficiency*: Sam Allis, "Closing the Gap," *Boston Globe*, June 27, 2004.

169 *"they'd still be in committee hearings"*: Maria Newman, "Newark School Shows Off Educational Approach," *New York Times*, March 30, 2000.

170 *Why does Kayla understand*: The students' names in this description are pseudonyms that come from a presentation that Doug Lemov gave about how to make diagnostic testing data useful using the example of an invented class of second-grade girls.

170 *at an education summit in 2006*: The slides from the presentation are available at http://www2.ed.gov/admins/tchrqual/learn/nclbsummit/lemov/edlite-slide002.html.

Chapter Six

174 *Driving home from Syracuse*: This chapter is based on extensive interviews by the author with Doug Lemov and his current and former students and colleagues between 2009 and 2013.

177 *challenging them to take the problem a step further*: The account of the car ride from Syracuse to Albany draws on interviews by the author with Doug Lemov (December 16, 2009) and Karen Cichon (January 27, 2010), as well as notes provided by Karen Cichon.

188 *to write down her thoughts on paper*: Doug Lemov, *Teach like a Champion: 49 Techniques That Put Students on the Path to College* (San Francisco: Jossey-Bass, 2010), 140.

188 *in order to chide another on her failure*: Ibid., 213.

190 *brutally specific about exactly what they wanted*: Ibid., 177.

191 *was less dismal and took up less time*: Ibid., 194.

193 *from about fifteen to more than a hundred*: Linda Brown, interview by the author, September 13, 2012.

Chapter Seven

196 *he was a true believer*: The following passage is based on extensive interviews by the author with Rousseau Mieze between August and December 2013.

196 *the most academically stimulating place he'd ever been*: This chapter draws on dozens of interviews by the author with no-excuses charter school teachers and leaders, as well as on many school visits and personal observations.

197 *because it serves your students*: Doug Lemov, *Teach like a Champion: 49 Techniques That Put Students on the Path to College* (San Francisco: Jossey-Bass, 2010), 175–76.

198 *the overall picture was shocking*: Fresno Unified School District, Chartering Authority, "Notice to Cure and Correct," sent to Nolan Highbaugh, General Counsel, KIPP California, December 11, 2008.

199 *"like a whipping and ball and chain"*: These comments were published in a private research report prepared for the Academy of the Pacific Rim in the 2002–03 school year and obtained by the author.

199 *their affection was always bracketed*: "love-hate": Millisent Fury Hopkins, interview by the author, September 2013.

200 *down from 58 percent the year before*: Academy of the Pacific Rim Charter School, "Annual Report 2002–03," 2.

200   *and 8 percent for black students*: Rebecca Gordon, Libero Della Piana, and
      Terry Keleher, *Facing the Consequences: An Examination of Racial Discrimi-
      nation in U.S. Public Schools* (Oakland, CA: Applied Research Center, 2000),
      http://www.arhsparentcenter.org/files/Racial-Discrimination-in-US-Public-
      Schools.pdf, p. 29.

201   *"And my teacher just assumed I did that on purpose"*: Chimel Idiokitas, inter-
      view by the author, September 20, 2013.

201   *but Kevin's were king's blue*: Kevin Thai, interview by the author, September
      2013.

201   *"just follow and follow and follow"*: These comments were published in a
      private research report prepared for the Academy of the Pacific Rim in the
      2002–03 school year and obtained by the author.

201   *"just a lot of pointless rules"*: Ibid.

201   *"grudging compliance"*: Jere Brophy and Mary McCaslin, "Teachers' Reports
      of How They Perceive and Cope with Problem Students," *Elementary School
      Journal* 93, no. 1 (September 1992): 14.

202   *to model his own devotion to his students on Mr. Phillips's example*: Kevin
      Thai, interview by the author, September 2013.

203   *"emotions that are counterproductive to learning"*: George G. Bear, "School
      Discipline in the United States: Prevention, Correction, and Long-Term
      Social Development," *School Psychology Review* 27, no. 1 (1998): 14–33.

203   *had only joined later on, in ninth grade*: The statistics are based on the recol-
      lections of two members of APR's first graduating class: Millisent Fury Hop-
      kins and Kevin Thai.

203   *to thirty-four in ninth*: Rousseau Mieze, interview by the author, September
      23, 2012.

203   *didn't make it to graduation was 21.6*: "Boston Public Schools 2007–2008:
      Student Dropout," Office of Research, Assessment, and Evaluation, February
      2009, http://www.bostonpublicschools.org/files/Dropout%20Rate%202007-
      08.pdf.

204   *"they had to stay because it would pay off"*: Chimel Idiokitas, interview by the
      author, September 2013.

204   *So they left*: The empirical research on charter school attrition is mixed.
      One study, of students in Texas, found that students across all racial and
      income groups leave charter schools at significantly higher rates than they
      leave noncharter schools, although the study did not investigate the rea-
      sons for the departures. Eric Hanushek et al., "Charter School Quality and
      Parental Decision Making with School Choice," *Journal of Public Economics*
      91 (2007): 823–48. However, other studies have found no significant differ-
      ence in charter and noncharter school attrition rates. See, for example, Scott
      A. Imberman, "Achievement and Behavior in Charter Schools: Drawing a
      More Complete Picture," *Review of Economics and Statistics* 93, no. 2 (May
      2011): 416–35; and Ira Nichols-Barrer et al., *Student Selection, Attrition, and*

Replacement in KIPP Middle Schools, Mathematica Policy Research Working Paper, September 2012.

204 *reports of bad behavior on the No Limits bus*: The following description of Rise Academy is based on multiple visits to the school by the author and on author interviews with Drew Martin, Shannon Grande, Ranjana Reddy, and more than a dozen other teachers and students at Rise Academy between December 2010 and February 2013.

206 *"may end in a trap"*: Ronald Wright, *A Short History of Progress* (New York: Carroll & Graff, 2004), 5.

208 *"and breaking of healthy adult bonds"*: American Psychological Association Zero Tolerance Task Force, "Are Zero Tolerance Policies Effective in Schools? An Evidentiary Review and Recommendations," *American Psychologist* 63, no. 9 (December 2008): 852–62.

208 *"time and opportunity to get a good education"*: Jay Mathews, *Work Hard. Be Nice.: How Two Inspired Teachers Created the Most Promising Schools in America* (Chapel Hill, NC: Algonquin, 2009), Kindle edition, location 2745.

209 *to the September 11 tragedy*: Interview by the author with the educator.

210 *"no practice interacting with other kids socially"*: Ranjana Reddy, interview by the author, November 10, 2012.

214 *"he gets it out, and he moves on"*: The descriptions of Shannon Grande's teaching are drawn from visits to her classroom in June 2011, September 2012, and February 2013, and from an interview with Shannon by the author, October 2011.

215 *more challenges than their more affluent peers face*: Paul Tough, *How Children Succeed: Grit, Curiosity, and the Hidden Power of Character* (Boston: Houghton Mifflin Harcourt, 2012).

216 *"we gave them tools, and they figured it out"*: Mariel Elguero, interview by the author, February 2013.

217 *"just throw [me] into a box and say go home"*: Kevin Thai, interview by the author, September 2013.

218 *to flesh out their culture conversations*: The KIPP character curriculum and its basis in research are described in Paul Tough's book, *How Children Succeed*.

218 *Chi changed—and so did his colleagues*: Chi Tschang, interview by the author, September 28. 2012.

219 *And it was much harder*: David Levin, interview by the author, December 18, 2013.

220 *"Expecting what you didn't think was possible"*: Mariel Elguero, interview by the author, April 2012.

222 *approaches to dealing with interpersonal challenges*: Bear, "School Discipline."

222 *"and of navigating obstacles"*: Carol D. Lee, *Culture, Literacy, and Learning: Taking Bloom in the Midst of the Whirlwind* (New York: Teachers College Press, 2007), 28.

222 *a girl named Taquisha*: "Taquisha" is a pseudonym created by Carol Lee.

222 *that morning's copy of the Chicago Sun-Times*: The following account draws on Lee, *Culture, Literacy, and Learning*, 132–41.

225 *and how the three can and cannot intersect*: Ibid., 118–23.

225 *"the ethical and moral" part of teaching*: Ibid., 128.

225 *"maladaptive coping strategies"*: Margaret Beale Spencer et al., "Vulnerability to Violence: A Contextually-Sensitive, Development Perspective on African American Adolescents," *Journal of Social Issues* 59, no. 1 (2003): 33–49.

226 *"a person who could have ideas"*: Magdalene Lampert, *Teaching Problems and the Problems of Teaching* (New Haven, CT: Yale University Press, 2001), 265–72.

227 *without asking Magdalene what to do*: Ibid., 278.

227 *"but not in a way that would be embarrassing"*: Ibid., 279.

228 *getting students to do "productive, positive work"*: Lemov, *Teach like a Champion*, 144–49.

Chapter Eight

230 *"I got a new class of fourth-graders," she says*: The description of Seneca Rosenberg's teaching and research career draws on interviews by the author in January, February, and March of 2013, and on e-mail exchanges with the author on July 1, 2013.

232 *looked for different strengths in teachers*: Brian A. Jacob and Lars Lefgren, *What Do Parents Value in Education: An Empirical Investigation of Parents' Revealed Preferences for Teachers*, NBER Working Paper, no. 11494 (Cambridge, MA: National Bureau of Economic Research, 2005), http://www.nber.org/papers/w11494.pdf?new_window=1.

233 *so that they wouldn't leave in the first place*: Jason A. Grissom and Michelle Reininger, "Who Comes Back? A Longitudinal Analysis of the Reentry Behavior of Exiting Teachers," *Education Finance Policy* 7, no. 4 (Fall 2012): 446.

233 *the "inconsistency" of "instructional guidance"*: D. K. Cohen and J. Spillane, "Policy and Practice: The Relations between Governance and Instruction," *Review of Research in Education* 18, no. 1 (January 1992): 17.

233 *"variability" or, more plainly, "incoherence"*: David K. Cohen, "Standards-Based School Reform: Policy, Practice, and Performance," in *Holding Schools Accountable: Performance-Based Reform in Education*, ed. Helen F. Ladd (Washington DC: Brookings Institution, 1996), 108–9.

234 *"You're also absolutely right!"*: Lee S. Shulman, *The Wisdom of Practice: Essays on Teaching, Learning, and Learning to Teach*, ed. Suzanne M. Wilson (San Francisco: Jossey-Bass, 2004), 102.

235 *more than fourteen thousand school districts*: "School Districts," U.S. Census Bureau, http://www.census.gov/did/www/schooldistricts, accessed November 2013.

235 *and nearly a hundred thousand schools*: "Educational Institutions," National

Center for Education Statistics Fast Facts, http://nces.ed.gov/fastfacts/display
.asp?id=84, accessed November 2013.

235 *"and go back to what you believe in"*: Lovely Billups, interview by the author,
February 4, 2012.

236 *like roads, bridges, and power lines*: *The American Heritage Dictionary of the
English Language*, 5th ed. (Boston: Houghton Mifflin Harcourt, 2011–13).

236 *exactly what students were supposed to learn*: David K. Cohen and Susan
L. Moffitt, *The Ordeal of Equality: Did Federal Regulation Fix the Schools?*
(Cambridge, MA: Harvard University Press, 2009), 3–4.

236 *"concerning teaching, learning and academic content"*: Ibid., 4.

236 *"standard operating procedures" outlining best practices*: David K. Cohen,
Teaching and Its Predicaments (Cambridge, MA: Harvard University Press,
2011), 56–57.

237 *"year-to-year road map for reaching those goals"*: Peter Meyer, "The Common
Core Conflation Syndrome: Standards & Curriculum," CUNY Institute for
Education Policy at Roosevelt House, June 12, 2013, http://roosevelthouse.
hunter.cuny.edu/ciep/the-conflation-continues-or-bring-on-the-comfederal
-stational-curstandalums.

238 *"best understood as a sort of exoskeleton"*: Cohen and Moffitt, *Ordeal of
Equality*, 10.

238 *more than ten thousand corps members*: Greg Toppo, "Teach For America
Turns 15," *USA Today*, October 6, 2005.

240 *about a month of extra instruction, by one estimate*: Paul T. Decker, Daniel
P. Mayer, and Steven Glazerman, "The Effects of Teach For America on Stu-
dents: Findings from a National Evaluation," *Mathematica Policy Research*,
June 9, 2004, 31.

240 *more than two and a half, by another*: Melissa A. Clark et al., *The Effectiveness of Secondary Math Teachers from Teach For America and the Teaching Fellows Programs* (Washington, DC: Institute for Educational Studies,
National Center for Education Evaluation and Regional Assistance, 2013).

240 *the corps members did no harm*: Steven Glazerman, Daniel Mayer, and Paul
Decker, "Alternative Routes to Teaching: The Impacts of Teach For America
on Student Achievement and Other Outcomes," *Journal of Policy Analysis
and Management* 25, no. 1 (Winter 2006): 75–96.

240 *"if it were settled easily or soon"*: Cohen and Spillane, "Policy and Practice,"
24.

241 *which snarled their efforts*: Cohen and Moffitt, *Ordeal of Equality*, 172.

241 *totaled only about seven thousand*: Toppo, "Teach For America Turns 15."

241 *less than 1 percent of the 3.6 million teachers*: National Center for Education Statistics, *Digest of Education Statistics*, Table 69 ("Public and Private
Elementary and Secondary Teachers, Enrollment, and Pupil/Teacher Ratios:
Selected Years, Fall 1955 through Fall 2020"), http://nces.ed.gov/programs/
digest/d11/tables/dt11_069.asp.

241 *almost forty-eight million in traditional public schools*: Ibid., Table 108.

242 *formal interviews with forty-one of them*: Seneca Rosenberg, "Organizing for Quality in Education: Individualistic and Systemic Approaches to Teacher Quality" (PhD dissertation, University of Michigan, 2012), viii.

242 *that had arisen so haphazardly for Seneca*: Steven Farr, *Teaching as Leadership: The Highly Effective Teacher's Guide to Closing the Achievement Gap* (San Francisco: Jossey-Bass, 2010).

242 *jugyokenkyu-style sessions for teachers*: Ibid., 136–41.

243 *to a formal coaching system*: Ibid., 148.

243 *"Look, this is how you're supposed to do it"*: Ibid., 246–47.

244 *"what America has never—or hardly ever—had"*: David Cohen, interview by the author, February 26, 2013.

244 *"might look like in the US context"*: Rosenberg, "Organizing for Quality in Education," 183.

245 *to get them to really understand*: Ibid., 170.

246 *"you're not sure how your kids are going to do"*: Ibid.

247 *"They came up with another plan that did work"*: The described exchange is based on recollections shared with the author by Magdalene Lampert in April 2012, July 2012, February 2013, April 2013, and August 2013; and on video footage from "Standards for National Testing and Exams," C-SPAN Video Library, July 19, 1991, http://www.c-spanvideo.org/program/Exams.

249 *"the work of teaching while students work independently"*: Magdalene Lampert, *Teaching Problems and the Problems of Teaching* (New Haven, CT: Yale University Press, 2001), 121.

250 *Out of $248 million*: NewSchools Venture Fund, "2012 Annual Report," http://issuu.com/nsvf/docs/2012annualreport?e=7139272/2303874, accessed February 2013.

250 *Achievement First received over $6 million*: "Venture Snapshot: Achievement First," NewSchools Venture Fund, http://www.newschools.org/venture/af, accessed February 2013.

251 *Uncommon Schools, more than $7 million*: "Venture Snapshot: Uncommon Schools" NewSchools Venture Fund, http://www.newschools.org/venture/uncommon-schools; "Venture Snapshot: Roxbury Preparatory Charter School" NewSchools Venture Fund, http://www.newschools.org/venture/north-star; and "Venture Snapshot: North Star Academy Charter School of Newark," NewSchools Venture Fund, http://www.newschools.org/venture/roxbury-preparatory-charter-school, both accessed February 2013.

251 *and KIPP, more than $6 million*: "Venture Snapshot: KIPP Foundation," NewSchools Venture Fund, http://www.newschools.org/venture/kipp-foundation; "Venture Snapshot: KIPP D.C.," NewSchools Venture Fund, http://www.newschools.org/venture/kipp-dc; "Venture Snapshot: KIPP MA," NewSchools Venture Fund, http://www.newschools.org/venture/kipp-ma; and "Venture Snapshot: TEAM Charter Schools," NewSchools Venture Fund,

http://www.newschools.org/venture/team-charter-schools, all accessed February 2013.

251 *"It was awesome"*: Magdalene Lampert, e-mail message to the author, February 14, 2013.

252 *And in math, they were worse*: Jesse Solomon letter to friends of Boston
Teacher Residency, December 14, 2011. The study was conducted by Harvard
University's Center for Education Policy Research at the request of the Bos-
ton Teacher Residency.

Chapter Nine

254 *if she still wasn't sure what to drink?*: Magdalene Lampert and Filippo Gra-
ziani, "Instructional Activities as a Tool for Teachers' and Teacher Educators'
Learning," *Elementary School Journal* 109, no. 5 (2009): 497.

254 *and got them to start over*: Ibid., 499–500.

254 *reminders and suggestions about how to proceed*: Ibid., 499–500.

255 *a discussion leading to the key mathematical idea*: Magdalene Lampert et
al., "Using Designed Instructional Activities to Enable Novices to Manage
Ambitious Mathematics Teaching," in *Instructional Explanations in the Disciplines*, eds. M. K. Stein and L. Kucan (New York: Springer, 2010), 136.

256 *five thousand worst-performing middle and high schools*: Michele McNeil,
"Tight Leash Likely on Turnaround Aid," *Education Week*, September 2,
2009.

256 *a fifteen-year veteran teacher*: Ilene Carver, interview by the author, April 23,
2013.

256 *The lesson began*: The description of this lesson is based on a video provided
by Magdalene Lampert and on interviews by the author with Magdalene
Lampert (April 2013), Ilene Carver (April 23, 2013), and Sabine Ferdinand
(April 23, 2013).

264 *"we're not where we want to be"*: The quotes from Heather Kirkpatrick in this
section come from an interview by the author on January 23, 2013.

268 *"that's why this evidence is so important!"*: The description of modeling is
drawn from the author's observation of a PLATO workshop for teachers led
by Pam Grossman, Michael Metz, and other colleagues in San Francisco on
March 14, 2013.

269 *between the neighborhoods of Watts and Compton*: Yvonne Divans Hutchinson, "About My School and My Classroom," Inside Teaching, a project of the
Center to Support Excellence in Teaching at Stanford, http://insideteaching.
org/quest/collections/sites/divans-hutchinson_yvonne/teachingcontext.
html, accessed November 2013.

269 *"I want to add to what (person's name) said"*: Yvonne Divans Hutchinson,
"Promoting Literate Discourse in the Classroom," Inside Teaching, http://

insideteaching.org/quest/collections/sites/divans-hutchinson_yvonne/ promlitdis.html, accessed November 2013.

270 *"they're much more apt to be engaged"*: Yvonne Divans Hutchinson, video-taped interview, http://insideteaching.org/quest/collections/sites/divans-hutchinson_yvonne/cleanwlfc.mov, accessed November 2013.

271 *and solicited comments on it*: Lisa Marie Barker, "Under Discussion: Improvisational Theatre as a Tool for Improving Classroom Discourse" (PhD dissertation, Stanford University, 2012), 16.

273 *notifying a student swiftly of her mistake*: Doug Lemov, *Teach like a Champion: 49 Techniques That Put Students on the Path to College* (San Francisco: Jossey-Bass, 2010), 267.

274 *couldn't be mapped back to a memorable race*: K. Anders Ericsson, William G. Chase, and Steve Faloon, "Acquisition of a Memory Skill," *Science* 208, no. 4448 (June 1980): 1181–82.

274 *what they knew about how numbers worked*: Thomas P. Carpenter et al., *Children's Mathematics: Cognitively Guided Instruction* (Portsmouth, NH: Heinemann, 1999).

275 *the abstract mental model that made sense*: Renee Baillargeon, "Physical Reasoning in Infancy," in *The Cognitive Neurosciences*, ed. M. S. Gazzaniga (Cambridge, MA: MIT Press, 1995), 190.

278 *"a normal and healthy part of the learning process"*: Lemov, *Teach like a Champion*, 222.

279 *only 4 percent of American public school students*: National Center for Education Statistics, *Digest of Education Statistics*, Table 108 ("Number and Enrollment of Public Elementary and Secondary Schools, by School Level, Type, and Charter and Magnet Status: Selected Years, 1990–91 through 2010–11"), http://nces.ed.gov/programs/digest/d12/tables/dt12_108.asp.

Chapter Ten

280 *"but what do you actually want to do?"*: Deborah Ball, interview by the author, June 2013.

282 *exactly what students are supposed to learn*: David K. Cohen and Susan L. Moffitt, *The Ordeal of Equality: Did Federal Regulation Fix the Schools?* (Cambridge, MA: Harvard University Press, 2009), 3–4.

282 *up from sixty-five thousand just twenty years earlier*: Richard Ingersoll and Lisa Merrill, *Seven Trends: The Transformation of the Teaching Force*, CPRE Report, no. RR-79 (Philadelphia: Consortium for Policy Research in Education, University of Pennsylvania, 2012), http://www.cpre.org/sites/default/files/workingpapers/1506_seventrendsupdatedoctober2013.pdf, 9.

282 *was now just one*: Thomas G. Carroll and Elizabeth Foster, *Who Will Teach? Experience Matters* (Washington, DC: National Commission on Teaching

and America's Future, 2010), http://nctaf.org/wp-content/uploads/2012/01/NCTAF-Who-Will-Teach-Experience-Matters-2010-Report.pdf, p. 10.

283 *and too few of Robert E. Lee*: Lynne Cheney, "The End of History," *Wall Street Journal*, October 20, 1994.

283 *a reading goal matched to third grade instead of first*: Phyllis Schlafly, "School-to-Work and Goals 2000," *Phyllis Schlafly Report* 30, no. 9 (April 1997), http://www.eagleforum.org/psr/1997/apr97/psrapr97.html.

283 *were important for teaching children to read*: National Reading Panel, *Teaching Children to Read: An Evidence-Based Assessment of the Scientific Research Literature on Reading and Its Implications for Reading Instruction* (Washington, DC: National Reading Panel, 2000), https://www.nichd.nih.gov/publications/pubs/nrp/Documents/report.pdf.

283 *Inevitable disagreements remained*: For a look at early push-back to the Common Core standards, see Stephanie Banchero, "School-Standards Pushback," *Wall Street Journal*, May 8, 2012.

283 *twenty-seven states had vowed to adopt the standards*: Tamar Lewin, "Many States Adopt National Standards for Their Schools," *New York Times*, July 21, 2010.

284 *"academic preparation of teachers more intellectually sound"*: Francesca Forzani, "The Work of Reform in Teacher Education" (PhD dissertation, University of Michigan, 2011), 206–22.

286 *"And thank you for always thinking of us. I love you"*: Charles Sposato, voicemail recorded in 2007 by Venecia Mumford and played for the author during an interview, June 2008.

287 *the kook became the establishment*: Eric Hanushek, interview by the author, October 25, 2012.

287 *or, at a school with thirty teachers, by firing two*: Eric A. Hanushek, "Teacher Deselection," in *Creating a New Teaching Profession*, eds. Dan Goldhaber and Jane Hannaway (Washington, DC: Urban Institute Press, 2009).

288 *"it's hard to imagine it ever being a useful thing"*: The complete discussant paper is Thomas J. Kane, "Improving Educational Quality: How Best to Evaluate Our Schools?" in *Education in the 21st Century: Meeting the Challenges of a Changing World: Conference Proceedings*, Conference Series (Federal Reserve Bank of Boston), no. 47 (Boston: Federal Reserve Bank of Boston, 2002). See also http://www.bostonfed.org/economic/conf/conf47/conf47p.pdf, accessed November 2013.

288 *the law "is likely to end as a fiasco"*: Thomas J. Kane and Douglas O. Staiger, "Rigid Rules Will Damage Schools," *New York Times*, August 13, 2001.

289 *"enough to close the black-white test score gap"*: Robert Gordon, Thomas J. Kane, and Douglas O. Staiger, "Identifying Effective Teachers Using Performance on the Job," Hamilton Project Discussion Paper 2006-01 (Washington, DC: Brookings Institution, 2006), http://www.brookings.edu/views/papers/200604hamilton_1.pdf, p. 8.

290 *"because they could save our lives"*: Tom Kane, interview by the author, April 17, 2013.

290 *"It's who their teacher is"*: Barack Obama, "Our Kids, Our Future" (speech, Manchester, NH, November 20, 2007), American Presidency Project, http://www.presidency.ucsb.edu/ws/?pid=77022.

291 *"or," he added, "with teachers"*: Nicholas D. Kristof, "Our Greatest National Shame," *New York Times*, February 14, 2009.

291 *performed well on achievement tests*: Robert Gordon, Thomas J. Kane, and Douglas O. Staiger, "Identifying Effective Teachers Using Performance on the Job," Hamilton Project Discussion Paper 2006-01 (Washington, DC: Brookings Institution, 2006), http://www.brookings.edu/views/papers/200604hamilton_1.pdf, p. 7.

292 *No meaningful exceptions emerged*: Jonah E. Rockoff et al., *Can You Recognize an Effective Teacher When You Recruit One?*, NBER Working Paper, no. 14485 (Cambridge, MA: National Bureau of Economic Research, 2008), http://www.nber.org/papers/w14485.

292 *had ever been deemed unsatisfactory*: Daniel Weisberg et al., *The Widget Effect: Our National Failure to Acknowledge and Act on Differences in Teacher Effectiveness*, 2nd ed. (Brooklyn, NY: The New Teacher Project, 2009), http://widgeteffect.org/downloads/TheWidgetEffect.pdf.

293 *$169,000 extra in each student's career earnings*: Gordon, Kane, and Staiger, "Identifying Effective Teachers," 14–15.

293 *by roughly $250,000 per classroom*: Raj Chetty, John N. Friedman, and Jonah E. Rockoff, "Measuring the Impacts of Teachers II: Teacher Value-Added and Student Outcomes in Adulthood," NBER Working Paper, no. 19424 (Cambridge, MA: National Bureau of Economic Research, 2013), http://www.nber.org/papers/w19424.

293 *"after they have started their jobs, not before"*: Malcolm Gladwell, "Most Likely to Succeed," *New Yorker*, December 15, 2008.

294 *a drop of 5 percentile points in academic performance rank*: Gordon, Kane, and Staiger, "Identifying Effective Teachers," 8.

294 *a new teacher could learn to help her students*: Donald J. Boyd et al., "Teacher Preparation and Student Achievement," *Educational Evaluation and Policy Analysis* 31, no. 4 (December 2009): 416–40.

294 *for the teacher certification exam as 92 percent*: John Hildebrand, "New Schools Chief Calls for Tougher Teacher Standards," *Newsday*, July 27, 2009.

294 *for the cosmetology certification exam was 59 percent*: Interview by the author with an employee of the New York Department of State, Division of Licensing Services, 2009.

295 *nearly 10 percent on time for teachers to learn*: *A New Vision for Teacher Professional Growth & Support: Six Steps to a More Powerful School System Strategy* (Watertown, MA: Education Resource Strategies, 2013), http://www.erstrategies.org/cms/files/1800-gates-pgs-white-paper.pdf, p. 33.

295 *"not someone, a group of really thoughtful people, did this"*: Joe Negron, interview by the author and Emma Sokoloff-Rubin, April 2013.

296 *called "Fractions and We Know Them"*: A rendition of the song is available in *Fractions and We Know Them*, YouTube, http://www.youtube.com/watch?v=lUygYN6tgyI, accessed October 2013.

297 *"having great teachers was the very key thing"*: Bill Gates, "Mosquitos, Malaria and Education" (TED Talk), TED 2009, February 2009, http://www.ted.com/talks/bill_gates_unplugged.html.

297 *"All you need are those top quartile teachers"*: Ibid.

298 *"development and evaluation systems"*: Vicki Phillips, interview by the author, October 14, 2013.

298 *"who aren't up to the job"*: Barack Obama, "Remarks by the President on Education" (speech, US Department of Education, Washington, DC, July 24, 2009), White House, http://www.whitehouse.gov/the_press_office/Remarks-by-the-President-at-the-Department-of-Education.

299 *"based on performance," meaning evaluation*: See for example, New York State's Race to the Top, Panel Review by Applicant for New York, Phase 1, http://www2.ed.gov/programs/racetothetop/phase1-applications/score-sheets/new-york.pdf, accessed September 2013.

299 *banned assessing teachers by students' test scores*: US Department of Education, "Final Priorities, Requirements, Definitions, and Selection Criteria," *Federal Register* 74, no. 221 (November 2009): 59692.

299 *that led several states to revise their laws*: Associated Press, "States Change Laws in Hopes of Race to Top Edge," January 20, 2010.

299 *could be denied tenure or fired*: Corinne Herlihy et al., "State and Local Efforts to Investigate the Validity and Reliability of Scores from Teacher Evaluation Systems," *Teachers College Record* (forthcoming).

299 *"the right people standing in front of the classroom"*: Gordon, Kane, and Staiger, "Identifying Effective Teachers," 5.

300 *"a teacher shall not be reemployed"*: Herlihy et al., "State and Local Efforts," 17.

300 *"very specific and actionable feedback to teachers"*: Ibid.

300 *after their teachers received focused evaluations*: Eric S. Taylor and John H. Tyler, "Can Teacher Evaluation Improve Teaching?" *Education Next*, Fall 2012.

301 *the skills students needed for English class*: The description of the PLATO group's research findings draws on Pam Grossman et al., "From Measurement to Improvement: Leveraging an Observation Protocol for Instructional Improvement" (paper presented at the annual meeting of the American Educational Research Association, April 20, 2013).

303 *could make words sing*: The preceding sequence draws on interviews by the author with Lorraine McCleod in March 2013, and on observations in her classroom.

303 *the average PLATO score had significantly improved*: Grossman et al., "From Measurement to Improvement," 12–17.

305 *from math to English to history to science*: Heather C. Hill and Pam Gross-

man, "Learning from Teacher Observations: Challenges and Opportunities Posed by New Teacher Evaluation Systems," *Harvard Educational Review* 83, no. 2 (Summer 2013): 379.

306 *the strategies that students needed to master*: Elizabeth Green, "Gates Foundation Study Paints Bleak Picture of Teaching Quality," Gotham-Schools, January 6, 2012, http://gothamschools.org/2012/01/06/gates-founda tion -study-paints-bleak-picture-of-teaching-quality.

306 *a better representation of dividing fractions*: Barbara Scott Nelson, Virginia C. Stimpson, and Will J. Jordan, "Leadership Content Knowledge for Mathematics of Staff Engaged in Key School Leadership Functions" (paper presented at the University Council of Education Administration annual meeting, November 2007).

306 *25 percent made only cursory references*: Lynn T. Goldsmith and Kristen E. Reed, "Final Report: Thinking about Mathematics Instruction," NSF grant EHR 0335384 (in preparation), cited in Hill and Grossman, "Learning from Teacher Observations."

306 *impressively predictive of a teacher's performance*: Jonah Rockoff et al., "Information and Employee Evaluation: Evidence from a Randomized Intervention in Public Schools," *American Economic Review* (forthcoming).

307 *who were destined for effectiveness*: The preceding calculations draw from Sean P. Corcoran, *Can Teachers Be Evaluated by Their Students' Test Scores? Should They Be? The Use of Value-Added Measures of Teacher Effectiveness in Policy and Practice*, Education Policy Action Series (Providence, RI: Annenberg Institute for School Reform at Brown University, 2010).

307 *"high-support policies that . . . help teachers learn"*: Hill and Grossman, "Learning from Teacher Observations," 382.

309 *They had to probe*: Deborah Loewenberg Ball and Francesca Forzani, "The Work of Teaching and the Challenge for Teacher Education," *Journal of Teacher Education* 60: 497–511.

309 *"it's individual, work on it, figure it out"*: Remarks by Deborah Loewenberg Ball at the launch of the Sposato Graduate School of Education, Boston, MA, September 21, 2012.

310 *"feedback" and coaching in addition to evaluation*: Bill Gates, "Teachers Need Real Feedback" (speech, TED Talks Education, May 2013), TED, http://www.ted.com/talks/bill_gates_teachers_need_real_feedback.html; Colleen Walsh, "Changing How Teachers Improve: Emphasis on Bettering Performance Rather Than Simply Rating Success," *Harvard Gazette*, February 3, 2011, http://news.harvard.edu/gazette/story/2011/02/changing-how-teachers-improve.

311 *"let them be themselves"*: Philip K. Howard, "Free the Teachers," *New York Daily News*, November 28, 2010.

311 *supported implementation of the new standards*: Brian Smith, "Common Core Standards Funding Officially Blocked in New Michigan Budget after Senate Vote," *MLive.com*, June 4, 2013.

311 *"I don't know what is"*: Sher Zieve, "Common Core Forcing Marxism/Nazism on America's Children," *Canada Free Press*, May 9, 2013.

Index